CHANGE OF PLANS

Towards a Non-Sexist
Sustainable City

CHANGE of PLANS

Towards a non-sexist sustainable city

Edited by
Margrit Eichler

GARAMOND PRESS

Cover illustration: Gail Geltner

Printed and bound in Canada

Garamond Press
77 Mowat Ave., Ste. 403,
Toronto, Ont.
M6K 3E3

Canadian Cataloguing in Publication Data

Change of plans : towards a non-sexist sustainable city

Includes bibliographical references and index.
ISBN 0-920059-33-3

1. Women and city planning. 2. Urban ecology.
I. Eichler, Margrit, 1942-

HT166.C53 1995   307.1'216'082   C95-931429-6

The publishers acknowledge the financial support of
the Canadian Studies Program of the Department of
Canadian Heritage, Government of Canada.

CONTENTS

vi   ACKNOWLEDGEMENTS

vii   THE CONTRIBUTORS

ix   FOREWORD
Margrit Eichler

I   DESIGNING ECO–CITY IN NORTH AMERICA
Margrit Eichler

25   DECONSTRUCTING THE MAN MADE CITY: FEMINIST CRITIQUES
OF PLANNING THOUGHT AND ACTION
Sherilyn MacGregor

51   SEEKING SHELTER: FEMINIST HOME TRUTHS
Sylvia Novac

71   AT RISK: THE PERSON BEHIND THE ASSUMPTIONS
Planning to Protect Human Health
Jeanne Jabanoski

89   WHAT DO YOU WANT TO DO? PAVE PARKS?
Urban Planning and the Prevention of Violence
Carolyn Whitzman

111   SOWING THE SEEDS OF SUSTAINABILITY: PLANNING
FOR FOOD SELF-RELIANCE
Connie Guberman

131   ACCESS OVER EXCESS: TRANSCENDING CAPTIVITY
AND TRANSPORTATION DISADVANTAGE
Sue Zielinski

157   PLANNING CHANGE: NOT AN END BUT A BEGINNING
Sherilyn MacGregor

169   REFERENCES

ACKNOWLEDGEMENTS

The folks at Garamond Press – Leslie McAfee, Bob Mawhinney, and Peter Saunders, and the copy editor, Anne Webb – have been wonderful to work with. Our collective thanks for a pleasant and expeditious process.

THE CONTRIBUTORS

Margrit Eichler is Professor of Sociology at OISE/University of Toronto. She has published widely on issues concerning women, family policy, non-sexist methodology, and reproductive technologies. She has lately been attempting to integrate a feminist perspective with an environmental perspective.

Connie Guberman teaches Women's Studies at Scarborough College, the University of Toronto, and co-ordinates urban safety initiatives for METRAC (Metro Toronto Action Committee on Public Violence Against Women and Children). She is a member of Grow TOgether community gardeners and is a keen organic gardener both inside and outside the city.

Jeanne Jabanoski, M.Ed. is an educator, researcher, and writer in the field of ecosystems and human health. Her research interests include community involvement in the resolution of environmental health issues, community-based health promotion on HIV and AIDS treatment, and the role of science in the formulation of environmental health policy.

Sherilyn MacGregor has an undergraduate degree in women's studies and a graduate degree in urban and regional planning from Queen's University.

Sylvia Novac recently completed a Ph.D. and is a visiting scholar at the Ontario Institute for Studies in Education. She is a research and housing policy consultant and lectures at Brock University.

Carolyn Whitzman worked for Women Plan Toronto, a feminist planning advocacy group, and for a non-profit housing resource centre before joining the Safe City Committee. As of July 1995, she will be commencing her Ph.D. at the Royal Melbourne Institute of Technology, in Australia.

Sue Zielinski works in the area of sustainable transportation and technology and holds a M.A. in environmental studies from York University in Toronto. She has written and co-produced numerous articles, videos, radio documentaries, and publications, including a recent book with Transportation Options and Steel Rail Press entitled *Beyond the Car*.

FOREWORD

Margrit Eichler

THIS BOOK had a very personal start. Early in 1994, I was invited by a team of architects to participate in a competition held by the province of Ontario to design an ecologically sustainable city. I accepted, for the fun of it, although city planning is not an area in which I had done previous work. When our team was one of three eventually selected to proceed with the design, I wondered what I had taken on. I was the only sociologist and the only feminist on the team. Our proposal stated that our design would be non-sexist. I thought the major contribution I might make would be to our achieving this goal. What, however, is a non-sexist city? And how does a non-sexist design interact with an ecologically sustainable design? Are they mutually supportive, neutral, or in conflict with each other?

A bit later, I was strolling around the publishers' exhibit at the Learned Societies meeting in Calgary. While I was talking with Peter Saunders of Garamond Press, he mentioned that he would be interested in a feminist book on the use of urban space. It occurred to me that editing a book on the subject of bridging feminist and sustainable approaches to city planning might serve several purposes at once: it would put me in contact with people who had thought about (at least some aspects) of this matter, thereby providing a positive influence on the Seaton project, and would generate a book that would be challenging, interesting, and worthwhile in its own right. It would also provide an opportunity to reflect on the city design process once it was finished but still fresh in my mind.

We, the co-authors of this book, came together five times to plan the content, and read and critique each other's papers. Some of us already knew each other before, some did not. One of the matters we had to clarify was whether we wanted to identify this as a feminist or non-sexist book. We all define ourselves as feminist (not surprisingly, this having been one of the criteria on the basis of which authors were invited to participate) and we are all committed – in varying, indeed quite different ways – to notions of sustainability. Clarifying the approach required identifying the audience, which we defined as primarily (but not exclusively) academic, in a broad range of disciplines and subject areas. We wanted the book to be useful as a supplementary text for a variety of courses. One consequence of this is that we decided not to assume that readers would be familiar with women's studies as an approach or discipline.

The relation between feminist and non-sexist research is a dynamic one. Feminist academic work has now been ongoing for about a quarter century, and the strides which have been made in that time are enormous. One of the earliest tasks for feminist scholars was to expose the sexism in established, mainstream, non-feminist scholarship. Hence an analytical vocabulary has been created that allows a precise analysis of the set of interrelated problems which comprise sexism.[1]

Identifying problems of sexism and working towards solutions are both part of the feminist enterprise. However, once solutions have been uncovered and shown to be of general applicability, their use should become part of mainstream scholarship. This book, then, is feminist in its impetus and the process which underlies it, but non-sexist in its applicability.

We each revised our chapter in light of the comments received from one another and the content of the other chapters. This benefited the cohesion and integration of the various chapters greatly. This book is, therefore, more a group product than is usual for edited books. On the other hand, although the chapters form a whole, each chapter also stands on its own, and each bears the distinct stamp of its author. Of course, we each take complete responsibility for the content of our individual chapters.

We hope that *Change of Plans* will raise some questions that are not commonly posed, suggest some new avenues for thought that might profitably be explored in city planning, and contribute to the growing literature on sustainability by merging it with a feminist approach.

Notes

1 See Margrit Eichler, *Nonsexist Research Methods. A Practical Guide* (New York: Unwin and Hyman, 1988; New York: Routledge, 1991); and Margrit Eichler, "Nonsexist Research: A Metatheoretical Approach," *Indian Journal of Social Work*, 53,3 (1992): 329–42.

DESIGNING ECO-CITY
IN NORTH AMERICA

Margrit Eichler

E VER SINCE I ceased being a student (at least in an official sense) all of
my academic and community work has been informed by a feminist
perspective. This encompasses, by now, a long period of time and work in
various substantive areas. Some years ago I felt it was impossible to continue to ignore the state of the environment. If our survival on this planet
is, indeed, threatened – which I believe to be the case – what help will
social justice be to us as we lie gasping for a clean breath of air on our dev-
astated earth? Is it worth continuing to do feminist work given the imme-
diacy and overriding importance of environmental issues? As I struggled
with these questions, I sought to integrate a sustainability perspective
into most of my activities. In doing so, I gradually came to see that not
only is the merging of these two concerns possible (though not always
easy), but that each is beneficial for the other. When I was invited to participate in a team that was to design an ecologically sustainable city, I accepted immediately. Here was a chance to find out in a planning context
to what degree ecological and feminist concerns can be mutually supportive, antagonistic, or merely additive.

The beginning

Early in 1994, the government of Ontario held a competition in which it
invited teams of architects and city planners to submit a proposal for designing an environmentally sustainable city. The city, Seaton, was to have
a population of about 90,000 and be located in the Greater Toronto Area.
Through a process of elimination, three teams were eventually chosen[1] to
develop their design. I was a member of one of these teams (Seaton Team
Dunker) – one of the few women to be involved in this or the other two

1

teams. It seems that women are largely excluded from the networks in which such projects materialize. Our task was to design a city from scratch, even though only on paper, that would be environmentally sustainable and, in particular, significantly reduce dependence on cars – cars being one of the environmentally more harmful agents in modern city life.

The background

About twenty-five years ago, the government of Canada decided to build a second airport for the Greater Toronto Area. It was to be located north of the town of Pickering. The Ontario government acquired a large swath of land (about eight thousand hectares, or just under twenty thousand acres) through expropriation and purchase, in the face of bitter resistance from farmers and others who were forced off their land. After the land had been assembled the airport idea was dropped due to consistent public opposition.[2] "People against Planes" was one of the rallying cries. The battle then switched to the question of what would happen to this assembly of land. The Ontario government had originally intended to establish a city of over 200,000 people in conjunction with the airport. However, citizens' groups opposed further urban sprawl. They formed themselves into the Seaton Community Group to push forward their own vision. Their report recommended that an innovative and compact community of 90,000 be established on a portion of the Seaton lands. The Ministry of Housing engaged in a lengthy public consultation process, the outcome of which was that the provincial government authorized a two-year planning and public consultation process which included, as one of its components, the Seaton Urban Planning and Design Exercise. For this purpose, 3500 hectares were set aside; the rest of the land became part of an agricultural preserve. However, a mega-dump is also planned for part of the same site as the proposed city. The struggle therefore continues.

The Urban Planning and Design Exercise was overseen by the Seaton Advisory Committee, consisting of citizens. An evaluation panel judged the twenty-three submissions made by teams that participated in the competition. Of these, ten were selected for a follow-up interview, and of these three were selected to engage in the planning exercise.

The teams received a detailed set of instructions and a large amount of information – maps, reports, etc. – about the area. Every team had to meet thirteen challenges. The values that the designs were to embody were specified by the community groups. They included:

- preserving the agricultural, natural, and cultural assets of the lands
- ensuring that the new community is respectful of its natural environment
- protecting and enhancing the natural and cultural heritage features, including the existing landscape character, wetlands, existing watercourses, woodlots, and hedgerows
- ensuring continued respect for the existing rural community fabric
- stimulating a sizeable and diverse range of employment opportunities in the community
- designing a compact urban form which is pedestrian-oriented and allows for mixed uses
- providing housing for individuals of all ages, income types, and family patterns
- enabling decentralized and accessible community services
- enabling community self-sufficiency and self-reliance
- encouraging ongoing community involvement in the process.

The parameters were therefore set. Our task was to find creative ways of implementing them.

The task

The task was largely to develop a vision, but the visioning took place under a tightly controlled set of conditions for a specific region with very particular geographic, biological, social, cultural, and political conditions. None of us had ever designed a whole city from scratch, and everyone was keenly aware that cities need to grow and develop. Designing a city that would become vibrant and be constantly evolving, while still meeting the values spelled out for us, was the major challenge.

The visioning we undertook was of a particular nature. It was neither an exercise in science fiction, in which one may adjust unpleasant facts of life in various ways, nor was it a normal exercise in city planning. For instance, we were explicitly told that we could ignore existing zoning regulations and by-laws, since the intent was to develop a "conceptual plan," that is, to generate creative ideas. The single most distinguishing feature of this particular site is that all the land, including all the environs, is in public hands. This allows a degree of control over land use that is unusual in modern times. Whether or not a city will actually ever be built is unclear at this moment. But, irrespective of any further developments, this was probably a unique exercise. It should therefore be instructive to examine some of the ideas that emerged.

The team

Our team consisted originally and officially of fourteen people.[3] Of these, two were women, and only one (myself) defined herself as a feminist. Of the two junior architects associated with the project throughout the entire process, one was female[4] and one was male.[5] One of the members – the only other sociologist – dropped out right from the beginning for personal reasons, and a substantial number of others were brought into the process at various stages. Towards the end another feminist sociologist[6] joined the team, after my desperate plea that I needed some support at the social end of things. In terms of their current geographical location, two team members were from Denmark, three were from the United States (not counting one member who during this period moved back to Canada from the United States), and the rest were from the wider environs of Toronto. However, in terms of cultural background, three were originally from Germany, one from Finland, two from Denmark, one from Australia, one from the Caribbean, one from England, one from India, and the rest from Canada. In terms of professional background, there were five architects, four engineers, three urban planners, two landscape architects, two sociologists, one environmentalist, and one developer.

The process

The process was interesting, intriguing, exhausting, fun, enervating, dismaying, inspiring, intensive, discontinuous for some of us, constantly in high gear for others. It was also an incredible learning experience. Even though some people were more familiar with city planning than others, all of us learned by listening to (and occasionally struggling with) the other team members and the many consultants who came to talk with us. All team members and consultants donated their time to the project.

There were four retreats: one in Toronto and three in a little town outside of Toronto where one of the team's architects lived. Each retreat lasted for four days. For the out-of-town meetings, we rented the community hall, in which we worked, ate, and talked, and we slept on couches, floors, and tents in the beautiful but small house and garden of the local architect. After the first retreat, some of the neighbours – who at the time were fighting the planned widening of a bridge which would have allowed through traffic to flow down the middle of this tiny and friendly village – offered up spaces for us to sleep. This was after several of the team's traffic experts had supported the villagers' efforts with various expert statements to the media about the bridge.

The team's output was defined by the competition guidelines. There were to be seven panels, of prescribed size and content, and a written report. Our report took the form of a handbook.[7] Towards the end, things became truly hectic. While some drew, others would re-write the handbook. In the last scramble, some pieces that probably would have been included, had there been more time, were lost in the shuffle while others were included that might have been excluded or better formulated.

For most of the time I was the only feminist sociologist on the team, with no particular expertise in the area of city planning. The rest of the team, conversely, had little or no connection with feminism, either as a social movement or as a scholarly perspective, or with sociology. This resulted in some translation problems. I would often find it difficult to relate to concepts that were taken for granted by other team members and, conversely, approaches, ideas, and concepts that are part of my daily bread were equally alien to them. However, in some way this was a problem shared by all. Everyone had to communicate across disciplines and areas of concern. Those of us from disciplines other than architecture or city planning had to find ways of communicating in a setting that was alien, while those for whom the setting was familiar had to cope with the unfamiliar concerns that were raised. For instance, the environmentalist in charge of meshing our planned city with animal pathways had to continuously work to make himself heard.

The approach

Was the overall approach a feminist one? Most definitely not. Neither the team composition, nor the types of people consulted allowed for that. On the other hand, I did raise the concerns consistently, and so they were, in a small way, a part of the group process. The greatest challenge was to defend a feminist approach against the charge of irrelevancy: "this is a nice idea but it is not part of city planning," would be the response when arguing, for instance, for certain social services. This is a problem feminists customarily encounter.[8] In contrast, no one felt any hesitation when it came to planning for physical structures that would guide social behaviour, such as streets that would attract people to walk rather than drive cars. Nevertheless, the *Seaton Handbook* does contain a section entitled "A Feminist Approach to Housing and Equity"[9] which deals primarily with the prevention of violence.

The planning exercise did allow us to spin out, in some concrete detail, what would make a city attractive to live in, environmentally sustainable, and possibly non-sexist. As the reports will all be published,[10] I will take considerable liberty here in drawing out those ideas that are of particular interest in a book that is trying to combine a sustainability and non-sexist perspective. Due to space considerations, many elements included in the *Handbook* have been left out of this chapter, in particular engineering aspects and the way in which the planned city fits into the existing landscape.

The outcome
Prefatory note

It was surprisingly difficult to come up with the appropriate subheadings for this section, the reason being that it was never quite clear under which heading a particular design feature fell. For instance, residential streets were designed to reduce car traffic, increase neighbourliness, integrate old and young, attract pedestrians and cyclists, be reflective of the existing hedgerows, potentially be part of an edible landscape, and so forth. So should they be discussed under reducing car dependency, designing for neighbourliness, facilitating alternative modes of transportation, or urban food production? In other words, the somewhat linear fashion in which the description is presented below, for the purpose of clarity and readability, is not reflective of the manner in which various features were conceived. Most quite deliberately serve more than one function.

A compact design

From the beginning, our design was for a highly compact city with high density but low-rise, human scale buildings, oriented around public transit, and encouraging cycling and walking as transportation options over the car. Our aim was to plan a city in such a manner that car use would on average be 50 per cent lower than is the norm in suburbia.

Designing for high density meant the largest possible tract of agricultural land was preserved for agricultural use, and urban sprawl was contained. The compactness of the design generated the density, and thereby the tax base, to enable us to plan for some innovative social services.

Reducing car dependency[11]

In order to reduce car use we needed to reduce the need for car travel, as well as present viable alternative transportation options. Both objectives are closely interrelated, although not identical. To reduce car travel, things must be conveniently located. We therefore planned the city so that schools, essential services, shops, and other amenities were located within easy walking distance in all residential areas.

One compelling reason for travelling by car is the need to go from home to one's place of paid work and back. Integrating work and family space, to the highest degree possible, is therefore an effective way of reducing car trips. We consequently planned for integrated neighbourhoods such that those jobs which do not interfere (through noise, pollution, traffic etc.) with the enjoyment of one's home would be available either within the home or in close proximity to it.

The home has often been advocated as the work location of the future. However, while it is attractive for some professionals to work in the comfort of their home (I am writing this at home), it is not necessarily a desirable, attractive, healthy, or efficient place of work for all workers. One recent study showed that many women working at home at secretarial functions combined childcare with their typing work. They had no appropriate work space, and were stressed, overworked, and without fringe benefits. Their working at home maintained a division of labour in which, in heterosexual couples, the woman was seen as responsible for childcare – while she worked for pay! – while the man worked in a physically different place. Where both members of a couple worked at home, the woman was still responsible for keeping the children from "disturbing" their father.[12]

To counteract these negative outcomes, yet still retain the benefit of close proximity between place of work and home, we planned for work stations in every street block to allow for telecommuting for all or part of the week. These work stations would also serve as meeting places and house some common services. In addition, it is important to recognize that people, whether female or male, who are working at a paying job cannot at the same time look after small children and do both well. We therefore also planned for daycare to be available within the same short distance.

Preferred transportation options include walking, biking, and public transit. We started with the belief that public transit should be easily accessible and affordable. In most cases, residents would be living no more than four hundred meters away from a transit stop. Public transit was planned for from the beginning, and will receive preferential treatment through exclusive right of ways. We found rail transit was too expensive to operate for a relatively small population, but planned for an integrated system of buses, minibuses, and taxis. We never settled the question of whether public transit for people with disabilities would run its own service or be integrated into the general system. Probably a combination of both would be optimal.

Increasing walking and cycling as means of transportation

If one wishes to encourage walking and cycling as forms of transportation, then obviously these two options must be made attractive to people.[13] This can be done through special networks of pedestrian and cycle lanes and a comprehensive all-weather policy. We discussed, for instance, that cycle lanes would have to be cleared of snow before the streets would be cleared, to allow for cycling in most winter conditions.

However, an issue that is just as important as the existence of networks of lanes is safety. People who want to walk need to be safe from other traffic as well as from violence. Safety from other traffic is achieved by designing streets on a grid system (a notion taken over from Toronto) and by dividing them into main streets and residential streets. Main streets carry the major vehicle traffic, and accommodate most of the businesses and some housing. On residential streets, cars are allowed but are clearly secondary. Their progress is impeded so that they have to crawl along. Anyone who wishes to drive through would therefore choose one of the main arteries and only enter a residential street if this was the desired end destination.

Safety from violence is best achieved through a high degree of interaction between residents.[14] In order to encourage this, residential streets are to be narrow, so that neighbours on both sides of the street find it easy to interact. Most interaction was visualized as occurring across the narrow street, rather than over the backyard fence, since the front is where people see each other, pass each other when walking and cycling, meet while observing their children play, and so forth. These streets, then, are primarily for the use of pedestrians, children playing, and cyclists. Street furniture invites residents to sit down and talk with each other, and forces cars to slow down. Soft edges of residential houses (e.g., through porches) and semi-public spaces invite social interaction without reducing the privacy of private spaces.[15]

Designing for neighbourliness

When Hayden[16] designed her non-sexist city, she visualized backyards being turned into communal spaces. Her plan was oriented towards reconceptualizing existing built forms. We had the luxury to plan for space that is basically free of buildings, and therefore were able to pick and choose how to build on it. Furthermore, given that the land is all in public hands, we could specify building conditions that do not normally prevail. Hence we planned for a public lot within each block (i.e., the two sides of a residential street facing each other). Costs of such public lots would be factored into the individual unit price. How exactly this communal space would be used would vary from block to block, and would depend on the residents – and presumably would change over time as the residents changed. We anticipated in most instances a built structure that might house the daycare centre, the work station (referred to above), a set of rooms for use by sick residents who needed some non-hospital care, a communal kitchen, the ubiquitous eco-deposit stations, common laundry facilities, and whatever else residents might want. Some blocks might prefer to maintain the common space as an outside facility only. In all instances, this would be a centre where something would be happening, people could congregate, and children could play.

In addition, each block had one landscaped square equipped with street furniture. This is in the centre of the street and would serve as a central play area for children and as a casual meeting place that most people would naturally pass by on the way to other locations.

Making the infrastructure visible and reducing wastage

A major factor in our current wasteful style of life is that we have organized our lives and our space in such a manner that a lot of the waste and consumption that occur remain invisible. Electricity and other forms of energy come into our houses and are used, usually without regard to the amount consumed. Our garbage is trucked away and we do not see it again – it simply vanishes from sight. Our sewage, in particular, literally goes down the drain and is gone, as far as most people are concerned.

In order to reduce waste and encourage better stewardship we planned on making the infrastructure more visible than is normal in Canadian cities. Consumption of all forms of energy is to be monitored in a ubiquitous and highly visible manner, e.g., through meters placed in strategic places, such as entrance doors. Heating is achieved through a district heating system, which would draw on various local clean energy sources. Sewage is handled by a series of "Living Machines" (invented by John Todd)[17] that would reclaim the sewage into grey water that could be used for various agricultural purposes or cleaned to such a degree that it could be safely returned to the ground. Since such grey water is rich in nitrogen, it would be very useful for intensive forms of urban and agricultural farming. Energy cycles could thus be closed by reutilizing the water for greenhouses and transitional cropping (described below). All compostables would be composted, and most other waste reused or recycled.

Providing housing for all

The type of housing built has major environmental implications.[18] Since we had decided, from the outset, on a highly compact design, we needed to plan for relatively high density and comparatively small lots. In order to create lively and heterogeneous neighbourhoods, we planned to mix the sizes of units.

We envisioned this city to have a higher proportion of various forms of collaborative housing than is usual. Such projects usually have to fight for appropriate zoning, whereas we would not only allow for it, but encourage it. We also envisioned that a number of groups interested in starting either co-operative or co-housing[19] complexes would be inspired to move to this city, precisely because they would find it easy to realize their particular building designs there. However, the difference between collaborative forms of housing and private dwellings is one of degree only. Since all dwelling units would share some communal space within their own street block, there would be some collaborative aspects for all residents.

For more formal collaborative housing arrangements we proposed a policy of zero tolerance of domestic violence. While, of course, one would want the entire city to be violence-free, it is harder to visualize an enforceable policy for strictly private dwellings. Therefore, first stage housing (shelters) and second stage housing for victims of violence is provided as well.

Encouraging social equity

Planning for social equity was an explicit goal. This implied equal access to all public spaces and amenities, whether indoors or outdoors, for women and men, but also for children and older people, and for people of differing abilities and of various cultural backgrounds. Signs on the streets are to be geared towards pedestrians, not cars, and are oriented towards being understandable by people who are visually or hearing impaired. All public and most private spaces are designed to be wheelchair accessible. Street paving will take the needs of wheelchairs – which are similar to the needs of people with children's strollers – into account. In addition, services for specific population groups are planned.

Providing a network of social services

We spent a considerable amount of time and effort planning for social services. In order to facilitate shopping on foot or by bicycle, and to make it possible for elderly people to remain in their own homes for as long as possible, we felt that it was imperative that all goods would be delivered to one's home on request. Likewise, there is need for sufficient public toilets and other amenities.

With respect to services, both crisis intervention and long-term care provided on a non-institutional basis are needed. We therefore adapted the idea of the municipal homemaker that has been tried out in various Finnish municipalities. These homemakers come into people's homes in cases of acute or chronic need (such as illness). Clients pay on a sliding scale according to capacity. For those below a certain income level, the service is free. For the women (and potentially men) who undertake this work it is not a dead-end job, but the first rung in a career ladder. They can work up to becoming a supervisor of other homemakers, and from there slide laterally into other municipal jobs.

We planned for daycare for all children. Part of this would be rendered by the municipality, and part of it could be arranged by the residents since public space is available in every block. All community centres would have daycare available. Such services both cost money and provide jobs for the staff employed. We anticipated that some of the services would be supplied by the municipality, and others by the private sector which would therefore have to be encouraged to provide them.

We consequently planned a tax rebate for businesses that met certain social service criteria. These criteria would ultimately have to be set by the community itself, but they would certainly include the delivery of goods, spaces for children – possibly shared between several businesses – to be dropped off while the parent is otherwise engaged, access to toilets, and so forth. We envisioned that businesses could earn a certain number of points that would entitle them to a partial or full tax rebate up to a set maximum. Part of the money would come by trading in the current subsidy provided for the use of chemical fertilizers. Since one of the major points of the scheme was to turn agriculture towards ecological forms of farming, organic rather than chemical fertilizers would have to be encouraged. Another source of financial flexibility is the public ownership of land. If businesses operate on long-term leases, part of the rebate can take the form of a lowered rent for the lease of the land (all buildings and improvements – including improvements to the land itself – would be owned by the lease holder).

A series of community centres would provide a focal point for all neighbourhoods. These would include a community organizer who would facilitate the formation of various groups around shared interests.

All of these ideas were contingent on Seaton having jurisdiction over local issues. We planned for local authority over local issues, such as local responsibility for managing sub-watersheds, the management of the "Living Machines," the administration of the social tax credit, and so forth.

Facilitating multiple uses of built forms

To provide built space for the various purposes already listed and others not yet mentioned is expensive. We therefore planned for all public buildings to play various functions at different times of the day and week in order to keep costs down. For instance, community centres are integrated with schools, and the public and separate school systems share facilities. The public library, a daycare centre, space for citizens' groups, and so forth are all part of the same complex. While not easy to realize, multiple use is possible. The planned (but never built) Ataratiri project, for instance, had integrated buildings for the public and separate school boards. Spaces for worship in Seaton are also planned as ecumenical buildings, in which various groups can worship according to their own fashion. This system allows the flexibility needed as the cultural composition of the city grows and changes with different waves of new residents.

The central community centre, with the largest array of services and functions, is to be located inside the beautiful greenhouse of the central "Living Machine." It is thus a place for recreation, as well as a highly visible and potent symbol of closed energy cycles.

A similar issue of use arises with respect to private spaces. While the use of private space will depend on the wishes and variable situations of the residents, we planned for easy conversions through zoning and building standards. What was built as one unit should therefore be relatively easily convertible into multiple units through additions. Similarly, we planned for easy conversions from office space to living space and back again.

Favouring small businesses over big businesses

A major source of potential employment in the area of Seaton is related to urban and rural agriculture. Agribusiness deals with food production as strictly a business, rather than as the production of the stuff we need to live. It is intrinsically unecological as it requires large-scale use of pesticides and chemical fertilizers. Ecologically sustainable forms of farming are more labour intensive and hence employ more people, but higher labour costs are offset through lower costs in other areas (no need for chemical fertilizers and pesticides, for instance). An ecologically sustainable form of farming sees agriculture not just as a profit-oriented business but as food production. Food produced for the local market is fresher, hence healthier, than food transported over long distances (which is the rule in agribusiness).

Hence, it is important to encourage local food production for local needs. We conceived of Seaton as a foodshed (analogous to a watershed) that is self supporting – not in the sense of producing all food needed, but in the sense of producing enough food for export so that the overall trade balance is positive or neutral.

With leaseholds, use of agricultural land can be steered in the desired direction. A belt of agri-gardens and diversified mini-farms using organic methods for food production is one important source of food and local employment. Community supported agriculture (CSA) is favoured, with conveniently placed pick-up points for produce. Various financing options, via peer group lending, a credit union, and other programs, are also to be put into place.

Local retailers have to sell local produce if local food production is to flourish. Large chain stores, however, are unlikely to use local produce. We therefore restricted the physical size of all local food stores. This makes operating in Seaton unattractive to mega-businesses, but attractive to local businesses. We do, however, allow some big box retail in goods other than food.

To stimulate local business we also invented, among other things, a local currency, the "Seaton Buck," which is pegged against some local product and floated on the market. The experience of other jurisdictions demonstrates that local currencies make every dollar circulate many times within a community, thus spreading wealth rather than drawing it out of the community.[20]

Urban agriculture

Urban agriculture can be an important source of self-provisioning, while at the same time it makes us aware of the yearly cycles, and connects us to what we eat.[21] If done collaboratively, it can also be an important source of solidarity. We therefore planned for roof gardens – on dwellings, garages, and other buildings – allotment gardens, greenhouses, and kitchen gardens. Air quality is decisively influenced by the amount of greenery around. When planting trees and other greenery in public spaces, one consideration is their food value – not just for humans, but also for various kinds of animals.

Transitional cropping

When the team first submitted its proposal, it included the idea of a tree farm, in which trees would be planted in the pattern in which the city would eventually grow. This idea was afterwards refined to a form of transitional cropping, in which various crops will be grown in the pattern of the city, with eventual streets kept free and bordered by trees. As sections are built up, the crops can be harvested. Crops include native wildflowers, potted trees (which use a lot of the grey water produced by the "Living Machines"), shrubs, and so forth. This provides a beautiful image of the completed town to be, generates some employment and profit from the beginning, and provides mature trees for the major streets.

The Seaton Institute for Sustainable Living

An eco-city would need a place of research and teaching to study solutions to particular problems, provide training for residents and students from elsewhere for transitioning towards sustainable ways of producing goods and of living, and help provide a focus for a new city. In the current political climate, it is unrealistic to assume that any government would finance an entirely new free-standing college. The Seaton Institute for Sustainable Living is therefore designed to draw on and co-ordinate existing facilities and resources, both human and otherwise, to achieve its goals.

An international exhibition

Finally, one major concern is, of course, how to generate knowledge and interest in a place like this. One way to stimulate public attention and to kick start the development would be an international exhibition. Internationally renowned architects would be invited to build ecologically sensible houses. These would be sold, but the tenants occupying them until that point could for a specified period of time – perhaps a year – live for free or against a low rent in exchange for letting the public view the houses. This would demonstrate various housing designs under realistic conditions, and allow businesses which serve visitors (cafes, restaurants, etc.) to find a clientele beyond the first residents. The publicity attending such a major exhibition would make the place known and attract further residents, thus speeding the process of city building.

Reflection

The above description is a very short summary sketch of some of the features of the city design of one of the three teams involved. Ironically, the general consensus was that the very best plan would be to build *no* city at all on the chosen site, but instead to integrate all the planned innovations into the Greater Toronto Area. However, the exercise had its own great rewards. How does it match with a feminist vision of a city?

The feminist city

In a recent article, Andrew (1992) pulls together a list of the features of a feminist city taken from the available literature. I will use this list as a convenient point of comparison.[22] A feminist city, then, would have the following features:

- a well-developed network of services dealing with the issue of violence against women and children;
- a wide variety of services;
- elimination of public violence against women through a public agency whose mandate it is to ensure this;
- friendly neighbourhoods through mixed use of space and lively streets oriented towards pedestrians rather than cars;
- a first-class public transportation system that is safe, cheap, and efficient;
- an active social housing policy which includes co-operative housing, housing for women leaving transitional homes, and special housing for women with disabilities;
- good daycare in a variety of forms, from drop-in centres to full-day care;
- active encouragement of community-based, economic development, with meaningful jobs for women, co-ordinated with daycare;
- a close physical relationship between services, residences, and workplaces, encouraged by mixed urban land use;
- a feminist planning process, working with the population rather than about the population;
- public art that is representative of women and women-centred activities.

To these points we can add from our considerations in this book:

- concern for a healthy environment;
- access to healthy food for all family members.

The match between the feminist and the sustainable city

Taking this particular vision of a feminist city and comparing it with the vision of a sustainable city as developed by the Dunker team demonstrates an extraordinary degree of overlap. Many design features are identical, although arrived at via different logics.

Transportation is a major concern for women, since women have less access to cars.[23] Easy, safe, and pleasant walking and cycling conditions and public transportation are therefore of particular interest. Safety – whether from domestic violence or in public spaces – has been and continues to be one of the greatest concerns for women. Being exposed to personal violence is intrinsically bad, freedom from it is intrinsically preferable. In that sense, safety needs no further justification as a feminist issue.[24] It becomes environmentally relevant when the presence or absence of the threat of violence affects our transportation choices. Women will use public transportation, walking, and cycling only if these options are safe. When these forms of transportation are unsafe, more people are pushed to use private cars.

A great deal of attention has been paid by feminist writers to the need for social services. In particular, the need for daycare and, increasingly, elder care and care for chronically ill people has been empirically demonstrated and theoretically argued. In so far as care work still remains women's work, it is disproportionately women who have to juggle paid work and unpaid family care work.

By contrast, much of the environmental literature fails to deal with social issues that are not directly related to physical features of our built and natural environments. However, if the intent is to design a city that will enable residents to rely much less on cars than is customary in North American cities, social services that are conveniently placed within walking distance become essential. The location of daycare is a case in point. Given that most mothers today are in the paid labour force,[25] driving children to daycare and picking them up has become a major activity for parents – particularly mothers[26] – of young children. Delivery service of goods is likewise closely related to transportation choices.

However, crisis intervention and long-term care provision are best justified on social, not environmental, grounds. Environmental and feminist perspectives do not necessarily overlap on this issue. It is possible to imagine an environmentally sustainable city (or society) that is based on a rigid hierarchy and in which no or few social services exist – what Robertson[27] refers to as the "Totalitarian Conservationist Future." It is simply not an attractive vision. In a more benevolent vein, a particular vision of a sustainable future may simply be naive with respect to social justice issues and feminist concerns in particular.[28] For environmentalists, it requires some concern with and consciousness of social justice issues – besides issues of sustainability – to plan for sufficient social services.

Housing policy is another area of considerable congruence. Novac[29] has outlined the major feminist issues surrounding it. As we have seen, environmental concerns lead to policies which are complementary to those proposed by feminists, although the overlap is not complete. Another important area of convergence concerns policies for economic development. For a variety of environmental reasons, it makes sense to foster small businesses over big businesses.[30] Women will profit from a policy that supports small businesses over big businesses, in so far as women are highly likely to start small businesses, and highly unlikely to partake in the profits of big business, or, indeed, to be involved in a leadership position in mega-businesses[31] – although they are highly likely to be clustered at the lowest level, and to suffer socially, economically, and health-wise through poor working conditions.[32]

Perhaps the area of greatest overlap concerns the physical relation between services, residences, and workplaces. An analysis of *why* paid work and home moved apart[33] and the tremendously negative effects on women of this spatial separation has long been a preoccupation of feminist writers.[34] It is also a major concern for environmentalists, who note the negative effects of travel to and from work and services, usually by private cars.

As far as public art that is representative of women and women-centred activities is concerned, this is a strictly feminist concern that does not necessarily overlap with an environmental concern, although there is certainly no mutual contradiction.[35]

There is also a long-standing feminist concern about a healthy environment for ourselves, our families and children,[36] and for access to healthy food.[37] Both of these are obviously concerns shared by environmentalists. Unfortunately, an environmentally sensitive planning process does not guarantee that it will also be feminist.[38] Conversely, however, a feminist process can reasonably be expected to yield many environmental benefits.

A strategic alliance

Feminism and environmentalism are in no way marching in lock step unison. Indeed, as Seager[39] has demonstrated, there has historically been considerable distrust between the two movements, for good reasons. It is only relatively recently that environmentalism as a social movement has been somewhat more sensitive to social justice concerns, and it is also relatively recent – with the important exception of ecofeminism – that environmental concerns have been seen as relevant to feminism.

Some of the features that environmentalists are turning towards today are inspired by past practices, such as the physical reintegration of residential and work places. However, these past times were certainly not good times for women. All western societies at the turn of the century were strongly patriarchal. In Canada and the US, a patriarchal family system kept women subjugated to their husbands and fathers, without many of the basic human rights we now take for granted.[40] Going back to the past therefore is not particularly appealing to women who are knowledgeable about women's position in the past.

Nevertheless, the overlap that has been demonstrated between environmental concerns and feminist concerns at the level of city planning is surprisingly large.[41] So far, we have found no areas of irreconcilable differences, although there are certainly different sensitivities, depending on whether one is dealing with an environmental or feminist approach, and some areas where the other approach is simply silent (e.g., with respect to feminist art on the part of environmentalists, or with respect to sewage disposal, energy conservation, heating systems, etc., on the part of feminists).

Both feminist issues and environmental issues are critical concerns of today. It would seem that a strategic alliance between the two movements might help both. This point has, of course, been made often by other writers. We now have considerable historical and conceptual evidence that patriarchal societies tend to dominate women and non-human nature at the same time.[42] We have demonstrated here that an alliance may, at least at the theoretical level, be possible in city planning. To what degree this is possible in practise is one of the questions that is addressed in the other chapters of this book.

I would like to thank Klaus Dunker for helpful suggestions on an earlier draft of this chapter.

Notes

1 The three teams were Dunker Associates (our team), Dunlop Farrow, and Van Nostrand.
2 Seaton Advisory Committee, *Seaton Planning and Design Exercise* Phase 3 Design Brief (draft, 4 July, 1994), p. 2.
3 Peter Bosselman, Jeffrey Cook, Klaus Dunker (team leader), Marjut Dunker, Margrit Eichler, Jan Gehl, David Gordon, Cameran Mirza, John Newton, Al Regehr, Charles Simon, Richard Soberman, Jeffrey Stinson, Ron Struys. Alan Powell, who is listed on the first submission, was unable to participate.
4 Heather Rolleston.
5 Ken De Waal.
6 Sylvia Novac. The other people that joined the team later were Henning Bang, James Floyd, and Paul Zabriskie. Others were involved in a number of ways.
7 The Van Nostrand team eventually was awarded first prize, the Dunker team second prize, and the Dunlop Farrow team third prize.
8 See Sherilyn MacGregor's chapter in this volume.
9 Seaton Team Dunker, *Seaton Handbook* (Toronto: Dunker Associates, 1994), pp. 2-15 to 2-18.
10 The Ontario government will publish the submissions of all three finalists in the competition.
11 The two major sources of direct pollution in Canada are car exhaust and household waste. Privately owned and operated cars in Canada are responsible for a significant portion of the nation's total annual air pollution (see Doug Macdonald, *The Politics of Pollution: Why Canadians Are Failing Their Environment* (Toronto: McClelland and Stewart, 1991). In addition, cars contribute to environmental deterioration through wasteful use of space for driving and parking in cities and businesses that depend on car transport, and in many other ways (see Wolfgang Zuckerman, *End of the Road: The World Car Crisis and How We Can Solve It* (Cambridge: Lutterworth Press, 1991).
12 See Margaret Oldfield's MA, thesis on homework, University of Calgary, School of Social Planning, 1990.
13 See Sue Zielienski's chapter in this volume.
14 This has been compellingly argued in Jane Jacobs, *The Death and Life of Great American Cities* (New York: Vintage Books, 1961).
15 Jan Gehl, *Life Between Buildings: Using Public Space* (New York: Van Nostrand Reinhold, 1987).
16 Dolores Hayden, "What Would a Non-Sexist City Be Like? Speculations on Housing, Urban Design, and Human Work," *Signs* 5,3 (Spring) 1980 Supplm., pp. S170-S187.

17 See Nancy and John Todd, *From Ecocities to Living Machines: Principles of Ecological Design* (Berkeley: Northatlantic Books, 1994).

18 Canada, *The State of Canada's Environment* (Ottawa: Minster of Supply and Services, 1991) notes that the one-family house is a heavy energy user which we can no longer afford as our major mode of housing with respect to the environmental costs it imposes. See Chapter 13.

19 Co-housing is a Danish housing concept that has been popularized in North America by: Kathryn McCamant and Charles Durrett, *Cohousing: A Contemporary Approach to Housing Ourselves* (Berkeley: Habitat Press, 1988); and Dorit Fromm, *Collaborative Communities: Cohousing, Central Living, and other New Forms of Housing with Shared Facilities* (New York: Van Nostrand Reinhold, 1991). By now, there are a considerable number of co-housing groups in the US and Canada, with a newsletter, *The CoHousing News*, and a computer bulletin board which has a lively and voluminous rate of exchanges.

20 See Marcia Nozick, *No Place Like Home: Building Sustainable Communities* (Ottawa: Canadian Council on Social Development, 1992).

21 See Guberman's chapter in this volume.

22 The formulation of this summary is mine, not hers.

23 See Zielinski's chapter in this volume.

24 See Whitzman in this volume.

25 In 1992, 56 per cent of all married women were employed in the labour force, compared to 71 per cent of all married men. Given the trend over the past few decades, it would seem we are rapidly approaching a time in which the rate of male and female labour force participation will be the same. The increase in labour force participation is particularly marked for married women with children. In 1992, 64 per cent of all married women with children under the age of sixteen were employed. (See Statistics Canada, *A Portrait of Families in Canada* Target groups project Cat. # 89-523E. (Ottawa: Minister of Industry, Science and Technology, [1993], p. 21 and 32).

26 Michelson has demonstrated in detail that mothers are responsible for most of the trips for childcare, and that this greatly increases the distances travelled by women (see William Michelson, *From Sun to Sun: Daily Obligations and Community Structure in the Lives of Employed Women and Their Families* (Totowa, NJ: Rowman and Allanheld, 1985), pp. 133-5.

27 James Robertson, *The Sane Alternative: Signposts to a Self-Fulfilling Future* (London: Villiers Publishing, 1978), p. 17.

28 For an example of this type of writing, see some of the publications of the Worldwatch Institute, in particular Lester R. Brown, Christopher Flavin, and Sandra Postel, "Picturing a Sustainable Society," in *State of the World 1990*, Report of the World Watch Institute, ed. Lester R. Brown et al. (New York: W.W. Norton, 1990), pp. 173-90 and 237-41.

29 See Novac in this volume. See also Gerda R. Wekerle and Sylvia Novac, *Gender and Housing in Toronto* (Toronto: City of Toronto, Institute on Women and Work, 1991).

30 For a devastating critique of big business' effect on the environment, see: Patricia Adams, *Odious Debts: Loose Lending, Corruption, and the Third World's Environmental Legacy* Probe International (London, Toronto: Earthscan, 1991); Susan Meeker-Lowry, *Economics as If the Earth Really Mattered* (Gabriola Island:

New Society Publishers, 1988); Maria Mies and Vandana Shiva, *Ecofeminism* (Halifax: Fernwood and London: Zed Books, 1993); Christopher Plant and Judith Plant (eds.), *Green Business: Hope or Hoax?* (Philadelphia: New Society Publishers, 1991); Joni Seager, *Earth Follies: Coming to Feminist Terms with the Global Environmental Crisis* (New York: Routledge, 1993); Vandana Shiva, *Staying Alive: Women, Ecology and Development* (London: Zed Books, 1989).

For compelling environmental arguments to support locally-based small businesses see: Marcia Nozick, *No Place Like Home*, 1992; and E.F. Schumacher, *Small is Beautiful: A Study of Economics as if People Mattered* (London: Arcus, 1978).

For many practical suggestions, see: Wayne Roberts, John Bacher and Brian Nelson, *Get a Life! A Green Cure for Canada's Economic Blues* (Toronto: Get a Life Publishing House, 1993).

31 See Helen Shaw, *Elite Women in Canada: A Study of Women in the Key Positions of the Corporate and Political Sectors of Canadian Society*, unpublished Ph.D. thesis, University of Toronto, Department of Educational Theory, OISE, 1994.

32 Barbara Rose Johnston and Gregory Button, "Human Environmental Rights Issues and the Multinational Corporation: Industrial Development in the Free Trade Zone," in *Who Pays the Price? The Sociocultural Context of Environmental Crisis*, ed. Barbara Rose Johnston (Washington, DC: Society for Applied Anthropology, Committee on Human Rights and the Environment, 1994), pp. 206-16.

33 See, in particular, Dolores Hayden, *Redesigning the American Dream: The Future of Housing, Work, and Family Life* (New York: W.W. Norton, 1986).

34 See MacGregor's chapter in this volume.

35 I personally put some effort into ensuring feminist-inspired public art was included in the Dunker team project, but regrettably this is not displayed in the final product due to time pressures at the end which made it impossible to integrate these concerns, either visually or in the *Handbook*.

36 Rosalie Bertell, *No Immediate Danger? Prognosis for a Radioactive Earth* (Toronto: Women's Educational Press, 1985); Irene Diamond and Gloria Feman Orenstein (eds.), *Reweaving the World: The Emergence of Ecofeminism* (San Francisco: Sierra Club, 1990); H. Patricia Hynes, *The Recurring Silent Spring* (New York: Pergamon Press, 1989); H. Patricia Hynes (ed.), *Reconstructing Babylon: Essays on Women and Technology* (Bloomington: Indiana University Press, 1991); Midge Stocker (ed.), *Cancer as a Women's Issue: Scratching the Surface* (Chicago: Third Side Press, 1991).

37 See Carol J. Adams, *The Sexual Politics of Meat: A Feminist-Vegetarian Critical Theory* (New York: Continuum, 1991); and Frances Moore Lappé, *Diet for a Small Planet*, revised edition (Toronto: Random House, 1982).

38 On this score, it would be very instructive to compare the three designs (which were the outcome of the competition) in terms of their sensitivity towards feminist issues.

39 Joni Seager, *Earth Follies: Coming to Feminist Terms with the Global Environmental Crisis* (New York: Routledge, 1993).

40 Margrit Eichler, "Family Policy in Canada: From Where to Where?" in *Justice Beyond Orwell*, eds. Rosalie S. Abella and Melvin L. Rothman (Montreal: Les Editions Yvon Blais Inc., 1985), pp. 353-63; Margrit Eichler, "Social Policy

Concerning Women," in *Canadian Social Policy*, ed. Shankar A. Yelaja, second edition (Waterloo: Wilfrid Laurier University Press, 1987), pp. 139-56; Margrit Eichler "Grasping the Ungraspable: Socio-Legal Definitions of the Family in the Context of Sexuality," in *Transactions of the Royal Society of Canada*, Series VI, vol. III, (Ottawa: Royal Society of Canada, 1993), pp. 3-15; Beth Light and Ruth Roach Pierson, *No Easy Road: Women in Canada 1920s to 1960s*, Documents in Canadian Women's History III (Toronto: New Hogtown Press, 1990).

41 This does not seem to be an artifact of the one particular plan under examination here. The only other description of feminist city planning that I have been able to find is also highly ecologically oriented, see Brigitte Karhoff, Rosemarie Ring, and Helga Steinmaier, *Frauen veraendern ihre Stadt. Selbstorganisierte Projekte der sozialen und oekologischen Stadterneuerung. Vom Frauenstadthaus bis zur Umplanung einer Grossiedlung*, Hrsg. by Feministische Organisation von Planerinnen und Architektinnen (Goettingen: Verlag die Werkstatt, 1993).

42 See Maria Mies and Vandana Shiva, *Ecofeminism*, 1993; Carolyn Merchant, *The Death of Nature: Women, Ecology, and the Scientific Revolution* (New York: Harper and Row, 1990); Carolyn Merchant, *Ecological Revolutions: Nature, Gender and Science in New England* (Chapel Hill: University of North Carolina Press, 1989); Vandana Shiva, *Staying Alive*, 1989; Marilyn Waring, *If Women Counted: A New Feminist Economics* (San Francisco: Harper and Row, 1988); Karen J. Warren, "Feminism and Ecology: Making Connections," *Environmental Ethics* 9, 1 (Spring 1987): 3-20; Karen J. Warren, "The Power and the Promise of Ecological Feminism," *Environmental Ethics* 12, 2 (1990): 125-46.

DECONSTRUCTING THE MAN MADE CITY: FEMINIST CRITIQUES OF PLANNING THOUGHT AND ACTION

Sherilyn MacGregor

A personal prologue

THIS CHAPTER is a product of my two frustrating years as a planning student. When I arrived at planning school in 1991, fresh out of a women's studies program, I was surprised to discover that issues of gender and sexism were matters of great controversy. My attempts to raise questions about how planning affects women's lives provoked much annoyance and eye-rolling amongst my colleagues ("Here she goes again..." they would often mutter). And when I had occasion to use the "f-word," feminism, I was met with the response that such a perspective was too political and narrowly-focused; in other words, it was inappropriate for the rational, technical field of planning. As very few of my courses offered any readings by or about women, I began an independent search for all the literature I could find on feminist critiques of planning and built environments. I was desperate for validation of my belief that a feminist approach to planning is both possible and necessary.

Since then, desperation has given way to optimism. Not only have I located and read a vast amount of feminist planning research, but I have also formed relationships with many feminist academics, practitioners, and activists who share a similar commitment to urban environmental change. These women, especially those I have come to know while writing this chapter, have inspired me to continue my efforts to work for change within the planning profession. The following chapter represents an attempt to understand and contribute to the development of feminist critiques of planning, a body of scholarship that radically challenges the way planners think and act.[1]

Introduction

For most people, "feminism" does not immediately evoke thoughts of curb cuts and zoning by-laws. Instead, we tend to think of freedom of re-productive choice, equal pay for work of equal value, and the fight against male violence as examples of "women's issues." It seems that few of us, committed feminists included, recognize that our struggles for equality take place within a built environment that has been quite literally man made. As a result, the built environment is often seen as a benign back-drop to the human drama rather than a force which shapes our lives in profound ways.

Since the late 1970s, however, a small group of feminist academics, planners, and activists in developed countries have been critically analyzing the role of the built environment in the perpetuation of gender inequality and other forms of social and environmental injustice. This "women and environments" critique has focused primarily on the sexist assumptions of professionals such as planners, architects, and urban policymakers, and has illuminated the harmful impacts of poorly planned cities on women. Most writers have argued that those who have been en-trusted to manage and design our buildings, neighbourhoods, and public spaces have served but a small segment of the population – namely white, affluent men.

As feminists have begun to deconstruct the built environment they have found many aspects of urban life that would look quite different if the needs of women and other marginalized groups were taken into ac-count. Many have suggested innovative alternatives to the present or-ganization of cities. The contributors to this book, for example, have done this with regard to transportation, housing, safety, food systems, and human health. The purpose of this chapter is to provide a context for these ideas by explaining the nature of feminist critiques of the built envi-ronment in general and the planning profession in particular.

It should be noted that the feminist literature to which I refer in this chapter comes primarily from Western, English-speaking countries, namely Canada, Australia, Britain, and the United States. As a result, my discussion is limited to the experiences of women in those over-developed countries. In addition, as I explain later in the chapter, the use of "women" as a category of analysis can be problematic in that it tends to mask the differences among women which stem from characteristics other than gender, such as race, ability, class, and age.

One of the basic premises of the women and environments critique is that most cities were designed to support a particular notion of family life which is no longer "the norm" in contemporary Western society.[2] Even though it is questionable whether the traditional, one-income family was ever the statistical norm, planning and architecture clearly have clung to this ideal despite the social, economic, and cultural changes that have taken place in recent decades. Thus, as more and more women take on so-called untraditional roles and activities, the concomitant changes in their needs are not easily met within the existing urban environment. This has been referred to as a "lack of fit" between the activities that women are trying to carry out and the environments in which they live.[3]

Specific examples of the problems women experience as a result of this lack of fit are discussed in the next section of this chapter. What is important to highlight here is the feminist claim that the planned environment not only reflects social inequality but also serves to reinforce (perhaps even produce) that inequality by making it difficult for women to participate equally in all spheres of life. As Greta Salem writes, "the built environment becomes an extension of the particular set of values operative at the time of its creation and continues to exert an independent influence on the activities that go on within it. It therefore functions as an instrument of social power and a force for the maintenance of the status quo."[4]

It might be considered unreasonable to blame planners and architects today for planning cities which were appropriate for yesterday. After all, how could they have known that social norms would undergo such dramatic changes? Or, one might argue that planners and architects have not intentionally sought to preserve male domination and female subordination; it is not about power at all, but rather about technical and rational decision-making in response to particular socio-economic conditions.

There are at least two types of arguments to counter these concerns. First, when feminists claim that planning has been instrumental in perpetuating gender inequality, most do not speak of intentionality or male conspiracy. In fact, some admit that women have been complicitous, both as producers and consumers, in the building of environments that cause them hardship and inconvenience.[5] Those feminists who analyse the power dynamics inherent in the shaping of the urban environment seem to focus on overarching social structures, namely the capitalist and patriarchal systems and, to a lesser extent, racism. In this sense, feminist analyses are similar to those of Marxist urban theorists such as Manuel Castells who contend that planning serves to further the interests of the capitalist class and perpetuate class inequality.[6] Planners usually work for the state and thus cannot legitimately work in opposition to state interests. Planning therefore serves to perpetuate the status quo, wherein existing power relations take on a "common sense" feel.[7] Simply stated, feminists involved in critiques of planning theorize about patriarchy and gender relations in much the same ways as Marxists do about capitalism and class relations. But they see systemic power as *both* capitalist and patriarchal; they see the interests of elite men as served by both public policy and governmental decision-making. Such an analysis leads necessarily to a view of planning as an inherently political enterprise.[8]

Feminist planning theorists also argue that planners have adhered to theories and conventions of practice that assume gender neutrality, that is, that women and men experience the urban environment in the same way. To the extent that planners have operated on the basis of planning theories that are "gender-blind,"[9] they have either failed to recognize the specific impacts of their plans on women or have made assumptions about what would be best for women based on narrow and rather stereotyped understandings of women's lives. Helen Liggett contends that planners have never planned environments that work well for women, even when traditional gender roles were more common, because "a notion of women's experience as a basis for making plans did not exist."[10] She goes on to provide this example:

... transportation facilities are geared to male commuting patterns. One can argue that streets last longer than social norms and that 'the working woman' places more and different demands on the transportation system than were dreamed of when it was devised. In those days, we may be reminded, women stayed at home in their communities. What then to make of the fact that the building of these roads destroyed communities where women were supposed to be safely at home living their spatially integrated lives.[11]

Arguments such as these underlie the majority of feminist critiques of the built environment and the planning profession. The following overview of women and environments literature is divided into three themes. One is the critique of the "products" of planning, that is, of the planned environment and its impact on women's lives. The second is the critique of the process of planning in terms of how and with whose participation decisions about the planned environment are made. These two types of critique predominated until recently and tended simply to argue for removing the obstacles to women's equal participation in urban life. As Leonie Sandercock and Ann Forsyth have commented, this literature did appear to "blame the men" because it gave little attention to the theoretical foundations of planning.[12] With the publication of their article entitled *Gender: A New Agenda for Planning Theory* the focus has begun to shift away from the effects of planning policy and practice to discussions of planners' values and underlying assumptions. These epistemological critiques constitute a third theme in the literature.

Feminist critiques of the planned environment

A central point articulated in women and environments literature is that the planned environment has acted as a barrier to women's struggles for equality. Much of the analysis has focused on urban land use and on the distribution and delivery of human services.

That the public and private spheres of life are gendered and unequally valued is a long-standing feminist argument. It is generally maintained that men have been associated with the public domain – the place of production, politics, and power – while women have been viewed as belonging in the domestic realm of family life and leisure. One manifestation of this arrangement, the sexual division of labour, has been analyzed by Marxists and socialist feminists.[13] In this division, male labour is productive and monetarily rewarded and female labour is reproductive (as in the reproduction and ongoing maintenance of human life and labour power) and unpaid. In fact, women's domestic work is not seen as work at all according to conventional economic definitions.[14] The acceptance of the sexual division of labour as natural is fundamental to modern capitalist societies and as such directly influences the decisions made by planners and other public decisionmakers.

Feminist discussions of planning almost always involve a critique of the spatial segregation of home and workplace as the most obvious translation of social arrangements into a physical form. Suzanne Mackenzie writes that "the history of the industrial city can be seen as a history of increasing spatial, temporal and functional separation between home and work, on a continuum which runs from the early industrial home workshop to the suburban home...."[15] The post-war development of suburbs has been given particular importance in women and environments literature because it created a lasting infrastructure for the division of labour. It has subsequently had profound implications for the organization of gender roles within households and for women's access to city life.

Commonly called "bedroom communities," suburbs originally were intended to be havens from the workplace for middle-class male breadwinners. The typical single family home was designed on the assumption of a male-earned family wage and full-time domestic maintenance.[16] Dolores Hayden has documented the economic and cultural processes that gave rise to the suburban housewife whose work was to make the home a happy and efficient place for male workers to come home to by, for instance, purchasing newly-invented consumer goods and labour saving technologies.[17] She writes:

> As women were ejected from wartime jobs, they moved into suburban married life and the birth rate rose along with mass consumption. Builders created millions of single-family houses that did not involve careful site planning, provision of community space, or any design input from architects. These houses were bare boxes to be filled up with mass-produced commodities.[18]

Little attention was paid to the personal needs of those women who lived and worked in the same environment, and who in essence never left "the bedroom." As a result, many accounts of women's lives in the suburbs describe isolation, mental illness, and violence.[19] In 1963 Betty Friedan, author of *The Feminine Mystique*, went so far as to call the home "a comfortable concentration camp."[20]

Many of the problems associated with suburbs today stem from the fact that most women who live in a typical suburban nuclear family context now have paid employment outside the home. But, as several studies have shown, they still carry more responsibility for household maintenance and care-giving than do men.[21] This has lead to theories about the "double day" of labour.[22] The dual responsibility for paid labour in the workforce and unpaid domestic labour is seen to underlie many of the problems women experience in the segregated urban environment. Perhaps the most explicit examples of this relate to the issue of public transportation.

Many researchers contend that women rely more heavily on public transportation services than men do for a variety of reasons, including the lower incidence of car ownership.[23] Time-budget studies, such as William Michelson's widely quoted 1985 study of daily obligations and community structure in the lives of employed women and their families in Toronto, indicate that women with children have different requirements of public transit and more complex travel patterns than men have.[24] Because of various domestic responsibilities, women tend to make more short trips at different times during the day to a number of spatially dispersed facilities such as childcare centres, grocery stores, and children's recreational activities. The fact that public transportation schedules have been designed to move large numbers of people at peak business hours, combined with the car-orientation of most urban and suburban environments, means that women with children (and those who are poor, elderly, disabled, or just car-less) are forced to cope with severe mobility constraints. These constraints present barriers to women's full participation in the public sphere.

Other criticisms of land use planning point to the hidden agenda of land use controls and exclusionary zoning policies. Marsha Ritzdorf's empirical research has been particularly important in demonstrating that municipal zoning regulations have not responded to changes in family and household structure. In fact, she found evidence of an "attempt to retrench land use policies in the traditional mode" making reforms almost impossible.[25] She and others have noted that zoning by-laws prohibit home businesses and thus discriminate against women as they are more apt than men to be involved in cottage industries.[26] There have also been complaints that current zoning policies in many North American municipalities are geared towards the traditional nuclear family and make the co-habitation of unrelated adults illegal.[27] This discriminates against many of the different household types that actually exist such as same-sex couples and single adults who live together in order to afford high rents. Further, Dolores Hayden has argued that single-use residential zoning has precluded the communalization of domestic tasks such as childcare, laundry, and food preparation, and thus serves to perpetuate the double burdening of women in families.[28]

The distribution and delivery of community support services has also been of interest to feminists. In particular, the lack of services available and the location of existing services produce undue hardships for many women. Childcare services are a good example. According to a 1991 Health and Welfare Canada study, only 15 per cent of children twelve years of age and under who required care for at least twenty hours per week were served by licensed childcare arrangements.[29] Despite this shortage, however, it seems that childcare has not been recognized as a necessary human service by planners. In fact, zoning by-laws in many municipalities prohibit childcare facilities in commercial or industrial zones. Michelson writes:

> ... the place of childcare in land use planning merits special concern but is seldom given explicit consideration. Instead, childcare is typi-cally one of the last land uses considered when land or buildings are allocated or constructed. Note how many day care centres end up in church basements because these are the only spaces available.[30]

That planners and developers do not place much importance on the provision of childcare facilities suggests that they continue to assume that children are cared for by a parent or in some other private arrangement during the day. It has already been noted that the placing of essential services away from residential zones often makes them inaccessible by mass transportation. Another problem is that most community service fa-cilities operate during the hours of the average work day and not on weekends. Again the assumption seems to be that one member of the household either has no other commitments during those hours or is able to take time off from their commitments in order to, for instance, take a child to a doctor's appointment.

In brief, the types of solutions to these problems that have been advocated by feminists are as follows: the integration of home, employment, and essential services through mixed-use zoning; building codes and zoning by-laws which permit more flexible housing designs so that varied familial arrangements can be accommodated; and public transportation systems which facilitate travel within cities at more times during the day. It is also important that support services which alleviate the double burden of women be implemented. It is believed that these changes would be expedited if women were better able to articulate their needs and if planners (most of whom are male, still) were more inclined to recognize their particular gender-based concerns. Unfortunately, feminist critics argue, the typical public consultation process has not been effective in facilitating input from women.

Feminist critiques of the planning process

Feminists likely have as many criticisms of the planning process as there are stages in the process itself. However, they have been particularly interested in critically examining the stages of needs assessment and citizen consultation in the conventional planning process.

The most general criticism is that the planning process aims to act in the best interests of a "public" which is defined in male terms. The generalized concept of "citizen" is based on male characteristics and concerns and "the public" tends to be made up of people who have in mind a life cycle which necessarily involves the traditional nuclear family.[31] Thus, when planners proceed with these generalized models when attending to functional categories such as housing, transportation, and community services, they tend to plan for the needs and desires of only a small segment of the population. Consequently, we end up with single family neighbourhoods with elementary schools but no employment opportunities, and business complexes with fitness rooms rather than childcare centres. As discussed above, this approach to planning for an undifferentiated public, conceived in supposedly gender-neutral but actually male-defined terms, creates many problems for the ever increasing numbers of people who do not fit into the assumed life patterns.

A related problem is that the citizen participation stage tends to exclude disadvantaged sub-groups such as women.[32] Most planning acts require citizen consultation through a series of well-publicized public hearings held by municipal authorities at various times throughout the planning process. But this process proceeds on the assumption that all members of "the public" have an equal opportunity to express their views and to have these views heard by municipal officials. As in so many other cases this liberal, "equality of opportunity" notion masks the power relations that exist in a politically and economically stratified society.[33]

Although planners may believe that public consultation processes are accessible to all citizens, in practice, more credence is given to powerful political and business interests.[34] A 1981 study by Blary-Charles concluded that "the institutionalization of participation may well discourage the ordinary citizen while the active urban agents (sellers) may well devise means of controlling the process."[35] Further, people who cannot read or speak either official language, or who do not understand the technical concepts and terms involved in planning proposals, are often excluded from meaningful participation in planning meetings. And, because the process tends to be adversarial, only those with substantive understanding of municipal planning policy and good argumentative skills are able to express their views effectively. It appears obvious to many critics that the hierarchical relationship that exists between planners, lawyers, and developers on the one hand and individual residents on the other tends to undermine the potential for productive and empowering dialogue.

Planning theorists working from a feminist perspective argue that women are particularly disadvantaged in the citizen consultation process for reasons arising from sexism and gender inequality.[36] It has been observed that women are less likely than men to express themselves in public meetings, and that this reluctance to participate is often an appropriate response to an environment that devalues and dismisses stereotypically feminine forms of communication. Further, a number of empirical studies have found that conventional political processes silence women through, for example, the monopolization of discussion by men and the bureaucratic jargon and adversarial models that are used.[37] Even women who do not conform to feminine stereotypes and participate alongside men in the political arena often find it difficult to get their views across to their male colleagues. As Beth Moore Milroy argues, "women simply are not heard or regarded as men [are] in public discourse."[38] Simply the scheduling and location of public meetings may inhibit women's participation, particularly if they have care-giving responsibilities or are afraid to travel in the city after dark. Moreover, it has been argued that the types of issues around which women tend to organize and express concern are rarely seen to be relevant to local politics by those in power.[39] This is due to the fact that their issues often are associated by this group with the private sphere, for example "safe neighbourhoods, decent housing, help for society's cast-offs, childcare"[40] – although in some cities there has been increased attention to these concerns in recent years.[41]

Thus, the conventional planning process begins with a predisposition to meet particular needs at the preliminary stages and then excludes the participation of those whose needs are often not met by plans and proposals at the later stages. Feminist critiques of the planning process suggest that this can only be rectified by adopting more participative and inclusive approaches and a recognition that among the diverse groups that exist in cities some are more able to articulate their needs than others. Some writers have suggested that a feminist advocacy planning approach be established wherein planners are assigned to address the specific gender-related concerns of women.[42] Still another solution is to establish grass-roots organizations which enable women and other marginalized groups to use the planning process as a means of improving the quality of life in their communities.[43]

Feminist critiques of planning epistemology

There has been growing interest among some planning theorists in the epistemological linkages between feminist theories and planning theories, and what feminist theorists have to contribute to planning theory. Robert Beauregard explains in a recent edition of *Planning Theory* that,

> as planning theorists, we seem suspended between out-moded and bankrupt positions [of] functional rationality, critical distance, universalizing stances, totalizing perspectives, apolitical practices and a variety of challenges emanating from postmodern, poststructuralist, hermeneutic, deconstructionalist, post colonial and feminist perspectives. Our epistemological base, our way of knowing, no longer supports our theoretical edifice.[44]

It seems that planning theorists are just beginning to contemplate the epistemological issues that feminists and other critical theorists have been writing about for years. Planning, as an academic discipline and a professional practice, appears to be at an intellectual turning point where theorists are re-examining the legitimacy of its methods, principles, and overriding purpose. John Friedmann has gone so far as to proclaim that "the old planning has died."[45] Indeed, the time seems to be ripe for introducing new paradigms into planning thought.

Feminist planning theorists have been contributing to the revisionist project with their critiques of planning theory. It is important to recognize that by challenging planning at its intellectual roots – its epistemology – feminists have gone beyond their argument that cities do not work for women because they were designed by men, for men, and that an analysis of gender must be inserted into existing planning theories and practices. Instead, their most recent critiques take issue with the very *raison d'etre* of planning and the types of values and assumptions that guide planners' work. Whether planners are male or female is of secondary importance because most planners are given a similar conceptual framework for professional practice through their education and the internal culture of planning organizations.[46] The central argument in more recent feminist planning literature is that planners' conceptual framework consists of Enlightenment values which are based on a male rather than female view of the world.[47] While this is a controversial issue within feminism, those planning theorists who advance this type of critique have embraced the epistemological arguments of feminists such as Carol Gilligan who contend that women speak "in a different voice" from men because of their different socialization and life experiences.[48] In that women value connection, caring, and contextuality, their "ways of knowing"[49] are in opposition to the dominant notions of reason and knowledge which are based on abstract principles, rationality, individualism, and objectivity.

Recent feminist literature is particularly critical of the popular assumption that planning decisions can be made through a process of rational decision-making wherein abstract principles are applied and costs and benefits are objectively measured. The rational decision-making model, which is defined as a scientific approach to analysis and a logical method of problem solving, is a cornerstone of conventional planning practice. According to Ernest Alexander, the model involves "the systematic consideration and evaluation of alternative means in the light of the preferred goals they are to achieve."[50] For example, in their work planners often employ tools such as cost-benefit analysis. Such methods are purported to provide objective assessments and quantitative measurements of the variables involved in, and the outcomes of, a decision-making process.

Several aspects of this rationalist planning framework are challenged by feminist critics. They have criticized the positivistic approaches of traditional social science for claiming to be objective while actually supporting the aims of those in positions of management and control in society. Many have underscored the claim that there is no such thing as value-free or neutral practice. For example, Janis Birkeland, Beth Moore Milroy, and Leonie Sandercock and Ann Forsyth have argued that because most conventional planning theories have incorporated the principles of instrumentalism, regulation, and market competition, the decisions of planners often help to perpetuate the domination of elite men and capital over other men, women, racialized groups, and the natural environment.[51]

The rational decision-making model uses scientific techniques and economic principles in order to evaluate the effectiveness of proposed plans. These techniques attempt to quantify and calculate the values of social and natural resources. Feminists have pointed out that capitalist and patriarchal interests play a significant role in deciding not only how much a resource is worth but also which resources are considered valuable at all.[52] An obvious example of an economic principle that supports male domination is the definition of work as that which is "productive" to the economy. Both Susan Fainstein and Beth Moore Milroy note that the accounting system inherent in planning's economic orientation is biased against women because it only recognizes their work when it is monetarily rewarded. As a result, the reproductive and community-building work of women (which basically allows society to function) is not considered in the calculations of planners.[53]

Perhaps the most radical critique of economics-oriented rationality in planning has come from ecological feminists. A less known branch of feminist theory, "ecofeminism," can be described as an amalgam of deep ecology, feminist theory, and moral philosophy which contends that there are fundamental connections between the oppression of women and the oppression of nature.[54] Those who have taken this approach argue that planning theory has an intellectual framework which is biased towards using women and the natural environment for the advancement of male interests. Janis Birkeland, for example, notes that the dominant planning paradigm, which she calls "the Power Paradigm," is "characterized by anthropocentric and instrumentalist concepts" which assign value to human and natural resources based on "the extent that they can be used for human purposes."[55] This notion of utility has been adapted by economists from Bentham's utilitarian calculus – which was based on maximizing happiness – to form a calculus based instead on maximizing consumer preference measured by willingness or ability to pay. Thus it is inherently biased towards the consumption of scarce resources by competing individuals and industries rather than their preservation for future generations. Birkeland argues that the practice of putting scientifically-derived numerical values on non-renewable resources or calculating acceptable levels of pollutants in the air are irrational and unethical because they ignore the ultimate outcome. As an example of this, she cites the Bruntland Report (entitled *Our Common Future*) and its recommendation to limit growth rates to 3 per cent of gross national product (GNP) in order to achieve "sustainable development":

> As indicated by that report, we are waiting for scientists to determine the "limits of growth". Such a limit can only be set scientifically if we accept the point of no return as the physical limit of growth or the point of inelasticity. This is irrational by any conception. Setting a limit that allows for life quality and human fulfilment therefore necessarily involves ethical, not technical, considerations.[56]

Additionally, Birkeland suggests that the tools and techniques used in resource allocation tend to further the immediate interests of industry rather than solve long-term social and environmental problems. For example, land use regulations which keep factories away from residential neighbourhoods do not really deal with the problem of air and soil pollution, rather they allow corporations to continue emitting harmful toxins under controlled, "out of sight out of mind" conditions. Similarly, as Jeanne Jabanoski discusses in this volume, the methods involved in health risk assessment not only use the male body as the norm, but they also aim to find acceptable levels of risk to human health (balanced against potential profits) as opposed to eradicating the danger altogether.[57] Such critiques of instrumental rationality have not only pointed out the difficulties inherent in quantifying and calculating essential aspects of life, but also have exposed the underlying biases involved in planning decisions which are supposed to be "objective."

Finally, many feminists criticize the concept of rationality because of its totalizing or one-dimensional discourse: it assumes that there is one reality or one way to understand the world.[58] In the rationalist paradigm, other forms of knowledge and understanding are considered less legitimate than scientifically tested and technically-derived facts. And these other forms of knowledge that lie outside the paradigm generally have been associated with feminine values and activities, such as intuition, experience, and emotionality. In response, some feminists have proposed alternative theories of knowledge that specifically describe "women's ways of knowing."[59] For example, Jane Braaten has theorized a "social intellectual virtue" which is derived from feminist values and involves traditionally devalued, stereotypically feminine abilities such as the ability to imagine another person's point of view or how she or he might feel about something; the ability to imagine a society based on a different, and perhaps better, set of norms and values; and "the ability to locate the sources of well-being and discord in relationships."[60]

In planning literature, theorists such as Sandercock and Forsyth, Friedmann, Fainstein, and Liggett have argued for a shift away from an epistemology based on an Archimedean position and towards the incorporation of alternative forms of knowledge into planning practice.[61] These ways of knowing can include talking/gossip, listening, creating symbolic forms to express ideas (i.e., pictures, poetry), intuition, and learning by doing.[62] They are important and relevant to planning, write Sandercock and Forsyth, because

> all of these ways of knowing are subject related. It is we who do the talking, listening, acting; which reminds us of the partially autobiographical and thus gendered nature of knowledge. And once we acknowledge the validity of other than scientific and technical ways of knowing, we have to rethink other methodological issues, such as how we go about research in planning.[63]

Examples of how other forms of knowledge have been used in planning decisions are discussed in Jeanne Jabanoski's chapter on health risk assessment. She describes one case in which local residents were able to contribute historical and experiential knowledge to the mixture of scientific data collected by government agencies in order to find acceptable solutions to a soil contamination problem in their community.

That conventional planning theory has adopted a one-dimensional approach to knowledge and rational decision-making is of great concern to feminists and to increasing numbers of theorists who share Beauregard's view that planning has lost its validity in a rapidly changing world.[64] However, there are limits to these critiques. For one, Susan Fainstein makes an important point when she argues that if feminists reject rationality they might as well forget planning altogether. She notes that at the very least, planning involves the integration of information and evaluation of possible courses of action – both of which are rational activities. She proposes instead that we try to transcend the dualistic notion that we can be *either* rational *or* non-rational, and reconstruct the rational decision-making model to include different types of rational action and ways of knowing.[65] For planning theory and practice to become more inclusive and better able to address the range of social problems that exist in a diverse society, it must accept a multi-dimensional paradigm: "An emancipatory planning calls for recognition of difference but within the context of an abiding hope for rationality."[66]

This new approach would presumably incorporate the feminist concerns for caring, connection, and context mentioned above. But even though these values stand in marked contrast to conventional planning epistemology, another question that must be asked is, how comfortable are we with the claim that they are "ways of knowing" specifically associated with women? There are no doubt women who do not place particular importance on listening, story-telling, and creativity; and there are many non-Anglo-European cultures in which these activities are central to both sexes (Aboriginal cultures, for example). More significantly, if these values and activities are deemed to be important for planning practice and community living, then they should be important for everyone – not just women. Breaking free of the binary oppositions that shape and constrain our thinking should be one of the principle goals of a feminist approach to urban environmental change.

There is a further epistemological concern that should be raised relating again to the issue of diversity. Recently, some feminist planning theorists have begun to consider how a poststructuralist perspective might help them to deal with the problem of difference in planning.[67] While many planning theorists are taking an interest in what feminist epistemology can contribute to planning theories, there are others who caution against assuming that there is *a feminist epistemology* and argue that we should not use "woman" as a unifying category of analysis.[68] The basis for this perspective is the recognition that until recently, feminist theories have been based on the experiences of white, Western/Northern, educated, heterosexual women. Since the early 1980s, women from non-Western/Northern cultures and marginalized groups in Western/Northern societies have challenged the legitimacy of feminist theories, claiming that they do not represent their particular histories, experiences, interests, and needs. This has lead to the realization that the category "woman" can be and has been exclusionary – not unlike the universal "man." As philosopher of science Sandra Harding explains:

> In trying to develop theories that provide the one, true (feminist) story of human experience, feminism risks replicating in theory and public policy the tendency in the patriarchal theories to police thought by assuming that only the problems of some women are human problems and that solutions for them are the only reasonable ones. Feminism has played an important role in showing that there are not now and never have been any generic "men" at all – only gendered men and women. Once essential and universal man dissolves, so does his hidden companion, woman. We have, instead, myriads of women living in elaborate historical complexities of class, race, and culture.[69]

It might be argued that there is a "universal woman" in the earlier women and environments literature and that she is a middle-class, white, heterosexual, able-bodied woman living in a large city. The centrality of the public-private dichotomy in that literature is clearly based on the plight of the suburban housewife who historically has tended to be white and middle class. There are and always have been many women whose lives are affected differently by the separation of home and workplace than are the lives of full-time homemakers. Inner city working-class and transient women, and of course rural farming women, are obvious examples of women whose concerns get little attention in the literature. In most cases, the earlier women and environments work does not seem to recognize the other sources of identity besides gender – such as race, class, sexuality, or ability – that have significant impacts on women's experiences of oppression.

The relevance of the poststructuralist feminist critique to planning theory and epistemology debates is as yet rather uncertain. Sandercock and Forsyth lament that poststructuralist feminism "has become increasingly esoteric, increasingly inaccessible for women who are not full-time theorists to read and integrate into our lives and feminist political projects."[70] At a basic level, however, they argue that poststructuralist perspectives point planning theory in the direction of developing a theory and practice of planning for multiple publics, wherein differences between and among people are recognized and even celebrated. They predict that this will become one of the most important themes in planning in the 1990s. Similarly, Moore Milroy suggests that if planning theory accepts poststructuralist, anti-racist/post-colonial, and lesbian feminist concerns for recognizing basic differences in people's experiences and subjectivities, then it will have no choice but to embrace "alternative images of the good life" and develop ways to work with many different images "while resisting the urge to reduce one to another."[71]

Conclusion

Although we are cast in the same mold, the mold is cracking. It is from our contemporary experiences that we must learn.[72]

Perhaps the most challenging task involved in deconstructing the man made city is to unearth and dispose of the assumptions that have misguided the planning profession for so long. As in many other disciplines, the focus of planning needs to be decentered. "The public," that amorphous blob of humanity in whose best interests planners are supposed to work, must be reconceptualized as "publics" with diverse experiences, needs, and aspirations. In light of profound demographic and cultural changes, what is classified as a "family" must become broad enough to encompass the many households and lifestyles that actually exist in our communities. The "average citizen," if we are to retain such a concept at all, must be based on the characteristics of the most vulnerable in society rather than those who dominate it. And what is most important, at least as far as women are concerned, is that planners must stop assuming that women will fill up the gaps in public policy by donating their time to keeping citizens healthy, happy, and housed.

One way to bring about such a change in thinking is to change what planners are taught in school. I began this chapter with a personal account of frustration about the absence of a gender analysis in my planning courses. The planning curriculum in my school seemed to be concerned more with producing "experts" with good computer and design skills than with preparing students for the social and political contexts in which they will ultimately work. It is undoubtedly important that planners be trained in the technical and physical aspects of planning so that they may be called upon to change the spatial organization of cities in ways that will make them greener, safer, and more accessible. But this training should be balanced with core courses in urban sociology (who lives in communities and how?); applied ethics; negotiation, participation, and qualitative research techniques; planning theories (both traditional and critical); and community development models. Also important is that book learning be augmented by experiential learning so that aspiring planners may gain insight into problems and lifestyles that they may never experience first-hand. For example, students could participate in safety audits, try to manoeuvre around the city in a wheel chair or with a child in tow, or facilitate a tenant's meeting in a social housing project. Above all, planning students should be encouraged to use their imaginations in the search for solutions to urban environmental problems. Only if the next generation of planners is equipped to understand and work with diverse communities will the profession contribute to a more just and sustainable future.

Somewhere in my search for intellectual reinforcement I discovered that women, most but not all of whom were feminists, have been the driving force behind the urban change movements of the last century. In fact, even though women were not admitted into the planning profession until the 1940s, through their clubs and charitable organizations in the 1890s they promoted the basic concepts of "municipal housekeeping" – a precursor to urban planning.[73] The group of women who have produced this book are clearly part of that legacy. In the chapters that follow, not only are the dominant planning assumptions dispelled, but a range of practical solutions to common problems are presented; these illustrate the power and promise of a feminist approach to planning.

That we are still arguing for "cities as if women counted" in 1995 may mean that the planning profession is as resistant to change as every other institution in patriarchal society. But for me this persistence is cause for celebration because it means that feminist urban visions are strong, innovative, and gaining validity at a time when our communities need them most.

Notes

1 As this chapter is derived from the literature review of my master's thesis, I would like to acknowledge the assistance and supervision of Professor Sue Hendler of the School of Urban and Regional Planning at Queen's University and Professor Roberta Hamilton of the Department of Sociology, also at Queen's.

2 See, for example, K. Hapgood and J. Getzels (eds.), *Planning, Women and Change* (Chicago: American Society of Planning Officials, 1974); D. Hayden, *Redesigning the American Dream* (New York: W.W. Norton, 1984); S. Mackenzie, "Women's Responses to Economic Restructuring: Changing Gender, Changing Space" in *The Politics of Diversity: Feminism, Marxism, and Nationalism*, eds. R. Hamilton and M. Barrett (Montreal: Book Centre Inc., 1986), pp. 81-100. For a critique of the nuclear family as norm, see M. Eichler, *Families in Canada Today: Recent Changes and their Policy Consequences*, second edition (Toronto: Gage, 1988).

3 G. Wekerle, R. Peterson, and D. Morley (eds.), *New Space for Women* (Boulder: Westview Press, 1980).

4 G. Salem, "Gender Equity and the Urban Environment" in *The Egalitarian City: Issues of Rights, Distribution, and Access*, ed. J.K. Boles (New York: Praeger Publishers, 1986), p.158.

5 S. Ahrentzen, "Introduction" in *New Households New Housing*, eds. K. Franck and S. Ahrentzen (New York: Van Nostrand Reinhold, 1989); D. Spain, *Gendered Spaces* (Chapel Hill: University of North Carolina Press, 1992).

6 M. Castells, *City, Class, and Power* (London: MacMillan Publishers, 1972). For a discussion of Marxist analyses of planning see J. Friedmann, *Planning in the Public Domain: From Knowledge to Action* (Princeton: Princeton University Press, 1987).

7 Here I refer to Gramsci's (1971) concept of "common sense" which means "an embedded, uncritical, mainly unconscious set of perceptions and understandings of the world which constitute a 'common' framework in a given era, culture, or social space," as quoted in L. Code, *What Can She Know? Feminist Theory and the Construction of Knowledge* (Ithaca: Cornell University Press, 1991), p. 196.

8 G. Salem, "Gender Equity and the Urban Environment," 1986.

9 L. Sandercock and A. Forsyth, "Gender: A New Agenda for Planning Theory," *Planning Theory* 4 (1990): 61-92.

10 H. Liggett, "Knowing Women/Planning Theory," *Planning Theory* 7,8 (1992): 24.

11 H. Liggett, "Knowing Women/Planning Theory" (1992): 21.

12 L. Sandercock and A. Forsyth, "Gender: A New Agenda for Planning Theory" (1990): 65.

13 See, for example, F. Engels, *The Origin of the Family, Private Property, and the State* (New York: International Publishers Co., 1942); M. Luxton, *More than a Labour of Love: Three Generations of Women's Work in the Home* (Toronto: Women's Press, 1980); P. Armstrong and H. Armstrong, *The Double Ghetto: Canadian Women and their Segregated Work*, third edition (Toronto: McClelland and Stewart, 1994).

14 B. Burnell, "Images of Women: An Economic Perspective" in *Foundations for a Feminist Restructuring of the Academic Disciplines*, eds. M. Paludi and G. Steuernagel (New York: The Hawthorne Press, 1990); B. Moore Milroy, "Taking Stock of Planning, Space and Gender," *Journal of Planning Literature* 6, 1 (1991): 3-15.

15 S. Mackenzie, "Women's Response to Economic Restructuring," 1986, p. 82.

16 For feminist critiques of the "bedroom community" concept, see S. Fava, "Women's Place in the New Suburbia" in *New Space for Women*, eds. G. Wekerle et al. 1980, pp. 129-50; K. Franck, "Social Construction of the Physical Environment: The Case of Gender," *Sociological Focus* 18,2 (1985): 143-60; S. Saegert, "The Androgenous City: From Critique to Practice," *Sociological Focus* 18,2 (1985): 161-76; and J. Little, L. Peake, and P. Richardson, eds., *Women in Cities: Gender and the Urban Environment* (London: MacMillan Publishers Inc., 1988).

17 D. Hayden, "What Would a Non-Sexist City Be Like? Speculations on Housing, Urban Design, and Human Work" in *Women and the American City*, ed. C. Stimpson et al. (Chicago: University of Chicago Press, 1980): 167-84; D. Hayden, *The Grand Domestic Revolution: A History of Feminist Designs for American Homes* (Cambridge: MIT Press, 1981); and D. Hayden, *Redesigning the American Dream*, 1984.

18 D. Hayden, *The Grand Domestic Revolution*, 1981, p. 23.

19 D. Rothblatt, D. Garr, and J. Sprague, *The Suburban Environment and Women* (New York: Praeger Publishers, 1979); D. Hayden, "What Would a Non-Sexist City Be Like?" (1980); B. Moore Milroy, "Taking Stock of Planning, Space and Gender" (1991).

20 B. Friedan, *The Feminine Mystique* (New York: Dell, 1963), p. 3.

21 Canadian Advisory Council on the Status of Women, *110 Canadian Statistics on Work and Family - Background Paper* (Ottawa: Canada Communications Group, 1994); M. Eichler, *Families in Canada Today*, 1988; P. Armstrong and H. Armstrong, *The Double Ghetto*, 1994.

22 G. Wekerle et al., *New Space for Women*, 1980; M. Luxton, *More than a Labour of Love*, 1980; W. Van Vliet, "Communities and Built Environments Supporting Women's Changing Roles," *Sociological Focus* 18,2 (1985): 73-7; S. Mackenzie, "Building Women, Building Cities: Toward Gender Sensitive Theory in the Environmental Disciplines" in *Life Spaces: Gender, Household, Employment*, eds. C. Andrew and B. Moore Milroy (Vancouver: UBC Press, 1988), pp. 13-30; J. Little et al., eds., *Women in Cities* 1988; P. Armstrong and H. Armstrong, *The Double Ghetto*, 1994.

23 M.K. Cichocki, "Women's Travel Patterns in a Suburban Development" in *New*

Space for Women, eds. G. Wekerle et al., 1980, 151-63; M. Ferrier, "Sexism in Australian Cities: Barriers to Employment Opportunities," *Women's Studies International Forum* 6,1 (1983): 73-84; F. Klowdawsky and A. Spector, "New Families, New Housing Needs, New Urban Environments: The Case of Single Parent Families" in *Life Spaces*, C. Andrew and B. Moore Milroy, 1988, 141-58; W. Michelson, "Divergent Convergence: The Daily Routines of Employed Spouses as a Public Affairs Agenda" in *Life Spaces*, eds. C. Andrew and B. Moore Milroy, 1988, 81-101.

24 W. Michelson, *From Sun to Sun: Daily Obligations and Community Structure in the Lives of Employed Women and Their Families* (Totowa, NJ: Rowman and Allanheld, 1985).

25 Quoted in L. Schneekloth, "Advances in Practice in Environment, Behaviour, and Design" in *Advances in Environment, Behaviour, and Design Vol 1*, eds. E.H. Zube and G.T. Moore, (New York: Plenum Press, 1987), p. 319. See M. Ritzdorf, "Zoning Ordinances Out of Touch with Changing American Demography," *Urban and Housing Research Report* 85,11 (1985a): 1; M. Ritzdorf, "Zoning Barriers to Housing Innovations," *Journal of Planning Education and Research* 4,3 (1985b): 171-84; and M. Ritzdorf, "Women and the City: Land Use and Zoning Issues," *Journal of Urban Resources* 3,2 (1986): 23-7.

26 See, for example, C. Moser, "Women, Human Settlements, and Housing: A Conceptual Framework for Analysis and Policy-Making" in *Women, Human Settlements and Housing*, C. Moser and L. Peake eds. (London: Tavistock Publications, 1987): 12-32.

27 D. Hayden, "What Would a Non-Sexist City Be Like?" 1980; M. Ritzdorf, "Women and the City" (1986).

28 D. Hayden, "What Would a Non-Sexist City Be Like?" 1980.

29 Health and Welfare Canada, *The Status of Day Care in Canada* (Ottawa: National Child Care Information Centre, 1991).

30 W. Michelson, "Divergent Convergence" 1988, p. 94.

31 J. Kaufman, "An Approach to Planning for Women" in *Planning, Women and Change*, eds. K. Hapgood and J. Getzels (Chicago: American Society of Planning Officials, 1974), 73-77; L. Sandercock and A. Forsyth, "Gender: A New Agenda for Planning Theory" (1990); B. Moore Milroy, "Taking Stock of Planning, Space and Gender" (1991); F. Klowdawsky and A. Spector, "New Families, New Housing Needs, New Urban Environments: The Case of Single Parent Families" in *Life Spaces: Gender, Household, Employment*, eds. C. Andrew and B. Moore Milroy,(Vancouver: UBC Press, 1988), 141-58.

32 For discussions of this point, see: J. Leavitt, "Feminist Advocacy Planning in the 1980s" in *Strategic Perspectives in Planning Practice*, ed. B. Checkoway (Lexington: Lexington Books, 1986) 181-93; C. Hjortland, A. Moflag, R. Skjerven, and A. Grimsrud, *Mobilizing Women in Local Planning and Decision-Making: A Guide to How and Why* (Oslo: Ministry of Foreign Affairs, 1991); B. Moore Milroy, "Taking Stock of Planning, Space and Gender" (1991).

33 See E. Frazer and N. Lacey, *The Politics of Community: A Feminist Critique of the Liberal-Communitarian Debate* (London: Harvester Wheatsheaf, 1993).

34 B. Moore Milroy, "Taking Stock of Planning, Space and Gender" (1991); L. Peattie, S. Cornell, and M. Rein, "Development Planning as the Only Game in Town," *Journal of Planning Education and Research* 5,1 (1986): 17-25.

35 Quoted in D. Piche, "Interacting with the Urban Environment: Two Case Studies of Women's and Female Adolescents' Leisure Activities" in *Life Spaces: Gender, Household, Employment*, eds. C. Andrew and B. Moore Milroy, (Vancouver: UBC Press, 1988), p. 170.

36 See, for example, M. Acklesberg, "Communities, Resistance, and Women's Activism: Some Implications for a Democratic Polity" in *Women and the Politics of Empowerment*, eds. A. Bookman and S. Morgan (Philadelphia: Temple University Press, 1988), pp. 297-313; L. Sandercock and A. Forsyth, "Gender: A New Agenda for Planning Theory" (1990); Moore Milroy, "Taking Stock of Planning, Space and Gender" (1991).

37 See, for example, D. Spender, *Man Made Language*, second edition (London: Routledge and Kegan Paul, 1985); and K. Ferguson, *The Feminist Case Against Bureaucracy* (Philadelphia: Temple University Press, 1984).

38 B. Moore Milroy, "Taking Stock of Planning, Space and Gender" (1991): 11.

39 L. Code, "Feminist Theory" in *Changing Patterns: Women in Canada*, eds. S. Burt, L. Code, and L. Dorney (Toronto: McClelland and Stewart, 1988); M. Acklesberg, "Communities, Resistance, and Women's Activism," 1988.

40 B. Moore Milroy, "Taking Stock of Planning, Space and Gender" (1991): 8.

41 For example, in Canadian cities such as Toronto, Ottawa, Winnipeg, and Montreal, safe city initiatives have been established to look at the problem of women's fear in public spaces. See C. Whitzman in this volume.

42 See, for example, K. Hapgood and J. Getzels (eds.), *Planning, Women and Change*, 1974; and J. Leavitt, "Feminist Advocacy Planning in the 1980s," 1986.

43 Women Plan Toronto is an example of such an organization. My master's thesis provides a case study of the group's work over a ten-year period: S. MacGregor, *Feminist Approaches to Planning Thought and Action: Practical Lessons from Women Plan Toronto*, unpublished thesis, School of Urban and Regional Planning, Queen's University, 1994. For a general discussion of feminist urban activism, see J. Gelb and M. Gittel, "Seeking Equality: The Role of Activist Women in Cities" in *The Egalitarian City: Issues of Rights, Distribution, and Access*, ed. J.K. Boles (New York: Praeger, 1986).

44 R. Beauregard, "Introduction" to "Planning Theories, Feminist Theories: A Symposium," *Planning Theory* 7,8 (1992): 9.

45 J. Friedmann, *Planning in the Public Domain: From Knowledge to Action* (Princeton: Princeton University Press, 1987), p. 416.

46 J. Leavitt, "Feminist Advocacy Planning in the 1980s," 1986; L. Sandercock and A. Forsyth, "Gender: A New Agenda for Planning Theory" (1990).

47 See, for example, M. Ritzdorf, "Feminist Thoughts on the Theory and Practice of Planning," *Planning Theory* 7,8 (1992): 13-19; H. Liggett, "Knowing Women/ Planning Theory" (1992); S. Fainstein, "Planning in a Different Voice," *Planning Theory* 7,8 (1992) 27-31; and L. Sandercock and A. Forsyth, "Feminist Theory and Planning Theory: Epistemological Linkages," *Planning Theory* 7,8 (1992) 45-9.

48 C. Gilligan, *In a Different Voice: Psychological Theory and Women's Development* (Cambridge: Harvard University Press, 1982).

49 M. Field Belenky, B. McVicker Clinchy, N. Rule Goldberger, and J. Mattuck Tarule, *Women's Ways of Knowing: Development of Self, Voice, and Mind* (New York: Basic Books, 1986).

50 E. Alexander, *Approaches to Planning: Introducing Current Planning Theories, Concepts, and Issues* (New York: Gordon and Breach Science Publishers, 1986), p. 12.

51 J. Birkeland, "An Ecofeminist Critique of Mainstream Planning," *The Trumpeter: Journal of Ecosophy* 8,2 (1991): 72-84; B. Moore Milroy, 1991; L. Sandercock and A. Forsyth, "Gender: a New Agenda for Planning" (1990), "Feminist Theory and Planning Theory" (1992).

52 See, for example, M. Waring, *If Women Counted: A New Feminist Economics* (San Francisco: Harper and Row, 1988).

53 S. Fainstein, "Planning in a Different Voice" (1992); B. Moore Milroy, "Taking Stock of Planning, Space and Gender" (1991).

54 For discussion of ecofeminism see: C. Merchant, *The Death of Nature: Women, Ecology, and the Scientific Revolution* (New York: Harper and Row, 1983); K. Warren, "The Power and Promise of Ecological Feminism," *Environmental Ethics* 12 (1990): 125-46; and M. Mies and V. Shiva, *Ecofeminism* (Halifax: Fernwood Publishing, 1993).

55 J. Birkeland, "An Ecofeminist Critique of Mainstream Planning" (1991): 73.

56 Ibid., 77.

57 See J. Jabanoski in this volume.

58 See, for example, C. Andrew and B. Moore Milroy, "Introduction" in *Life Spaces: Gender, Household, Employment*, eds. C. Andrew and B. Moore Milroy (Vancouver: UBC Press, 1988); M. Ritzdorf, "Feminist Thoughts on the Theory and Practice of Planning" (1992); S. Fainstein, "Planning in a Different Voice" (1992); L. Sandercock and A. Forsyth, "Gender: A New Agenda for Planning (1990), "Feminist Theory and Planning Theory (1992).

59 See, for example, M. Field Belenky, et al., *Women's Ways of Knowing*, 1986.

60 J. Braaten, "Towards a Feminist Reassessment of Intellectual Virtue," *Hypatia* 5,3 (1990): 8.

61 L. Sandercock and A. Forsyth, "Gender: A New Agenda for Planning" (1990), "Feminist Theory and Planning Theory" (1992); J. Friedmann, "Feminist and Planning Theories: The Epistemological Connection," *Planning Theory* 7/8 (1992): 40-3; S. Fainstein, "Planning in a Different Voice" (1992); and H. Liggett, "Knowing Women/Planning Theory (1992).

62 L. Sandercock and A. Forsyth, "Gender: A New Agenda for Planning" (1990), "Feminist Theory and Planning Theory" (1992).

63 L. Sandercock and A. Forsyth, "Feminist Theory and Planning Theory" (1992): 46.

64 R. Beauregard, "Introduction" (1992).

65 S. Fainstein, "Planning in a Different Voice" (1992).

66 Ibid., 31.

67 For a helpful discussion of the links between feminism and poststructuralism, see C. Weedon, *Feminist Practice and Poststructuralist Theory* (Oxford: Blackwell Publishers, 1987).

68 See, for example, L. Sandercock and A. Forsyth, "Gender: A New Agenda for Planning" (1990), "Feminist Theory and Planning Theory" (1992); and B. Moore Milroy, "Some Thoughts about Difference and Pluralism," *Planning Theory* 7/8 (1992): 33-8.

69 S. Harding, "The Instability of the Analytical Categories of Feminist Theory" in

Feminist Theory in Practice and Process, eds. M. Malson, J. O'Barr, S. Westphail-Wihl, and M. Wyer (Chicago: The University of Chicago Press, 1986), p. 16.

70 L. Sandercock and A. Forsyth, "Feminist Theory and Planning Theory" (1992): 47.

71 B. Moore Milroy, "Some Thoughts about Difference and Pluralism" (1992): 38.

72 J. Friedmann, "Educating the Next Generation of Planners," paper presented at the 34th Annual Association of Collegiate Schools of Planning (ACSP) Conference, Columbus, Ohio, (October 1992).

73 E. Ladner Birch, "From Civic Worker to City Planner: Women in Planning, 1880-1980" in *The American Planner: Biographies and Recollections*, ed. D.A. Krueckeberg (New York: Methuen Inc., 1983).

SEEKING SHELTER:
FEMINIST HOME TRUTHS

Sylvia Novac

HOUSING POLICIES may appear to be gender-neutral, but their effects are not. Broad patterns of social inequality are reflected and reinforced by policies that ignore or uphold structural and systemic dynamics of gender, "race,"[1] and class relations.[2] This is evident in recent research on gendered patterns of inequity in housing tenure, affordability, security, and control. Framing such inequities as a problem only of poverty detracts attention from questions of how male dominance and racism interact with the labour market (including immigration control) and the housing market to organize hierarchies of advantage within our housing system.

Policy context

Compared to other levels of government, it is federal policies that most powerfully affect the housing system. These policies (which include not only housing programs, but housing-related aspects of the tax system as well) have consistently supported market-driven development, provision, and allocation of housing,[3] with a residual allocation of non-profit housing programs to deal with some of the effects of obvious market failures. This means that the built form, location, and context for housing production is decided by market mechanisms, and that the ability to pay for available housing options largely determines housing status. For women, labour market position interacts with family status to account for notable differences in terms of housing tenure and affordability among women, and between women and men. Especially for the increasing number of sole-support women with low incomes, the availability, cost, location, physical condition, and social relations of housing provision are major determinants of their quality of life, independence and, as we used to call it, liberation.

Social rights and the welfare state

Ann Orloff has argued that along with access to paid work, women's capacity to form and maintain an autonomous household is a significant indicator of women's social rights of citizenship and of the emancipatory potential of the welfare state's provisions.[4] Women's subordination underpins the gendered politics of both intra-household relations and household formation. That is, there is a crucial dynamic between women's ability to sustain equitable relations within male-dominated households and their ability to establish a separate household. We can also frame this within Sylvia Walby's analysis of a historic move from private patriarchy (where the father/husband is the primary oppressor and beneficiary of the oppression of women) to public patriarchy (where women are subordinated within public arenas, e.g., by the state, employers, and property owners).[5] Throughout this century, women have struggled for increased access to employment to improve their economic independence, and also a welfare state that meets their needs, especially to guarantee assistance so that they can survive and support their children without having to marry, or stay married, to gain access to a male breadwinner's income. Access to housing that is affordable, suitable, and secure is a fundamental component of this independence.

Housing "the" family

As an analytical framework, women's capacity to form and maintain autonomous households is, to me, an intriguing one, for I have been exploring the interrelation between women's family status and housing position, and how women-headed households are disadvantaged. Inadvertently or otherwise, housing policy is family policy – for what does a house/*hold* if not a family?[6] Such thinking still dominates, despite the fact that, in 1991, almost a quarter of households in Canada had a single occupant.[7] This is the result of fewer and later marriages, more divorce, and increased longevity. In terms of household demographics, the single-person household is the fastest growing form, nearly tripling their numbers since 1971. And single-parent households more than doubled during that period, while the number of couples with children grew by less than a quarter.[8]

Not only do such demographic changes only slowly lead to new thinking about planning, but we must continue to adapt current with past decisions. The halcyon decade of the 1950s epitomized the "cult of domesticity" that extolled a suburban version of the nineteenth century North American ideal of a self-sufficient cottage/house set in a garden and inhabited by a Christian god-fearing father-dominated family with an angelic mother responsible for inspiring appropriate moral (including sexual) control.[9] Our society may have never come closer to emulating that model than when the post-World War Two industrial economy was booming and the dream of material wealth expansion was truly expected, if not realized, by much of the working class. The consequent sprawl of suburban growth was underwritten by a deplorable waste of resources. Dolores Hayden has carefully outlined how post-war development of suburban areas, predicated on the continued and unproblematic use of cheap fossil fuels and the production of domestic appliances, was based on strong government support for home-ownership, with zoning restrictions that both assumed and reinforced a "male breadwinner with housewife" family form.[10] Low density and single use neighbourhoods promoted the exclusion of "other" household types, either by legislative means or the straightforward "price-sorting" of the marketplace, combined with discriminatory practices by banks and property owners.[11]

This post-war era was also marked by the attempt to rationally or scientifically satisfy a residual housing need for poor and destitute households through the provision of large modern public housing projects, now avoided and dangerous "dead spots" in a city's fabric that are roundly pronounced planning failures. These soulless environments constitute our residual (last resort) housing sector and are increasingly home to female-headed, minority, and immigrant households.[12] They are modern poor-houses for women and children with no option but to live on the streets; many women living in them try desperately to get out. In the meantime, however, their lives are truncated by fear. Anti-social messages punctuate the carefully planned turf of projects like those concentrated in the Jane-Finch area of Toronto.

We can catch a glimpse of life in these projects from one woman's childhood memories of a particularly harrowing scene of imminent violence that has hardened her resentment against police who have harassed and assaulted her brothers on various occasions. Many Caribbean-

Canadians, like her, believe that their neighbourhood has been designed to maximize social control and that the police have brought more risk to their lives than protection.

> *There were about 5 undercover cops outside the door. I looked through the peephole, and they were standing there with their guns pulled. And I froze, I totally froze... I didn't know what to do. My sister was upstairs, and we had some friends over, and my brother wasn't there.... All I remember is them jumping over the balcony, there were about 10 of them, with machine guns – big rifles, like a real SWAT-team style. I stood there, and I started screaming.... From the time the police officers were coming through the back, the ones in the front pushed us out of the way.... And they came in, and they started searching all through the house.*

Heavy-handed policing has become the norm in neighbourhoods with concentrations of low-income, "black," female-headed households, making this form of state-subsidized housing an encampment of mistrust, racial tension, and fear that even taxi drivers avoid entering at night.

Women as "squatters" in housing literature

When, in 1984, Janet McClain and Cassie Doyle reviewed policy-directing housing reports and government documents from the previous fifteen years, they found almost no reference at all to women.[13] Households were taken to be homogeneous entities of consensual relations, designated simply as family or non-family; women were rarely mentioned, except to note their prevalence as consumers of public housing, although there has been no investigation of the reasons for this, or their predominance in the rental sector as a whole.

What are the implications of women's invisibility in housing policy? For one, women's views of security which incorporate the gendered realities of woman abuse have no profile. For another, statistical data on women's housing conditions has not been available in published form as they are, for instance, on women's labour market status. Clearly, women's housing issues are assumed to be addressed in the emphasis on housing families. In fact, women have obtained access to housing largely on the basis of their familial roles as wives and mothers, so that housing access and security for women has been tied to marital relations with men and to their work in the unpaid domestic economy. These assumptions have led to some largely unexamined situations. For instance, until 1988, Canadian women who met the residency requirement in Ontario were eligible for public housing only as mothers of dependent children (and as people who were elderly or had disabilities). Further, as the term "Canadian" implies, women without Canadian citizenship or landed immigrant status were ineligible on any basis until 1991, and refugees without status remain excluded.

Gender and housing status

The discovery by McClain and Doyle, that the silence on gender extended to the availability of any published statistics on the basis of sex, motivated them to dig up and analyze the available raw data themselves. They demonstrated that women's lower incomes are reflected in their housing tenure profile, such that women-headed households are largely renters and, regardless of tenure, pay a much higher proportion of their income on housing costs than male-headed households. Even women who own their own house tend to have less available income to support themselves, so that more women than men homeowners rely on government transfer payments and pension funds to pay their mortgage and other housing costs.[14] Older women's capacity to maintain their homes as they age is still a largely unassessed housing issue.

There are several factors that account for women's disadvantaged housing status:

1) their positions in a segmented labour market (shaped by sexism and racism); 2) their positions in families with unequal divisions of labour and power, including responsibility for the care of other family members; and 3) widespread discriminatory practices, along with harassment and woman abuse.

The proportion of women among Canada's poor has not changed since 1975; it remains at about 60 per cent, despite the increase in women's labour force participation (which is in part due to higher housing costs).[15] The National Council of Welfare attributes women's higher risk of poverty to childcare responsibilities, labour market inequities, marriage breakdown, and widowhood. In other words, women are at a disadvantage in the market of paid labourers, and their material support as family workers is contingent on access to their husband's income. Since this family exchange usually vanishes when husbands leave or die, women who spend many years raising children and doing unpaid work in the home are at a high risk of living in poverty. In fact, the poverty rate for female heads of single-parent families in Canada is 58 per cent.[16] In poor households, shelter costs are usually given the highest priority, so that there are inadequate funds for other essentials, such as transportation, clothing, and even food. Thus, the now commonplace food banks have become a necessity for some women living in urba areas with high housing costs.[17]

An understanding of women's housing conditions requires analysis of how male dominance shapes our domestic relations and the setting for those relations – the private home. Family structure plays a strong role in determining women's housing status. For women living in the Toronto area, a study of gender, family, and housing status found that almost three-quarters of women with male partners (73 per cent) are homeowners, compared to about a quarter (28 per cent) of single women, and less than half (44 per cent) of single mothers.[18] The presence of a male partner affected not only housing tenure, but also affordability. Among homeowners, 10 per cent of women with male partners have affordability problems, compared to 20 per cent of single mothers and 29 per cent of single women. For those renting, the situation is worse for women in general, but the family status pattern holds: 21 per cent of married women have affordability problems, compared to 44 per cent of female-headed households (both single mothers and single women).[19]

As Morris and Winn have pointed out, a housing policy that encourages home-ownership assumes that households will have a full-time (male) wage-earner with an uninterrupted working career.[20] The pattern of gendered housing inequality found in Canada is common in the advanced capitalist countries. Even in Australia, where housing policy is being used as a vehicle for deliberate wealth redistribution, the actual impact on women-headed households demonstrates a similar pattern of disadvantage for single mothers, particularly those in the private rental sector.[21]

Over the last decade, since McClain and Doyle's first analysis, this situation has not changed. Among renters in 1991, female-headed households were still at great risk of being in housing need, based primarily on affordability difficulties,[22] although since 1986 slightly more single women have become homeowners.[23] The small increase in single female homeowners may reflect a higher proportion of elderly women living alone in houses they have inherited.

Although most single men also rent, they are far less likely than female-headed households to experience affordability problems, regardless of tenure. Also, the likelihood of home-ownership is less for racial minority households, yet the gendered pattern still holds, so that 64 per cent of racial minority wives are homeowners, compared to 34 per cent of single mothers, and 21 per cent of single women.[24]

There has been almost no research on the effects of racism on housing status and conditions in Canada,[25] not even on the deplorable situation for First Nations peoples, both on reserves and in urban areas. The analysis that is available ignores gender. In fact, the frequency of affordability problems is extremely high for female-headed households, regardless of whether they are racial majority or minority, immigrant or Canadian-born, although many immigrant and racial minority women also face complex problems of settlement and racism.[26]

Cycles of family status

To some extent, there is a life-cycle progression operating across these family and household statuses. Most of the women who are single parents were once married and, as they get older, the vast majority of women end up living alone. McClain and Doyle found that women's home-ownership rate doubles after age sixty-five.[27] This suggests that women do not obtain this tenure form on the basis of their own earnings, but via their family status through inheritance. Older women homeowners are also far less likely to have mortgages – even if inherited, the very low income of many older women makes it difficult for them to retain a mortgaged property. Women over sixty-five years of age are also more likely to be living in older housing stock with high maintenance needs. This is an additional burden, especially for disabled or frail women, which frustrates the desires of many older women to age-in-place and avoid institutional care.

These analyses of women's family or household status and housing tenure make it clear that women's home-ownership is related to their family status. As young wives, they are quite likely to be owner-occupiers, a tenure that they are unlikely to sustain should they divorce. Despite changes, ostensibly more favourable to women, in divorce and family law relating to division of property, they are unlikely to retain ownership of the family house: in one study, only 29 per cent of women kept the marital home upon divorce.[28]

The family home

Men dominate housing policy and planning decision-making, not only in their persons, but in a way of thinking about housing that is profoundly shaped by the ideological foundations of traditional patriarchal thought: women are sequestered at home, there is a gendered division of labour, household equals family, and "the" family is male-dominant. From this flows the strong association between "home" and women, an association that reinforces the secondary status of women's public roles.

Such a family structure has been built into our housing, community, and urban structures, not only conceptually, but materially and by design. One example of this is the use of exclusionary zoning mechanisms that have operated (with the effect, if not the intention) to exclude from designated neighbourhoods low-income and non-nuclear family households. As a result, separated and divorced women, for instance, are unable to cover housing costs by living with non-family members or subdividing their houses to create a separate housing unit.

Dominant views of "the" family have been subjected to feminist critiques, the implications of which have not yet been integrated in housing research and policy frameworks whose assumptions about rational and harmonious intra-household relations belie the actual politics of family and private life. The problem of domestic violence against women and children raises a crucial question: for whom is home a safe haven? And the view that women labour in the home out of "love" privatizes not only the politics of familial relationships, but also the political economy of childrearing, food preparation, personal care, laundry – in short, the reproduction of life in broad terms. Feminists have long been aware that home is a site in which a great deal of valuable and necessary work is accomplished by women, and that the neighbourhood and community context greatly affects women's ability to access services, employment opportunities, and social support.[29] Black feminists have also stressed home as a site for resistance to the racist hegemony of a "white"-dominated society.[30]

Feminists have critiqued the assumption of consensual family relations and pointed to the differential distribution of power and benefits within households, and the inherent conflict and violence that ensues. The literature on household decision-making has not been integrated with the literature on violence against women and children; we lack empirical research on social relations within households that connect issues of power and control of quality of life. The lack of affordable and appropriate housing alternatives is a major factor keeping women (and other dependents) in abusive relationships with men where at least they have a roof over their heads.[31] This explains, in part, why so many women who enter shelters for abused women later return to their abusive partners.

The economic consequences of divorce are such that, on average, men's standard of living improves slightly and that of women and children plummets. Finnie's major longitudinal study demonstrates that women's incomes (adjusted for family size) drop over 40 per cent after divorce, while men's incomes rise slightly. More importantly, he concludes that "women who face the greatest impoverishment upon divorce are less likely to split," meaning that the negative effects of divorce are underestimated in his study.[32] This suggests that poor and working-class women are more likely to put up with unsatisfactory relationships with male partners to sustain their relative economic security. The combination of responsibility for children, poverty, and the lack of affordable housing almost seals the choice for many women. Gendered relations of power may override even the benefits of shared residential property ownership for women whose personal safety is threatened by controlling or abusive male partners. While men's homelessness is attributed primarily to unemployment, for women it is more likely to be family breakdown, and abuse by a husband or father.[33] The difficulty of finding alternative housing has been portrayed as "one of the solid walls of the little family prison."[34]

The security of home

Popular imagery of house and home is replete with assumptions of personal sovereignty, at least for men (e.g., "a man's home is his castle"), while women are associated with a consoling sanctuary, in opposition to the dangers of the public sphere. The sanguine reality is that one in six women have reported violence by their current spouse; and one in two have reported violence by a former spouse.[35]

Home is usually assumed to be the site for maximal personal control and security, but for many women that control and security is severely diminished by interpersonal violence. Recent indications of the prevalence of sexual harassment of tenants, and female tenants' fears suggest how women's autonomy is curtailed, not only by men with whom they are intimate, but also by housing gatekeepers and neighbouring tenants. The actual degree to which women's housing options are limited by these experiences has yet to be fully acknowledged, never mind measured.

In an investigation of how women understand and describe their experiences of sexual violence, Liz Kelly found that coercive relations were frequently taken for granted when women had little choice or were making the best of their options.

> *When I was living with Mark, I'd come home from work and I'd be shattered. I'd just want to go to bed and sleep. He'd start cuddling up and touching me and I'd think "oh here we go again". It was like a duty, that was sort of paying the rent. I had a roof over my head and that was what I was expected to pay.*[36]

Women live with contradictions between personal safety and housing security. Their greater fear of crime and violence "out there" tends to strengthen the association of home privacy with safety. Women tend to restrict their activities, for instance, by staying home and by avoiding going out alone at night because of their fears, yet violence against women occurs primarily in the home, and is a factor contributing to women's homelessness.[37]

For low-income women, finding alternate housing means dealing with discrimination and even harassment in the rental housing market. There is little public acknowledgement of these practices against women. For instance, the problem of sexual harassment of tenants (by "landlords," to use the legal term, their agents, and neighbouring tenants) is one which women deal with in personal isolation.[38]

Restricting women's access

Although the private rental sector is the primary source of housing for women-headed households, we have little systematic Canadian data on how women are treated by private property owners and their agents. Several women's groups active in the Toronto area have reported incidents of property-owner discrimination and abusive control of women tenants. Some property owners do not consider sole-support women desirable tenants because they have low incomes, because they have children, or because they receive social assistance. Perhaps because they face this more often, or are motivated by desperation and anger at their limited housing options, further curtailed by gatekeepers who are determined to "cream" for the most profitable and compliant tenants,[39] women are more likely than men to fight back against housing discrimination and to lay formal complaints.[40]

Housing discrimination was reported by half of the respondents to a survey of female tenants undertaken by a women's community group in the city of Montreal,[41] and by almost a third of respondents to an Ontario survey.[42] Property owners discriminate for a variety of reasons, some of which are not immediately evident. In the course of many housing searches, one woman reported experiences of discrimination on the basis of her youth, the source of her income, being a single mother, and having no credit history. These reasons were more or less explicitly revealed by the private sector housing gatekeepers. What was not so explicitly expressed was racist discrimination. This incident shows how it commonly occurs:

> *I spoke to the man on the phone, and he seemed very nice. I explained my situation – I was a young mother, and I said I was on welfare, and she would be going to daycare and I would be going to a course or something. It was fine, great, and he sounded really positive. I got out there and he looked at me like he was dumbfounded. I thought after, the way he kept looking at me, it's because of the colour of my skin, it's because I'm black.... I asked to see the place. He said, 'Well, I'm kinda in a hurry now,' after I already made the appointment, so of course it was because of my skin colour. It was a race issue.... I was really upset.*[43]

Not only does discrimination limit women's housing options, it can escalate to include harassment.

Harassment and sexual harassment

Almost half of the Montreal study respondents said they had experienced some form of harassment, usually by the property owner or an agent, taking a variety of forms. A quarter of the women reported unscheduled visits when they were absent or without adequate notice; a quarter also reported prying questions and comments about their personal life; insults and verbal abuse were reported by a tenth; 9 per cent reported eviction threats; and 7 per cent reported threats to cut services and refusals to make urgently needed repairs.[44] A quarter of the Ontario survey respondents also reported harassment by property owners or their agents, and 16 per cent were harassed during their housing searches.[45]

There are indications that tenants are susceptible to harassment from property owners who plan conversion or major renovations, or because they are actively organizing within the building.[46] In the case of women organizers, the harassment can be sexually explicit,[47] demonstrating how sexual harassment is part of a struggle for power and control.

Experiences of explicitly sexual harassment were reported by 12 per cent of the women in the Montreal study. In the Ontario study, which focused on this problem, 25 per cent of respondents reported such harassment, yet very few formal human rights complaints are laid on these grounds. Like the findings in workplace settings, more severe forms of sexual harassment, like sexual assault, occur least frequently (2.5 per cent of all respondents), while less severe forms, like degrading remarks, occur most frequently (18 per cent). Five per cent of female tenants have experienced classic quid pro quo sexual harassment, i.e., sexual bribery.[48]

Some women believe that the increasing number of female households necessitates adjustments to property owners' expectations that a man will sign the lease and pay the rent. The expectation of female economic subordination within the household is extended so far by some property owners that it violates women's autonomy and privacy.

If you're working, at least you should be able to go pay your rent without the landlord giving you a hassle. And some landlords – because they know you're single – they want to come into your apartment just about any old time. That's out of order.[49]

Illegal entry by property owners and superintendents was reported by 29 per cent of women, and is frequently coincident with attempts to sexually harass.

Clearly, sexual harassment detracts from women's housing security; it also affects their housing choices. A leering male superintendent will prompt a woman to look elsewhere, but so may a building's design, such as a poorly lit, isolated laundry room. One woman commented on the greater opportunity for men to harass women in confined spaces that foster proximity with strangers, relative anonymity, and no surveillance. Because of this, she avoids living in buildings with elevators, despite the limits this places on an already difficult housing search.

They won't rent to you because you're a woman.... I've got four boys, and I have to have some place to live. As a matter of fact, I'm looking for somewhere to live. And, Lord help me find somewhere without an apartment [building], because I don't like living in an apartment. Because when you're a woman, you go up on the elevator – guy sees you, and wants to come and pinch your bum.[50]

Previous experiences of abuse increase women's anticipation and fear, not only when going out, but also when home alone.[51]

Tenant concerns

Women are more concerned than men about some, but not all, potential sources of danger. Among low-income tenants living in municipal non-profit housing in Toronto, there were no significant gender differences in responses to the following concerns: vandalism, building security, pet/animal control, racial problems, youth/teens, loitering residents, and loitering strangers. Yet there were gender differences in responses to the potential of verbal assault, physical assault, sexual harassment, and family violence. Concerns about drug and alcohol use were also greater among women, possibly because alcohol and drugs are frequently used by aggressors to justify and accompany acts of violence against women. Women living in poverty (categorized by their receipt of a housing subsidy) also reported higher levels of concern in general.[52] When women feel vulnerable, it is not because they are feminine wimps; their fear is grounded in experience and knowledge of the potential for abuse, and abuse with impunity.

Discussion

All of the issues raised have the greatest impact on poor and working-class women with attendant implications for what Orloff calls the state-market-family relations dimension. For the welfare state to alter gender relations requires at least the adequate provision of social housing. Not the residual form we have in large public housing projects, but a non-profit housing sector for an income mix of residents, not just the most needy or "deserving." Orloff suggests that the state must do more by compensating women also for marriage failures and raising children alone.

According to Orloff, the capacity to form and maintain an autonomous household, along with access to paid work, is the appropriate basis for eliminating the compulsion to enter or stay in marriages in order to obtain economic support, and parallels (historically, male) workers' demands for jobs through full employment and active labour market policies. Development of this analysis and strategy will require a full review of family and tax legislation, a variety of social assistance programs, and an explicit focus on adequate housing provision, rather than continued favour for a market housing system as is currently the case in Canadian government policies.[53]

Strategies for change

Needless to say, many women have not had to wait for the results of research to understand their own position within the housing system, nor are they holding their breath waiting for government intervention. Their efforts to promote change are extensive and vary from highly specific policy initiatives to comprehensive development of housing projects. I will briefly refer here to a few examples of political housing action.

Advocates with the battered women's movement in Ontario have lobbied effectively for specific policy changes designed to assist women in crisis due to male violence. The realization of a priority placement within public housing is one of their successes. Since 1986, the Ontario Ministry of Housing has maintained a policy of special priority for assaulted women that allows women whose safety is in jeopardy from an abusive partner to jump the queue of public housing applicants,[54] shortening the wait from several years to several months. A monitoring system and evaluation of the policy's effectiveness is in place internally, but the results are not made publicly available. And there are obvious limitations to a remedy that waits for criminal assaults to occur.

Women abused by male intimates usually lose their housing and have to move. Concerned members of a housing co-operative drafted a corporate by-law that allows a victimized member to evict an abusive spouse and keep her home, thereby declaring itself the first domestic violence-free zone in Canada.[55] A resolution encouraging all co-operatives to declare themselves domestic violence-free zones was overwhelmingly approved by the national federation a year later, and since then many individual co-operatives have adopted such a by-law. Some are undertaking additional efforts, such as community education and the provision of safe houses.[56] The by-law mechanism (which deals with eviction of an abusive spouse, emergency subsidy, and referrals to existing community supports) requires that a board of directors consider evidence that there is abuse and act on it. It remains to be seen whether this policy will accommodate the complex family dynamics of wife or child assault and be carried out justly, but it is encouraging to note the potential for an effective community response that may better protect women's housing security and mitigate their dependence on abusive partners. Only the existence of collectively-managed housing makes this kind of response even possible. It is likely that the popular education and consciousness-raising that accompanies such a by-law will have as much impact as the eviction provision.

Some women have also taken another approach which is more holistic and separatist. In Canada and Australia,[57] advocates, activists, service providers, and consumers have become housing developers, using state funding for community-based housing development designed and controlled by women residents. There has been tremendous growth in the number of such projects in Canada; there are now close to one hundred. What distinguishes them, besides the emphasis on women's control and the provision of subsidy, is their efforts to develop supportive community, either as post-crisis transitional or permanent housing, and their responsive diversity. There are projects designed for teenage mothers, single mothers, Aboriginal women, and immigrant and racial minority women; housing co-operatives have been developed by and for lesbian women and women over forty.[58]

These projects represent significant feminist spatial claims on the urban landscape, where the commodification of housing is bent to the desires of women with modest incomes. Women's interpretation of housing security goes well beyond the legislated codes in "landlord" and tenant law. Financial support is necessary to bridge the gap between women's earning power and housing costs, as women householders are highly susceptible to displacement and economic eviction; management control allows for more innovative ways to prevent sexual discrimination and harassment; and design input makes it possible to better match needs to unit layout (e.g., large kitchens to accommodate more than one worker, foster social connection, and allow for the supervision of children) and territorial control between the project and the neighbourhood (gates, signs, fences, and other markers), and between personal and public spaces (solid locks on doors and windows, off-grade building openings, communication mechanisms for entry control).

The demand for affordable urban housing is compatible with both the needs of low-income women and the objectives fostered by increased environmental awareness: an energy- and resource-efficient design addresses both. Multi-unit buildings and smaller unit size reduce land and infrastructure costs; however, the conservation of natural resources must not become another excuse to force poor and working-class people into smaller and less marketable sites (usually due to inconvenient locations or health hazards).[59] There are many ways in which construction costs can be reduced and energy efficiency increased,[60] but rigid government restrictions for "modest" housing projects have already blocked women's ability to realize their plans for integral community and economic activities, such as collective childcare and the development of businesses and employment, due to the lack of office space, meeting space and collective space.[61]

Co-operatives house a higher proportion of female-headed, racial minority, and immigrant households than exists in the general population.[62] And, there are signs that they have already adopted "green" thinking. This becomes more feasible when residents can control the building design and pool their efforts to reduce, reuse, and recycle. If we can adjust housing programs and policies to more equitably distribute the country's housing assets, and allow people with low-incomes control over their own living environments, both feminists and environmentalists will stand a better chance of altering housing inequities and wasteful ecological practices.

Notes

1 By the use of quotation marks, I want to indicate the dilemma of referring to the real and material results of racism while discrediting the socially constructed, but scientifically invalid, notion of "races" of people except as a mechanism for creating and sustaining inequality. See Robert Miles, *Racism* (London: Routledge, 1989).

2 See David Clapham, Peter Kemp, and Susan J. Smith, *Housing and Social Policy* (London: Macmillan Education, 1990); Moira Munro and Susan J. Smith, "Gender and Housing: Broadening the Debate," *Housing Studies* 4 (1989); Susan Smith, "Income, Housing Wealth and Gender Inequality," *Urban Studies* 27 (1990); Fran Klodawsky, Aron Spector, and Damaris Rose, *Single Parent Families and Canadian Housing Policies: How Mothers Lose* (Ottawa: Canada Mortgage and Housing Corporation, 1985); and Jenny Morris and Martin Winn, *Housing and Social Inequality* (London: Hilary Shipman, 1990).

3 John Bacher, *Keeping to the Marketplace: The Evolution of Canadian Housing Policy* (Montreal: McGill-Queen's University Press, 1993).

4 Ann Shola Orloff, "Gender and the Social Rights of Citizenship: The Comparative Analysis of Gender Relations and Welfare States," *American Sociological Review* 58 (1993): 303-27.

5 See Sylvia Walby, *Theorizing Patriarchy* (Oxford: Basil Blackwell, 1990), p. 178, where she states:

> In private patriarchy it is a man in his position as husband or father who is the direct oppressor and beneficiary, individually and directly, of the subordination of women. This does not mean that household production is the sole patriarchal structure. Indeed it is importantly maintained by the active exclusion of women from public arenas by other structures. The exclusion of women from these other spheres could not be perpetuated without patriarchal activity at these levels.
>
> Public patriarchy is a form in which women have access to both public and private arenas. They are not barred from the public arenas, but are nonetheless subordinated within them. The expropriation of women is performed more collectively than by individual patriarchs. The household may remain a site of patriarchal oppression, but it is no longer the main place where women are present.

6 For more on housing policy as family policy, see Gillian Pascall, *Social Policy: A Feminist Analysis* (London: Tavistock Publications, 1986), p. 132; and Sylvia Novac, "Not Seen, Not Heard: Women and Housing Policy," *Canadian Woman Studies* 11 (1990): 53-7.

7 Statistics Canada, *Housing Costs and Other Characteristics of Canadian Households* (Ottawa: Minister of Industry, Science and Technology, 1993), p. 8.

8 Canada Mortgage and Housing Corporation, *Changing Canadian Households, 1971-91*, Issue 14 (Ottawa: Research and Development Highlights, March 1994).

9 Clifford E. Clark, Jr., *The American Family Home, 1800-1960* (Chapel Hill: The University of North Carolina Press, 1986).

10 Dolores Hayden, *Redesigning the American Dream: The Future of Housing, Work, and Family Life* (New York: W.W. Norton, 1984).

11 Jane Jacobs uses the term price-sorting to refer to the segregation of households according to their income levels and housing costs.

12 Robert Murdie, *Social Housing in Transition: The Changing Social Composition of Public Sector Housing in Metropolitan Toronto* (Ottawa: Canada Mortgage and Housing Corporation, 1992).

13 Janet McClain and Cassie Doyle, *Women and Housing: Changing Needs and the Failure of Policy* (Ottawa: Canadian Council on Social Development and Lorimer, 1984), p. 10.

14 Ibid., p. 12.

15 National Council of Welfare, *Women and Poverty Revisited* (Ottawa: Minister of Supply and Services, 1990), p. 1.

16 National Council of Welfare, *Poverty Profile 1992* (Ottawa: Minister of Supply and Services Canada, 1994) p. 30.

17 See Connie Guberman in this volume.

18 Gerda Wekerle and Sylvia Novac, *Gender and Housing in Toronto* (Toronto: Equal Opportunity Division, Institute on Women and Work, 1991).

19 The threshold for housing affordability was based on the conventional standard of paying less than 30 per cent of household income on housing.

20 Morris and Winn, *Housing and Social Inequality*, 1990, p. 149.

21 Smith, "Income, Housing Wealth and Gender Inequality" (1990).

22 Canada Mortgage and Housing Corporation, *Low Income, Labour Force Participation and Women in Housing Need, 1991*, Research and Development Highlights, Issue 16 (Ottawa: Canada Mortgage and Housing Corporation, 1994), p. 2.

23 Sylvia Novac and Associates, *A Place To Call One's Own: New Voices of Dislocation and Dispossession* (Ottawa: Advisory Council on the Status of Women, forthcoming).

24 Ibid. The designation of racial minority used for this analysis is based on the Statistics Canada variable "visible minority," the definition of which is drawn from Employment and Immigration Canada (this includes ten groups: Black, Indo-Pakistani, Chinese, Korean, Japanese, South East Asian, Filipino, Other Pacific Islanders, West Asian and Arab, and Latin American. It does not include Aboriginal peoples).

25 See Frances Henry, *Housing And Racial Discrimination in Canada: A Preliminary Assessment of Current Initiatives and Information* (Toronto: Equal Opportunity Consultants, August 1989); and David Hulchanski, "Barriers to Equal Access in the Housing Market: The Role of Discrimination on the Basis of Race and Gender," (A Report Prepared for the Ontario Human Rights Commission, June 1993).

26 Sylvia Novac and Associates, *A Place To Call One's Own*, forthcoming.

27 McClain and Doyle, *Women and Housing*, 1984, p. 16.

28 Dana Stewart and Freda Steel, *The Economic Consequences of Divorce on Families Owning A Marital Home* (Ottawa: Canada Mortgage and Housing Corporation, 1990).

29 Dolores Hayden, *Redesigning the American Dream*, 1984; and Caroline Andrew and Beth Moore Milroy, *Life Spaces: Gender, Household, Employment* (Vancouver: UBC Press, 1988).

30 bell hooks, *Yearning: Race, Gender, and Cultural Politics* (Toronto: Between the Lines, 1990), pp. 41-9.

31 The Ontario Association of Interval and Transition Houses, "Balance the Power: Background Report, Annual Lobby," unpublished report (November, 1990), p. 28.

32 Ross Finnie, "Women, Men, and the Economic Consequences of Divorce: Evidence from Canadian Longitudinal Data," *The Canadian Review of Sociology and Anthropology* 30 (May 1993): 228.

33 Stephanie Golden, *The Women Outside: Meanings and Myths of Homelessness* (Berkeley: University of California Press, 1992), p. 159; and Elliot Liebow, *Tell Them Who I Am: The Lives of Homeless Women* (New York: The Free Press, 1993).

34 Michèle Barrett and Mary McIntosh, *The Anti-Social Family* (London: Verso, 1982), p. 57.

35 Statistics Canada, "The Violence Against Women Survey," *The Daily* (18 November, 1993).

36 Quote from research participant cited in Liz Kelly, *Surviving Sexual Violence* (Minneapolis: University of Minnesota Press, 1988), p. 110.

37 Sophie Watson with Helen Austerberry, *Housing and Homelessness: A Feminist Perspective* (London: Routledge & Kegan Paul, 1986).

38 Sylvia Novac and Associates, *The Security of Her Person: Tenants' Experiences of Sexual Harassment* (Toronto: Ontario Women's Directorate, 1994).

39 W. T. Stanbury and John D. Todd, "Landlords as Economic Prisoners of War," *Canadian Public Policy* (1990) pp. 399-417.

40 Gerda Wekerle and Sylvia Novac, *Gender and Housing in Toronto* (Toronto: City of Toronto, Equal Opportunity Division, 1991), pp. 38-9.

41 Comité Logement Rosemont, *Discrimination, Harcèlement et Harcèlement Sexuel*, (Montréal: Front d'Action populaire en réaménagement urbain, Avril 1986).

42 Sylvia Novac and Associates, *The Security of Her Person*, 1994.

43 Sylvia Novac and Associates, *A Place to Call One's Own*, forthcoming.

44 Comité Logement Rosemont, *Discrimination, Harcèlement et Harcèlement Sexuel*, 1986.

45 Sylvia Novac and Associates, *The Security of Her Person*, 1994, 115.

46 Social Planning Council of Metropolitan Toronto, *Losing a Home: Experiences Under Ontario's Rental Housing Protection Act* (Toronto: Federation of Metro Tenants' Associations, 1988).

47 Sylvia Novac and Associates, *The Security of Her Person*, 1994.

48 Ibid., 115.

49 Ibid.

50 Ibid., 67.

51 Statistics Canada, *Violence Against Women Survey*, 1993, p. 9.

52 Wekerle and Novac, *Gender and Housing in Toronto*, 1991, p. 43-4.

53 Orloff, "Gender and the Social Rights of Citizenship" (1993): 319.

54 Ministry of Housing of the Province of Ontario, *Special Priority Policy for Assaulted Women: New Revised Guidelines and Implementation Strategies* (Toronto: Tenant Support Services, Ministry of Housing, 1990).

55 Howard Goldenthal, "Declaration Makes Co-op Violence-Free," *Now* (22-8 November 1990): 27.

56 Co-operative Housing Federation of Canada, "Members To Take On Domestic

Violence," *Co-opservations* (September 1991): 5; "Oak Street Co-op Takes Action Against Domestic Violence" *The Circuit* 14 (Summer 1992): 1; and Julie Cool, "Co-ops: Creating Violence-free Communities," *Vis-A-Vis: A National Newsletter on Family Violence* 12 (Fall 1994): 1,4.

57 Sophie Watson, *Playing the State: Australian Feminist Interventions* (London: Verso, 1990), p. 18.

58 See Gerda Wekerle and Sylvia Novac, "Developing Two Women's Housing Cooperatives," in *New Households, New Housing* eds. Karen Franck and Sherry Ahrentzen (New York: Van Nostrand Reinhold), 1989; and Gerda Wekerle, "Responding to diversity: housing developed by and for women," in *Shelter, Women and Development: First and Third World Perspectives*, ed. Hemalata Dandekar (Ann Arbor, MI: George Wahr Publishing, 1993), pp. 178-86.

59 See Jeanne Jabanowski in this volume.

60 See Canada Mortgage and Housing Corporation, *Sustainable Residential Developments: Planning, Design and Construction Principles (Greening the "Grow Home")*, Research and Development Highlights, Issue 15 (Ottawa: Canada Mortgage and Housing Corporation, July 1994).

61 Wekerle and Novac, "Developing Two Women's Housing Co-operatives," 1989, pp. 223-42.

62 Mary Anne Burke, "People in Co-operative Housing," *Canadian Social Trends* (Autumn 1990): 27-31.

AT RISK:
THE PERSON BEHIND
THE ASSUMPTIONS

Planning to Protect
Human Health

Jeanne Jabanoski

THE ORIGINS of this chapter are rooted in my discovery a few years ago that as a woman I was not one of the people who was being "protected" in health risk assessments. I was not assured when I was told that in some planning decisions women are considered a sensitive "sub-population." When I discovered that these decisions also exclude a number of other people, I began to wonder whose health was being "protected" and how these decisions were being made. This chapter is my attempt to begin to answer those questions.

Whose risk? Whose benefit?

In the planning of our communities, whether for housing, parks, or transportation, environmental health questions enter into our decisions. These questions are often raised in a context that is specific to a site or project, to determine whether the development will have an adverse impact on human health and the environment. But such questions are usually raised after the project plan has been developed to the point where modifications would be difficult and expensive. They are rarely raised at the beginning or asked in the affirmative to consider how a development could improve human health and the environment. One of the principal ways in which planners and other officials attempt to answer these questions is by assessing the health impact of environmental factors, such as soil contamination or air quality, to determine whether they fall within current Canadian guidelines. These guidelines are based on scientific information culled from a range of sources. The information is used in health risk assessment (as well as other terms for similar processes such as ecological risk assessment, quantitative risk assessment, etc.) which purports to determine the point at which a particular contaminant might pose a risk to human health.

Within the literature that provides a running critique of the assumptions, methodology, and findings of health risk assessment, a central criticism is that the "universal person" who is being "protected" is a healthy male of 150 pounds with a life span of seventy-three years. While there is a growing awareness that this assumption leaves out a large portion of the population, including women, children, seniors, and people with disabilities, this oversight is often addressed by the consideration of these sectors as special groups. This usually occurs in relation to specific sites with a proposed use such as a daycare, or in the case of specific contaminants, such as lead with its documented impact on the health of children. Members of these groups are rarely considered the "universal person" that these guidelines are intended to protect.

This and other shortcomings of health risk assessment call into question the usefulness of depending on the guidelines intended to ensure that a project does not have a negative impact on people and the environment. The deficiencies also expose the way in which one form of specialized and quantified knowledge has achieved dominance in decision-making over other forms of knowledge. Furthermore, one must question whether establishing levels of "acceptable risk" to the environment or human health will help us achieve an ecologically sustainable city.

In this chapter I consider some feminist critiques of the assumptions and limitations of science, particularly as the basis for environmental health and planning considerations. I review the critical literature that deals with health risk assessment to determine the usefulness of this method and whether it could be made more effective by recalibrating some of its basic assumptions. Some principles and practices that could make environmental health planning a more integrated process that protects human health are also explored.

Science through a feminist lens

Feminist critics have posed a strong challenge to the dominance of the natural or physical sciences. Carolyn Merchant was one of the earliest feminist theorists to consider the social construction of science and its connection to environmental issues. She lays many of the ecological and social problems we face today at the feet of a science which allows us to gather ever-increasing information about the parts of everything but fails to connect these parts to each other, or say anything meaningful about the whole ecosystem.[1]

Merchant makes the point that women have been seen as both historically and socially connected to nature. While not accepting that connection as a given, she maintains that it has been possible for a mechanistic science, derived from these gendered constructions, to reinforce the domination of both nature and women.[2] Vandana Shiva blames mechanistic science for international "maldevelopment" and claims that Third World women and "tribals" have a special relationship with nature. She argues for a people's knowledge that will dislodge the dominant scientific paradigm.[3]

Other theorists, such as Margrit Eichler and Joni Seager, dispute the assumption that women have a special relationship with nature. As Seager points out, "not all women are naturally equity seeking and life enhancing, nor can it be assumed that they would be so if removed from the constraints of patriarchy. Men may treat nature as a woman and a woman as nature, but this does not mean that all women actually experience a closeness to nature."[4]

One of the central points of the feminist critique of science is that it has been produced largely by white, middle-class men.[5] As Sandra Harding points out, an outcome of this has been that

...what we took to be humanly inclusive problematics, concepts, theories, objective methodologies, and transcendental truths are in fact far less than that. Instead, these products of thought bear the mark of their collective and individual creators, and the creators in turn have been distinctively marked as to gender, class, race and culture.[6]

On the other hand, just ensuring that more women enter the physical sciences would not necessarily result in a more emancipatory kind of knowledge seeking. Evelyn Fox-Keller observes, "to be a successful scientist, one must first be adequately socialized. For this reason, it is unreasonable to expect a sharp differentiation between women scientists and their male colleagues, and indeed, most women scientists would be appalled by such a suggestion."[7] The same argument is made for the planning profession by Sherilyn MacGregor in this volume.

Many feminist theorists[8] argue that a reliance on the physical sciences to delineate and shape our understanding of society has led science to be used as an instrument of control by the state. Harding suggests:

> social policy agendas and the conceptualization of what is signifi-
> cant among scientific problems are so intertwined from the start
> that the values and agendas important to social policy pass – unob-
> structed by any merely methodological controls – right through the
> scientific process to emerge intact in the results of research and im-
> plicit and explicit policy recommendations.[9]

Seager argues that scientific certainty is an inadequate base upon which to build action or change, calling uncertainty "central to the nature of science."[10] As she points out,

> because environmental problems are characterized as physical dis-
> ruptions in the biosphere, governments increasingly rely on scien-
> tists to determine whether environmental problems exist in the first
> place, and, if so, what to do about them. Environmental impacts are
> measured on a scientific yardstick, and regulatory standards are sci-
> ence-driven.
>
> Exclusive reliance on scientific "rationality" is a slippery slope. In
> the first place, this regulatory stance presupposes that "science"
> CAN define acceptable environmental quality; it also presupposes
> that scientists are disinterested, neutral players who can arrive at
> "objective" truth. Both of these presumptions are seriously flawed.[11]

In a similar vein, Janis Birkeland, a critic of planning theory and practice, argues that science is too narrow a base from which to derive planning decisions. She argues that "planning techniques, which are modelled upon science, have therefore been centred on prediction rather than prevention, as a means of coping with uncertainty. Thus, only things that can be predicted will be prevented." As an example, she points out that since it is not possible to measure the synergistic effects of chemical compounds in the environment, they are not considered a problem.[12]

Birkeland states clearly that planning regulations do not prevent environmental damage. She says that one of the reasons is that land, water, and other natural resources are not considered "public goods" when regulations are developed. She explains:

> They are still treated as raw materials (of no intrinsic value) which can be compensated for or traded off by cash contributions or development impact fees. In short, our regulatory devices do not protect the public domain and public health, but merely exact a tax or royalties on their degradation.[13]

Birkeland goes on to argue that from a number of perspectives planning as it is currently constituted cannot protect the environment. One of the many difficulties she discusses is the process "whereby human and natural resources are construed as having value to the extent that they can be used for human purposes."[14] This means that often the only entry point planners and other municipal officials have to improve environmental conditions occurs when a site becomes available for development.

Many feminist theorists argue for a more holistic science that would include knowledge in different forms and from different sectors.[15] Fox Keller calls for the "reclamation, from within science, of science as a human instead of a masculine project, and the renunciation of the division of emotional and intellectual labor that maintains science as a male preserve."[16] In arguing for a broadening of the science used to address environmental issues, Eichler makes a case for the greater involvement of the social sciences, particularly sociology, in what are "at their root, social problems."[17] Specifically, she concludes:

> Our environment has reached a critical point, at which we cannot take continued human (and other) life for granted, unless we engage in a drastic reversal of our behaviour. This would involve placing all social processes and structures in relation to environmental degradation and asking the question whether any given social process or structure speeds, retards, or reverses environmental degradation.[18]

Assessing risk

Many of the criticisms made by feminist theorists of science are also made by critics of health risk assessment. Health risk assessment is a process that was developed in a specific historical context; it derives many of its current assumptions and practices from this context. Its genesis was during the introduction of pesticides for use on crops in the 1920s in the United States when people began to ask questions about the effects these chemicals would have on human health.

Scientific testing of chemicals was undertaken on laboratory animals to determine the highest concentration of the chemical that these animals could tolerate without an adverse health effect. This is called the no-observable-effects level or NOEL.[19] Regulators then suggested that the safety factor for these same chemicals in humans should be one hundred times lower than the NOEL for animals. Most of the testing was carried out on male animals, largely because the hormonal fluctuation in female animals was believed to interfere with testing conditions. These animal test results were then extrapolated to the entire US adult human population of women and men. As is the case in medical research, this method of testing has raised a significant question around the relevance of the results to females, children, older people, people with disabilities, etc., in the human population.[20] There has also been an ongoing critique, largely from the industrial sector, that the extrapolation of animal test results to humans is overly conservative and scientifically indefensible.

During this same era, people began to question whether a NOEL could apply to substances that cause cancer, and by 1950 the US Food and Drug Administration had ruled that no safety factor could be justified for a carcinogen. Cancer became the focus of attention because standardized test data had only been developed for cancer at that time.[21] US legislation was passed in the late 1950s that forbade the addition of a chemical carcinogen to the food supply. This is called the "zero tolerance" or Delaney rule.[22]

As public concern over environmental contaminants increased in the 1960s and 1970s, it became difficult to gain public acceptance for the introduction and release of chemicals into the environment. Given this difficulty, attempts on the part of government and industry to move beyond zero tolerance and estimate an "acceptable" level of risk for cancer began in earnest. These mathematical models often attempted to balance the health risks of additional chemicals in the environment against the benefits that they might generate. As Wartenberg and Chess point out,

> by comparing risk of lives lost with the potential for dollars gained, many regulators thought they had derived a fundamental basis for decision-making on public policy. Critics, including labor unions and environmentalists, assailed the comparisons, arguing that there was more to human life than simple dollar values and pointing out that the people who stood to profit were rarely the ones at risk.[23]

While there has been some tinkering with risk assessment over time, as well as some waxing and waning in its popularity, it remains the basis for determining health risks and setting regulatory limits for environmental contaminants.

The risk in risk assessment

Critics, including many within the academic and scientific sectors, have raised questions regarding health risk assessment that tread several well-travelled paths. Many believe that health risk assessment can lead to at least a partial understanding of the risks posed by environmental contaminants to human health. These same critics, however, object to the way it has been set out as a definitive answer to a complex and changing question. Ginsburg describes how risk assessment is considered "the greatest scientific tool for making 'objective and sound' health policy decisions since the first canary was taken into a mine or the first rat used for toxicity testing."[24]

One of the recurring criticisms of risk assessment is that it depends "on highly uncertain and subjective assumptions."[25] In effect, depending on who is doing the assessing and the assumptions they build into the process, the levels of health risk determined can vary greatly. Some critics contend that they can vary by many orders of magnitude.

Another criticism concerns the positioning of risk assessment as "'good science' that gives 'objective' (as opposed to the hysteria of citizen groups) and 'scientific' evaluations of contamination problems."[26] By focusing on science, numbers, and a complex mathematical modelling that is the purview of "specialists" within government, industry, and academia, knowledge that may exist in various communities is largely excluded. As

Wartenberg and Chess suggest, "residents and workers often know the history and variability of contamination that scientists cannot easily reconstruct or measure."[27]

Critics also dispute the emphasis on cancer in health risk assessment. Increasingly, research shows that cancer may not be the most sensitive indicator of health risk. The effects of environmental contaminants on reproduction, the nervous system, or the immune system may be greater than the risk of cancer at the same level of exposure. As Ginsburg points out,

> while it is valid to argue whether or not the calculation overstates the risk of cancer, it says almost nothing about other health effects or the likelihood of any *meaningful* adverse health effect (including rashes, headaches and dizziness, breathing disorders, allergies, liver and kidney effects, reproductive effects, and so forth) showing up in the exposed population.[28]

Birkeland also argues that this kind of assessment rarely includes a calculation of the extent to which chemicals interact with each other or how they add to a burden of contaminants that may already exist in a given environment.[29] According to Ginsburg, "the calculation does not usually take into account simultaneous exposure to the same or similar substances from adjacent sources or through various routes of exposure (such as contamination of food, air, and water)."[30]

These calculations also do not calibrate, except under special circumstances and with certain substances, the differences among people that can lead to very different "acceptable" exposure estimates for an environmental contaminant. Some critics argue that worst case scenarios for risk assessment should be modelled with infants, or "sensitive sub-populations."[31] People with disabilities or sensitivities may have a very different susceptibility to environmental contaminants than the supposed "universal person" in the health risk assessment. That is also true for people who, because of ethnic and socio-economic factors as well as the work they do, are more exposed through food or personal activities to certain environmental contaminants.[32] As an example, "acceptable" average estimates for levels of contaminants in vegetables may not take into account the impact on strict vegetarians.[33]

Why then, given these limitations, does health risk assessment play such a major role in environmental regulation and guideline setting? Ginsburg argues that government and industry are committed to "controlling release rather than protecting public health by controlling production and generation of toxic substances." He argues that this is "a sophisticated form of the dilution solution" which presupposes that the environment has an infinite carrying capacity for substances as long as they are diluted to small quantities.[34]

Ginsburg, echoing many of the feminist theorists, suggests that a public health approach would be aimed at preventing exposure through a dialogue that would attempt to prevent contaminants from entering the environment and humans as a first principle.[35] Mary O'Brien advocates an alternative to health risk assessment which she calls the "assimilative capacity approach":

> The alternative process, the one I join others in urging, is based on the precautionary principle. It asks different questions. It asks, "What is the least tinkering we can do with earth's life systems? What opportunities do we have to eliminate discharges of toxic chemicals into the environment?"[36]

Recalibrating risk assessment

While there are some recalibrations of the assumptions in risk assessment at the macro level – largely for specific substances known to have effects on certain groups or to cause specific health problems – in general governments attempt to protect the whole population rather than its more vulnerable parts. Some site-specific risk assessment is taking into account "sub-populations," such as women, children, and people with disabilities. This tends to occur if the planned use of a site is one in which these people will be on or near the site for prolonged periods of time. One of the inherent difficulties with site-specific assessment is that it considers the health impact for a contained geographical location, not for the environment as a whole. This results in an arbitrary definition of the site as well as a delimiting of other factors, such as off-site air sources, which may also add to the burden of contaminants experienced by people.

In Toronto, this kind of risk assessment occurs most frequently if a site is to be developed for such uses as daycares, schools, or workplaces. In these instances, women, particularly those of child-bearing age, and children are considered as special cases. Key points in considering children's exposure to environmental contaminants are that they breathe more frequently than adults, their body weight is lighter, and their bodies are still being formed. The impact of most contaminants is therefore greater for children than adults.

One example of a Toronto development project that has included site-specific health risk assessment is the proposed expansion of a fire department installation. An assessment was carried out of the cancer risk of polyaromated hydrocarbons in the soil by estimating the chemical intakes of on-site employees and averaging their chronic daily intakes over a seventy-year lifespan. Site-specific assessments have also been conducted for a proposed service centre facility, a proposed recycling facility, and a proposed park. In the case of the proposed private-sector service centre on an old industrial site, estimates were made of the health risk to future users of the site, such as office workers and maintenance workers. There were also calculations made of the health risk to pregnant female workers, given that some chemicals can be transferred through the placenta and affect the developing fetus. Other estimates were made of adults and children who might use a near-by area for recreational purposes. Based on these calculations, consultants concluded that no special precautions were needed to reduce health risk on the site.

While it may be helpful, at a theoretical level, if site-specific risk assessments are inclusive of people other than the universal male person, a review of these cases does not indicate that these calculations are having a significant impact on the remediation of these sites. This may be because the difference is slight or because the retooling of assumptions is not extensive enough to result in a numerical difference. It may simply speak to the limitations of health risk assessment in making these types of determinations. The focus on the universal male person therefore stands as just one example of the inadequacy of complex modelling as the sole basis on which planning decisions are made about human health and the environment.

Beyond health risk assessment

Given the limitations of health risk assessment in evaluating the impact of planning on human health and the environment, to what extent are we wedded to the guidelines that flow from these assessments, and what other models might we use at both the policy and practical levels? One approach in the city of Toronto has been to enshrine statements and policy objectives that value human health and the environment in documents that affect the planning process, such as *Cityplan*, the *Toronto Declaration on the Environment*, *Healthy Toronto 2000*, and the *Zero Discharge Statement of Principles*.

These documents are no panacea in and of themselves. Many of them contain policy statements which are general, lack implementation plans, are not subject to monitoring, and can easily be overlooked. However, the existence of these broad statements of intent has made it possible for planners and other municipal officials, as well as community residents, to argue that human health and environmental concerns should be embraced as general principles in planning an ecologically sustainable city.

The *Toronto Declaration on the Environment* commits the city to principles designed to enhance the sustainability of the environment, human health, and cultural heritage. It calls for the development of an implementation plan that will allow citizens to evaluate the policy and program directions of the City of Toronto. This implementation plan will include corporate codes of practice, environmental audits, targets, and monitoring systems.

Some important guiding principles in the *Declaration* are:

– To take preventive action in future planning;
– To make polluters responsible for environmental damage;
– To provide the community with information to make informed choices on environmental issues;
– To encourage public participation in the development of policies and programs.[37]

Healthy Toronto 2000 sets out a blueprint for public health until the turn of the century, including a number of recommendations to preserve the environmental health of the city.[38] The *Zero Discharge Statement of Principles* defines zero discharge as "ending the use, the production and, thus, the disposal of persistent and/or bioaccumulative toxic substances."[39]

Cityplan, which constitutes Toronto's official plan, has sections that deal with water quality and quantity, waste, contaminated soils, and the protection of environmentally significant areas. Some of these provisions include reduction targets, such as the goal of reducing carbon dioxide in the city by 20 per cent of the 1991 levels by the year 2006.[40] Another provision calls for the reduction of the use of chemical herbicides and insecticides within Toronto by 50 per cent of 1991 levels by the year 2001.[41]

One of the areas of *Cityplan* that affects development in Toronto, where most available land was previously the site of industrial activity, is the provision for the remediation of contaminated soil. The provision specifically states that:

> Council shall seek to ensure in cooperation with the appropriate government authorities, if necessary, that contaminated soil and groundwater do not create a hazard for the health of natural ecosystems or the people who live, work or play within the City.[42]

So, given these principles, how are the on-the-ground planning decisions made in a city like Toronto and to what extent are they influenced by these policies? The answer is mixed. When sites become available for redevelopment, the imperative to generate economic activity often swamps other considerations. On the other hand, there are projects that demonstrate how many of the principles enshrined in these policies get taken up at the site-specific level.

One of the best examples is the remediation of the Toronto Refiners and Smelters site which had been polluted by lead and other contaminants during forty years of industrial activity. Toronto City Council ensured that the community, represented by the Niagara Neighbourhood Association, had the funding to carry out its own evaluation of scientific documents and educational activities within the neighbourhood. The association hired a lead decommissioning expert to provide information on remediation of other sites in North America, and a community liaison person who was on the site during the entire decommissioning process.

Residents were able to bring to the remediation planning historical knowledge of the operation of the industry on the site, knowledge that was largely undocumented by government agencies. Knowing about the operation of the industry over time gave investigators clues as to where to sample on the site as well as to what they might expect to find.

Citizens also provided observational data by monitoring activities on the site. Citizens were able to set standards such as "zero discharge," meaning no contaminants could be discharged, either by air, water, or other sources, during the site clean-up. This resulted in effective air monitors and other provisions which prohibited the release of contaminants into the community. As an example, citizens were concerned about the lead-contaminated dust that might be raised as the trucks moved on and off the site. To deal with this issue, a truck washing system was put in place to ensure that all trucks moving off the site were as clean as possible.

The citizens involved in this remediation were also very familiar with analytical data given their lengthy history of trying to reduce lead emissions from this industry. They made an important contribution to the remediation by reviewing levels of contaminants on site and decommissioning options. While this project occurred during an era in the city's history when economics made much of this possible, it remains an important model to keep in mind when considering what a broadening of involvement and expertise might look like. It includes knowledge beyond physical science through drawing upon the lived experience of residents, and attempts to include people in the process of making community decisions which effect their own lives.[43]

Another case is the Ataratiri project. Eighty acres of industrial land in downtown Toronto were to be used to increase the supply of affordable housing in the city. Although the project was never built, largely because of the cost of remediating soil and implementing flood-proofing measures, the planning process incorporated a variety of methods to ensure that members of the public were heard. Some of the issues raised by citizens were noise and vibration, transportation, air quality, soil and groundwater management, health risk, and flood risk. The greatest number of questions posed concerned soil and groundwater management and health risk:

On the issue of soil and groundwater quality, questions were raised concerning the expected level of soil quality after remediation, how soil guidelines that are proposed for the site were established, how remediation decisions will be made and the location of contaminated soil and groundwater. In the area of health risk, there were questions on cumulative exposures, on what would happen if new, more stringent guidelines were developed, and on establishing a system for on-going monitoring of health and health-related concerns of residents.[44]

It is clear from these comments that the issues that citizens raised speak directly to their concerns about the sustainability of the environment and the impact of contaminants on human health.

Another example of both a policy and practice that operates outside the framework of scientific certainty and risk assessment is the way in which the City of Toronto Department of Public Health deals with electric and magnetic fields (EMFs). Electric power in North America creates two types of fields: electric fields result from the strength of a charge and magnetic fields result from the motion of the charge. Some studies have demonstrated a connection between EMFs and changes at the cellular level, while other studies have suggested they may be linked to cancer promotion. Some cancers associated with EMF exposure in both residential and occupational studies are childhood and adult leukemias, central nervous system cancer, and male breast cancer. Other studies have not been able to measure a health effect.[45]

Despite the lack of scientific agreement, public awareness and concern has continued to grow. Citizens in Toronto demand changes to existing structures and raise objections to new development near EMFs. The Department of Public Health has adopted a policy of prudent avoidance, which advocates limiting exposure to electric and magnetic fields where practical and feasible at little or no cost. Working with the Departments of Planning and Development, and Parks and Recreation, guidelines have been developed to deal with the siting of community gardens, utilities, and new land developments.[46]

This approach demonstrates that it is not necessary to achieve a level of scientific certainty before actions can be taken. Where there is a high level of scientific uncertainty, it is still possible to develop policy alternatives that result in practical and cost effective solutions. These should be undertaken routinely, whether public concern is high or not.

Conclusions

A feminist analysis of the social construction of science unveils gender-based assumptions which also permeate the science-derived practice of developing guidelines through health risk assessment. Except in a few special cases, assessment is based on a universal male person with set characteristics; little consideration is given to women, children, seniors, or people who are not considered part of the general population. In fact, when we look around us in our communities and workplaces, it is clear that this focus is not the result of a neutral position, but is a position that is willfully blind to the reality of most of our lives.

Health risk assessment in and of itself is part of a reductionist science which, using complex mathematical modelling, gives us a great deal of information about the parts and little about the whole. It also, as its critics point out, relies on a series of uncertain assumptions that can change over time and is very narrowly focused on outcomes such as cancer. It leaves out important considerations that fall outside this kind of modelling, including the social sciences with their potential to reveal the structural underpinnings of environmental degradation. It also works against the concept of pollution prevention and remediation by determining an "acceptable risk" for individual environmental contaminants.

The reliance on such guidelines to assess human health and environmental quality largely leaves out people who should be protected, and provides only a narrow base of knowledge from which to build an ecologically sustainable city. While this numerical information may be useful to consider when reaching a decision, it is limited in many ways and should be augmented by the development of policies and practical solutions which include other forms of knowledge, including the social impact of proposed projects.

Federal, provincial, and municipal policies that value the environment and human health are prerequisites to planning an ecologically sustainable city. Federal and provincial policies are particularly important since they set a broad direction for the country and province that could ensure environmental and health equity for all. This is critical at a municipal level. Industries and other potential polluters will often move to another municipality or province to avoid stringent policies and regulations concerning the discharge of contaminants into the environment.

These policies, because of their broad-based approach, should start from the point of "assimilative capacity" that O'Brien describes.[47] They should set broad policy direction for the city and its inhabitants as a whole which, as Birkeland suggests, will protect both "the public domain and public health."[48] They should be made operational to provide guidance to planners and community residents who often enter the picture only at the point where a specific site has been slated for redevelopment. In site-specific assessments, the most vulnerable people should be included in calculations of health risk. Data pertaining to social and economic considerations should be weighed alongside the data generated by the physical sciences. Community residents with their historical, observational, or analytical data should also be involved in order to ensure that decisions are made with all relevant information at hand. This is particularly important since citizens, either because of their geographical proximity to a site or their specialized interest, often have information that is not available to officials or consultants.

As a guide to people who are involved in the day-to-day decisions about what an ecologically sustainable and non-sexist city might be, the following principles should be kept in mind:

- health risk assessment, and the guidelines and regulations that flow from it, may not be inclusive or sensitive enough to protect those with the highest health risk;
- policies that define an ecologically sustainable city should be developed to provide a context for decision-making that is broader than specific developments and immediate economic considerations;
- a range of scientific information, including social science as well as the historical and observational data generated by community residents, should be part of planning decisions for an ecologically sustainable city;
- community residents and others with important information to contribute should be included at an early stage in order to work in concert with the development of environmental and human health sustainability principles.

Finally, it is important that environmental planning and risk assessment, at both the macro and micro levels, begin to take into account the varied persons who make up the population. In a very real sense, if we ensure environmental and human health for the most sensitive among us, we will ensure them for all.

Notes

1 Carolyn Merchant, *The Death of Nature: Women, Ecology and the Scientific Revolution* (San Francisco: Harper and Row, 1990), pp. 290-94.

2 Ibid., xvi, xxi.

3 Vandana Shiva, *Staying Alive: Women, Ecology and Development* (London: Zed Books, 1989), p. 46-7.

4 Joni Seager, *Earth Follies: Coming to Feminist Terms with the Global Environmental Crisis* (New York: Routledge, 1993), p. 246.

5 See, for example, Evelyn Fox Keller, *Reflections on Gender and Science* (New Haven: Yale University Press, 1985); Sandra Harding, *The Science Question in Feminism* (Ithaca: Cornell University Press, 1986); Seager, *Earth Follies*, 1993.

6 Harding, *The Science Question in Feminism*, 1986, p. 15.

7 Fox Keller, *Reflections on Gender and Science*, 1985, p. 173.

8 See, for example, Fox Keller, *Reflections on Gender and Science*, 1985; Harding, *The Science Question in Feminism*, 1986; Seager, *Earth Follies*, 1993.

9 Harding, *The Science Question*, 1986, p. 77.

10 Seager, *Earth Follies*, 1993, p. 91.

11 Ibid., 163.

12 Janis Birkeland, "An Ecofeminist Critique of Manstream Planning," *The Trumpeter, Journal of Ecosophy* 8, 2 (Spring 1991): 76.

13 Ibid., 82.

14 Ibid., 73.

15 See, for example, Merchant, *The Death of Nature*, 1990; Fox Keller, *Reflections on Gender and Science*, 1985; Margrit Eichler, "Umwelt als Sozologisches Problem," *Das Argument. Zeitschrift fuer Philosophie und Sozialwissenschaften* 36, 3 (1994): 359-76; Seager, *Earth Follies*, 1993.

16 Fox Keller, *Reflections on Gender and Science*, 1985, 178.

17 Eichler, "Umwelt als Sozologisches Problem" (1994).

18 Ibid.

19 Daniel Wartenberg and Caron Chess, "The Risk Wars: Assessing Risk Assessment," *New Solutions: A Journal of Environmental and Occupational Health Policy* (Winter 1993): 17.

20 Eichler, "Umwelt als Sozologisches Problem" (1994).

21 Robert Ginsburg, "Quantitative Risk Assessment and the Illusion of Safety," *New Solutions: A Journal of Environmental and Occupational Health Policy* (Winter 1993): 10.

22 Wartenberg and Chess, "The Risk Wars" (1993): 18.

23 Ibid.

24 Ginsburg, "Quantitative Risk Assessment" (1993): 10.

25 Ibid.

26 Ibid., 9.

27 Wartenberg and Chess, "The Risk Wars" (1993): 23.

28 Ginsburg, "Quantitative Risk Assessment" (1993): 10.

29 Birkeland, "An Ecofeminist Critique of Manstream Planning" (1991): 76.

30 Ginsburg, "Quantitative Risk Assessment" (1993): 12.

31 Wartenberg and Chess, "The Risk Wars" (1993): 20.

32 Mary H. O'Brien, "Alternatives to Risk Assessment: The Example of Dioxin,"

New Solutions: A Journal of Environmental and Occupational Health Policy (Winter 1993): 40.

33 Wartenberg and Chess, "The Risk Wars" (1993): 20.

34 Ginsburg, "Quantitative Risk Assessment" (1993): 12.

35 Ibid., 14.

36 O'Brien, "Alternatives to Risk Assessment" (1993): 39.

37 City of Toronto, *Toronto Declaration on the Environment* (Toronto: City Council, July 1991).

38 Healthy Toronto 2000 Subcommittee, City of Toronto, *Healthy Toronto 2000* (Toronto: Board of Health, September 1988).

39 City of Toronto, *Zero Discharge Statement of Principles* (Toronto: City Council, June 1991).

40 City of Toronto Planning and Development Department, *City of Toronto Official Plan Part 1 – Cityplan* (By-law 423-93) (Toronto: City Council, 20 July 1993), p. 2.2.

41 Ibid., 2.3.

42 Ibid., 2.5.

43 Jeanne Jabanoski, "CITIZEN SCIENCE: The Toronto Refiners and Smelters Site Remediation Project," presentation to the Ministry of Environment and Energy Conference (Toronto: November 1994).

44 Jane Weninger, "Public Participation in Decommissioning and Site Clean-up: A Look at the Ataratiri Project," presented at the symposium sponsored by the Institute for Social Impact Assessment (Toronto, 1990), p. 11.

45 City of Toronto Department of Public Health, *Policy Respecting Electric and Magnetic Fields (EMFs)* (Toronto: Board of Health, 6 October 1993).

46 Ibid.

47 O'Brien, "Alternatives to Risk Assessment" (1993): 39.

48 Birkeland, "An Ecofeminist Critique of Manstream Planning" (1991): 82.

WHAT DO YOU WANT TO DO?
PAVE PARKS?

Urban Planning and
the Prevention of Violence

Carolyn Whitzman

FIRST OFF, a bit of background. Since 1989, I have been the co-ordinator of the City of Toronto Safe City Committee. The Safe City Committee works with the municipal government to prevent violence against women and other vulnerable groups such as children and the elderly in our homes, our workplaces, and on the streets. The Committee is staffed by the Planning and Development Department, which also provides staff for a number of other community service initiatives, including a bicycle safety co-ordinator and an accessibility consultant for people with disabilities.[1]

Safety from violence, whether it be in the home, in the workplace, or on the street, has not generally been a consideration in post-war urban planning. This chapter makes the case that the prevention of violence is a legitimate, and in fact should be a central, concern of urban planners. It reviews current planning trends and their impact on crime and violence. Its focus is the Toronto example of planning for a safer city, whose principles can be summarized as:[2]

- Safer for women, safer for everyone: Treat "crime" and "fear of crime" as gendered phenomena, and treat public violence as part of the continuum of acts that harm women and other vulnerable groups.
- The process shapes the result: Rely on a participatory research and evaluation process, that will allow the people who are most affected to define the problem and participate in solutions.
- There are no simple answers: integrate design improvement and community development. Do not expect overnight miracles.

Why should personal safety be an urban planner's responsibility?

When I speak about the promotion of personal safety being an urban planner's responsibility (as opposed to fire and traffic safety, which are relatively established issues in the North American planning discourse), I often receive blank stares. The question that was often asked in my early days as a student was simply: "why should safety from violence be of concern to urban planners?" I hear this question much less now, as poll after poll shows crime and violence to be the number one concern of city-dwellers, ahead of such traditional concerns as unemployment, high taxes, and sufficient green space.[3] Even if the human and fiscal costs of crime are not apparent to urban planners, the pressure from politicians and the public to "do something" certainly is noticeable.

There are, however, a number of frequently stated concerns that remain with integrating personal safety issues within planning. I still hear, "*I* feel safe," with the implication being that those who do not should perhaps be sent to a re-education camp. I have also heard: "I don't think that planning has anything to do with crime"; this is certainly an arguable point, though the sentiment is often articulated by people who think urban planning will lead people to buy more, change their aesthetic sensibilities, or live happily ever after. I sometimes hear, "whaddya wanna do, pave parks?" to which I have often wished to reply, "only if you are part of the foundation, sir." Finally, I continue to hear, often from women, "why do you talk about women all the time? Don't you care about violence against everyone?"

So here are some answers to these concerns.

Yes, many people do feel safe using all public spaces all day and all night. In 1987, I interviewed a number of women in a rather rough part of downtown Toronto. Half answered that they felt "safe" or "very safe" walking alone on their neighbourhood streets after dark, which is consistent with Canadian statistics on fear of crime. Among the women who felt safe, a nun I spoke to felt safe because she knew everyone along her usual 6 a.m. walk to work on a street sometimes known as "skid row." Several women said they felt perfectly safe, but then added: "of course, I don't go out at night without my husband," "I'd never walk in this park after dusk," and even, "I don't get out much any more."[4] When you talk with people who say they feel safe, you often get variations on these answers. People feel safe within an ever-decreasing set of self-imposed time and place limitations. This is not safety, and it is not the freedom that urban dwellers deserve.

In 1992, 39 per cent of Torontonians (and 34 per cent of Canadians) said they did not feel safe walking alone on their neighbourhood streets after dark. To be more specific, 50 per cent of Canadian women said they did not feel safe, more than three times the rate of men's fear.[5] The difference in the fear level between women and men is consistently greater than any other single difference, although age, socio-economic status, marital status, race, and location of residence are also important factors affecting the level of fear.[6]

This climate of fear has tremendous implications for individuals. Fifteen years of research in this area details the psychological stress, the loss of social and job-related opportunities, and the general impact on people's ability to use allegedly "public" resources that are due to fearing crime in public places. The impact differs along gender lines: women are far more likely to take precautionary measures such as avoiding places or activities that they feel are unsafe; men are more likely to use a more proactive and expensive precaution, such as taking a self-defense course or buying a dog.[7] A British study found that 90 per cent of women aged sixteen to twenty-four habitually take precautionary measures, ranging from avoiding certain streets to not going out at all.[8] A survey of High Park, Toronto's largest green space, found that twice as many men as women use the park during the day, with the ratio rising to three to one in the evening. Of the users concerned about their safety, 93 per cent are women.[9]

"What's wrong with these women anyhow?" was the implication of research in the 1970s and 1980s which sought to explain the irrational fact that women were less likely to be victims of a reported crime, yet feared and avoided public places more. This research question ignored some essential facts:

1. The crime women most fear is rape. The crime men most fear is robbery. Robbery is a bad thing to have happen to you. Rape is worse.

2. Rates of certain crimes, such as sexual assault, were grossly underreported in the 1970s. At least some of the recent increase in reported sexual assault rates is due to some limited reforms which make it slightly easier to report and prosecute the offense. But the latest survey of violence against women made it clear why statistics based on reported crime do not work: one in two Canadian women reported hav-

ing suffered some form of physical or sexual violence since the age of sixteen, but only 14 per cent had gone to the police.[10]

3. Men are most likely to be assaulted outdoors and the perpetrator is most likely to be a male stranger. In contrast, the majority of assaults against women occur in homes, and the majority of offenders are men known to the victims. Assaults by a stranger are more likely to be reported, which is part of the reason why there were more reported assaults against men than women in the 1970s and 1980s. However, the impact of *all* assaults includes a greater fear of crime than experienced prior to being assaulted, which is part of the reason why women are more fearful.[11]

4. By 1991, women's equality had progressed to the point where we are equally likely to be the victim of a *reported* violent crime. Given rates of reporting discussed in the second point, this indicates that a woman is more likely to be the victim of a violent crime.[12]

In short, women's fear is highly rational.

There is surprisingly little good research available on the social and economic impacts of crime and violence. In the 1991-92 fiscal year, the direct cost of the Canadian criminal justice system was $9.2 billion. This tally includes only police, correctional institutions, courts, and legal aid. The same Canadian study places the indirect cost of crime at $6.7 billion, including property loss, security services, insurance fraud, volunteer services, and crime-related hospitalization.[13] Even this figure is a gross underestimation of the true costs of violence to the public, which would include other forms of health care, children's aid, criminal injuries compensation, welfare, lost work days, and many other untallied indirect costs. The indirect costs of fear of crime should also be included: one study by the well-known accounting firm of Peat, Marwick in Nottingham, England – a city of 300,000 people – indicated that the cost of fear of crime to the central shopping district was in the order of $45 million annually.[14] Universities, apartment buildings, hotels, and workplaces in the United States have been sued by victims of violence who successfully argued that the managers did not take sufficient precautions to protect the users.[15]

The cost of intolerance in society is hard to calculate, yet it is at least partly attributable to crime and violence. Certainly, 53 per cent of Torontonians felt that prejudice against minority groups was increasing at the same time as fear of crime,[16] although it could be argued that media coverage of crime makes it seem more acceptable to articulate existing prejudices. Fear of crime has been posited as a major reason for "white flight" from American inner cities, a phenomenon that has had a muted echo in Canadian equivalents. The suburbs have proven to be an illusory refuge: one-third of all new housing developments in the United States' fastest growing cities consists of "gated communities," where private residential streets are surrounded by locked fences and patrolled by private security companies.[17] There are at least two gated communities that have recently been built in the Greater Toronto Area. A new "prototype" series of shopping centres is appearing in Los Angeles, heavily subsidized by the US National Institute of Justice: eight-foot-high security fences with three remote-controlled gates for auto entry surround these centres, and shoppers are frisked for guns at the entrance.[18]

If urban planners are at all concerned about the economic viability, sociability, and general liveability of the spaces they help to create, they need to be concerned about crime and violence. If planners wish to be effective in their measures to reduce insecurity and promote safety, they need to take gender into account.

What can urban planners do?

What can urban planners do to reduce violence and make cities safer? The point of departure in any response usually considers planners' direct impact on the form and design of the city. Whether working for government or private concerns, planners help create public and private urban spaces.

Although some people disagree, I would certainly argue that design and crime do not have a simple causal relationship. Bad design does not create bad people. However, the evidence that does exist suggests that planning can have an impact on opportunities for crime as well as opportunities for successful defense, especially in the case of crimes occurring in a public space. For instance, a 1982 study of sixty-five rape sites in Seattle public places indicated that certain design factors were characteristic of sites where the rapes had occurred.[19] Interestingly, studies from Canada and England of design factors that make women feel unsafe turn up nearly identical indicators.[20] The possibility of entrapment near a pedestrian route; isolation found in places such as multi-storey parking garages and parking lots; factors which reduce visibility such as poor lighting, signage, and "blind corners"; and obvious signs of "not caring" such as poor maintenance and graffiti, signal to criminal and potential victim alike that a particular site might be appropriate for an assault.

These physical design factors are combined with knowledge of local residents' behaviour patterns among assailants who commit crimes in their own neighbourhood, including many if not most robbers and serial "stranger" rapists. The presence of people who will intervene when they see a perceived criminal activity is one major social factor that deters criminals, but the "neighbourliness" of a neighbourhood may, in turn, be influenced by design features.[21]

Urban planners need to recognize that post-war urban development trends have done a great deal to make cities less safe. Extreme separation of land uses is the trademark of the typical suburban neighbourhood plan, with its border of arterial roads, shopping plazas with huge parking lots, industrial parks, and high-rise housing, and its interior of circuitous inner streets with single family houses, centred around a school surrounded by a large playing field. Informal surveillance by shopkeepers and passers-by, getting to know your neighbours through hanging out on the front porch or sidewalk, and achieving a clear mental map of the area, are all near impossible due to the physical design of these neighbourhoods. The ghettoization of the poor in huge isolated public housing projects can be seen as the natural progenitor to the voluntary imprisonment of the rich behind closed gates. Zoning that disallows basement apartments and two single parents to share a house (these discriminatory zoning practices are not allowed in the new Ontario Planning Act) made affordable private-sector housing for low-income women and children escaping violent men virtually unattainable in many municipalities.[22]

Urban planners must also recognize that their role goes far beyond the zoning and land-use issues that have dominated the work of post-war planning departments. New developments and land use changes all have an impact on the need for social services. The adequacy of social services, in turn, has an impact on safety that may be at least as important as more traditional planning concerns. Schools, community health centres, parent-child drop-ins, specialized legal clinics, community economic development "incubators," and ethnospecific agencies have all been sites where violence prevention initiatives have flourished. Merely by providing a place where people in fear or under stress can find counselling, individual advocacy, and referral, these services work to prevent violence. But these services are also increasingly involved in public education and policy development around violence prevention. Schools and recreation centres are providing conflict resolution training to young people and staff alike, parent-child drop-ins are providing education to vulnerable parents on how to handle stress, community centres are providing programs to help women start small businesses and obtain some measure of economic independence, and ethnospecific agencies are developing pamphlets and videos against wife assault. While the responsibility for funding these services cannot rest with the local level of government, urban planners can ensure that accessible and affordable space is provided in new and existing neighbourhoods.[23]

Ideally, design improvement would be coupled with community development to make places safer. A sophisticated understanding of safer cities recognizes that violence prevention does not mean creating barriers that will guard against a singular violent event. Rather, violence is something that goes on every day, in popular culture, in people's homes, within workplaces, and on the street. Preventing violence can mean preventing the same kind of domestic assault from occurring the thirty-first time through helping a woman or child reach help. It may mean teaching a child or adult that there are other alternatives to reacting violently to a threat. It may mean assisting a community to do something to improve their neighbourhood. Whether you look at urban safety from the perspective of the potential victim or the assailant, from the perspective of what people want or what seems to work, you find the complex interaction of social control and opportunity reduction, and a need to promote both together.[24]

Missing the boat

Unfortunately, a divisive twenty-year debate has raged over "design versus social" change. In the United States and Britain, and to a lesser extent in Australia and Canada, researchers have expended far too much time and energy trying to prove one another "wrong," instead of bringing their particular perspectives together.

There are a number of reasons why the war has been waged. First, there is both too much money and too little money being put into crime prevention. Alice Coleman, an influential "Crime Prevention Through

Environmental Design" (CPTED) theorist, has been given several million dollars by the British government to carry out a longitudinal project that she hopes will "prove" that design improvement is more important than community development.[25] Apparently, the earlier public housing projects where her recommendations were carried out were tainted by having community development projects going on at the same time. When less than 1 per cent of the total Canadian budget for police, courts, and corrections is going into primary prevention initiatives,[26] and the figure is not much better in any other country, this kind of money going into social experimentation with the lives of poor people in Britain is pretty hard to swallow.

Ideological differences underlie the rivalry. Alice Coleman's argument that the existence of public housing itself is wrong plays well with the British Conservative government. Oscar Newman, author of the influential 1972 CPTED book *Defensible Space*,[27] is the American equivalent of Alice Coleman. Newman portrays himself as a liberal, but criticism directed at him comes largely from the American liberal left. CPTED has been developed by people with academic backgrounds in geography and architecture; the critics of CPTED and the promoters of crime prevention through social development tend to come from the disciplines of sociology, anthropology, and other "softer" social sciences.

Both streams of crime prevention have been criticized by feminists who are concerned that the focus of crime prevention on "public" crime by strangers leaves out the majority of crimes against women. It is true that from a reading of the major texts on crime prevention of the 1970s and 1980s, public concern and private pain stems from vandalism, break-ins, robbery, and in the case of Alice Coleman, littering. Gender gets left out, and with it, specific concern about rape as the most feared crime, or any analysis that might link woman abuse in private space with urban decay. Even when "domestic violence" is included within a general discussion of crime, many feminists argue that the gesture smacks of co-optation by mainstream crime prevention organizations, rather than a genuine understanding of the causes of violence against women. Feminists are also concerned that the current trendiness of community and locally-based strategies undermines federally-funded organizations, and represents the senior level of government passing the buck to local governments and voluntary organizations, without actually passing the bucks.[28]

In response to this, there has been parallel development of initiatives to prevent violence against women and initiatives to prevent crime. Thus, Australia had a contemporaneous National Crime Prevention Commission and a Commission on Violence Against Women; Canada had a national Panel on Violence Against Women touring the country at the same time as public hearings were held on a National Crime Prevention Council. These "women's issues" initiatives were both critically under-supported by the governments that created them, and wracked by dissension within feminist organizations as to their effectiveness. In contrast, high-ranking feminist staffers of "mainstream" British crime prevention organizations such as Crime Concern have propelled these organizations to include a gender and race analysis, and to promote domestic assault prevention as an integral part of local strategies.[29] Many British "safe community" schemes, funded by the national government, have placed women's safety foremost among their concerns.[30] It is to be hoped that the Canadian Crime Prevention Council, with staff and Council members who have considerable experience within feminist organizations, will do the same.

Another criticism of crime prevention policy comes from the left, with the question of whether urban planners can have any meaningful impact on cities at all. The implication of a book like *City of Quartz*, by Mike Davis, is that market forces, including the powerful gun lobby in the United States and the burgeoning security and prison businesses, are far more powerful than any local government or private planning concern. The popularity of "gated communities" is not a result of any coherent planning theory (though certain elements of the Crime Prevention Through Environmental Design literature certainly support them[31]), but is the manifestation of a marketing device used by private housing developers to play on people's fears. Although some cities have implemented planning policies that take prevention of violence into account (a simplified planning process for emergency shelters, or "planning for a safer city" guidelines), these have a limited impact on a small number of new buildings.

At the same time, in Toronto at least, there have been scores of small-scale "success stories" where neighbourhood organizations and private developers have taken the safety and liveability of cities into account. Whether it is creating a community barbecue in a park, painting a mural on a parking lot wall, turning a concrete school yard into a community gardening project, hiring a youth development worker in a mall, or starting a women's group in a public housing project, these small changes have been as meaningful to people's right to live free from violence and fear as broad planning policies. None of these projects, significantly, was initiated or even given staff support by the planning department. This can be seen as a manifestation of local planning departments' reaction to the 1990s recession, which is to cut back to the "basics," that is, reviewing development proposals by applying the necessary provisions of the Planning Act and relevant by-laws. Staff who focus on policy issues such as emerging community service needs, program funding for community organizations, and community development initiatives are seen as concerned with "frills": nice when the money is around, but not necessary to the planners' mission, which is to review plans. Perhaps the field of urban planning is now reactive and ineffective in dealing with any emerging urban concerns, of which safety is merely an example.[32]

The Toronto example

I would like to use the example of Toronto as a model, however flawed, of the integration of design and community improvements in planning for a safer city, and of the integration of a feminist analysis into crime prevention initiatives.

Two organizations have been critical to the development in Toronto of a set of internationally known crime prevention initiatives. The Metro Toronto Action Committee on Public Violence Against Women and Children (METRAC) was created as the result of a metropolitan government taskforce in 1984. Its initial mandate was broad. It was to oversee the implementation of recommendations regarding education, the police, legislation, victim services, urban planning, and the control of pornography.[33] The Safe City Committee came about four years later as the City of Toronto's municipal response to public violence against women. As the City of Toronto has more limited powers than the metropolitan government, with no direct say over policing, public transportation, or social service funding, the recommendations focused on local government strengths such as planning, parks, and public health.[34] METRAC was created as an autonomous organization, funded by Metro Toronto, but with an independent board of directors. The Safe City Committee, in contrast, reports to Toronto City Council, and is made up of the mayor, local councillors (currently four) and representatives of community organizations (currently twenty).

These two organizations have in turn worked with and been informed by a multitude of community groups, including Women Plan Toronto, a feminist planning advocacy group, Metro Men Against Violence, and the DisAbled Women's Network.

METRAC's *Women's Safety Audit Guide* has successfully been used by hundreds of community organizations around the world to pinpoint specific design elements that make places unsafe. With the Toronto Transit Commission (TTC) and the Metro Toronto Police Force (MTPF), two reports on the safety of the subway system and the safety of transit stops, especially in suburbs, have led to many concrete improvements, including designated waiting areas in subway stations, better signage throughout the system, and staff training to better respond to the public's – and TTC workers' – safety concerns.[35]

The Safe City Committee hosted "Green Spaces /Safer Places," a forum on making parks safer for women, that was the first event to bring together professionals and community people on the subject of park safety.[36] And the City of Toronto now has a policy in its comprehensive plan that states:

> It is the goal of Council to promote a City where all people can safely use public spaces, day or night, without fear of violence, and where people, including women and children and persons with special needs, are safe from violence.
>
> Accordingly, Council shall adopt development guidelines respecting issues of safety and security and shall apply these guidelines in its review of development proposals.[37]

These two organizations have also broadened the concept of "urban safety." METRAC has worked with professional organizations such as the College of Physicians and Surgeons to develop standards related to abuse of power and sexual assault. METRAC's work with campuses and hospitals has also encompassed policies and procedures, as well as design improvement. The Safe City Committee has sponsored several initiatives related to education in workplaces on violence against women and the prevention of workplace harassment and assault. The provision of free women's self-defense classes in recreation centres as the result of a Safe City Committee recommendation, has helped to prevent date rape and wife assault as well as stranger assaults.[38] A major focus of advocacy in recent years has been the establishment of the "Breaking the Cycle of Violence" grants program, which has in its two years of existence disbursed nearly one million dollars to nearly one hundred community groups. The money has gone to improve resources, public education, and counselling for the prevention of violence against women and other vulnerable groups.

While a full-scale evaluation of these initiatives is only underway now, it is indisputable that these Toronto safe city groups have inspired other Canadian examples. The Ottawa-Carleton Women's Action Centre Against Violence, established in 1992, has sponsored safety audits, professional education for planners, developers and architects, and a coalition on workplace harassment. The Edmonton Safer Cities Initiative projects include six comprehensive neighbourhood safety audit projects; several programs for youth at risk; co-ordination, advocacy and follow-up on family violence; and the promotion of more affordable housing, including second stage housing for women and children escaping abusive men. Montreal's CAFSU (Comite d'Action Femmes et Securite Urbaine/ Women's Action Coalition for Urban Safety) has, in addition to the ubiquitous safety audits, embarked on an ambitious campaign to educate men about men's violence against women. Winnipeg's Taskforce on Violence Against Women and Children, the Saint John Safe City Committee, and Vancouver's Safer City Taskforce have also recently embarked on urban safety initiatives informed by the needs of the most vulnerable populations.[39]

In all of these initiatives, planners have been the promoters, the staff people, and the mediators. Planning departments, however, have hardly been the leaders. In Winnipeg, the Taskforce was co-ordinated by the Social Planning Council. The Montreal initiative grew out of a women and planning advocacy group. Staffing for the safety audits, the professional education, and the policy changes has come from the respective planning departments, but only after political pressure.

100

Including urban safety in the planning curriculum
and in planning practice

In the course of writing this article, I surveyed the department heads of seven university planning degree programs in Ontario. Only one program offers an elective course on "planning for a safer city." While several program heads pointed to a growing number of students (mostly female) who are writing theses or major papers on safety or related topics, urban safety and violence prevention issues are relegated to being occasionally discussed in a social planning course, or a one-off workshop.

An interesting question arises. If planning can work to prevent violence, why is the study of "safer cities" not part of the core curriculum in urban planning programs? Why are selections from the large and growing body of books, magazine articles, and reports on the issue not likely to show up on course reading lists?[40]

One might well look at who is in charge at planning schools. As in most of academe, the majority of planning professors, especially those with tenure and those who are heads of departments, are white, able-bodied men. It is quite possible that their personal experience has not included being terrified while working alone in a basement student room at 3 a.m. or getting hassled on the street or at work. It is also possible, given statistics about the prevalence of woman abuse in the larger population, that some of these male professors are themselves hitting their wives, harassing their students, or not taking no for an answer.

The gender or experience of teaching staff might be one reason for the resistance to including "safe city" ideas in teaching. A more fundamental source of resistance to including any "women's issues" in the planning curriculum is the tension between planning for social change and planning for economic efficiency. In this, planning schools accurately reflect the situation in the "real world of city planning."

The conflict within planning between "higher" social, philanthropic aims and "base" money-generating schemes has existed since the beginning of the profession. When urban planning was first being promoted in the late nineteenth century, health and welfare concerns sat uneasily with the goals of protecting rich homeowners' property values and increasing cities' "beauty" and marketability.

There is a myth that the 1960s and 1970s saw a golden era of planning, when community development was "king," planners were radicals in jeans and sandals, and the dragon of rampant highway expansion was slain. In Toronto at least, this was not the case. There were some cases of working-class neighbourhoods successfully curbing the destruction of their communities, especially in Toronto's east end. There were also some examples of mostly middle-class neighbourhoods stopping mid-town expressways or especially egregious examples of high-rise disasters. Particularly in the central city, there were examples of small social housing projects, integrated within neighbourhoods, and new neighbourhoods that stressed humane, mixed-use development. But the 1960s and 1970s were also the decades when Toronto's downtown pedestrian amenity was sorely challenged by the creation of a huge mall, the Eaton Centre; when the working-class houses saved from the wrecker's ball became financially inaccessible to lower income people; and when the urbanized area expanded to new suburbs where highways, highrises, and homogeneity reigned unchallenged.

If a planner goes to a Canadian planning school in the 1990s, she or he can be expected to find courses on real estate law, a descriptive rather than critical study of zoning, and case studies that focus on winning at the Ontario Municipal Board rather than on conflict resolution skills when negotiating between different community stakeholders. If that planner had gone to the same school two decades earlier, the curriculum would not have been that different. The difference is that the 1970s planner was as likely as not to have obtained a degree in urban studies or sociology, or no degree whatsoever. The 1980s and 1990s have seen a growing professionalization of the planning field, that is, the creation of a "turf" where the cross-disciplinary nature of the best urban safety work may not be welcome.

Another barrier to the introduction of the complex issues surrounding urban safety lies, I think, in the quest for "planning perfection."[41] Major influences on the twentieth century profession, such as Ebenezer Howard and Le Corbusier,[42] were utopians of the highest order. They advocated a kind of scorched earth policy of starting from scratch, whether it be in Howard's Garden City new towns, or Le Corbusier's Paris rising from the ashes of its former self. In this, they shared commonalities with other twentieth century professions, such as psychiatry and sociology. Psychiatry held that if we unlocked the secrets of the psyche we could create a generation of mentally healthy individuals. Sociology taught that if we developed a good society, then people would be good. Even some influential for-profit developers articulated their aims in terms of utopian ideals: what was the aim of Levittown if not to create the ideal setting for the ideal family?[43]

Some "postmodern" reformers of the environments created by the earlier generation of reformers are no better. To a lesser extent in Oscar Newman and to a greater extent in Alice Coleman, there is the underlying message that if we replace "bad" design with "good" design, we can recreate a (mythical) earlier generation of poor people who strive to better themselves along socially respectable lines as defined by the middle class.

Meanwhile, the initiatives in Toronto have been a messy amalgam of social planning, advocacy, and community development. They are hard to evaluate. They are based in complex communities. They are not particularly expert-based. In this, they run against some of the current trends in planning.

Conclusion: Safety and "a healthy city"

Perhaps the coming of the millennium will bring the development of mixed-use, heterogenous neighbourhoods throughout Canada's urbanized regions. Certainly, issues that previously were unheard of in the planning discourse, such as accessibility for elderly people and people with disabilities, and environmental sustainability, are beginning to be discussed by students and professionals.

But counter-pressures exist. Streamlining the development process, a current concern across Canada, may mean dropping some issues and trying to reduce other complex issues, such as urban safety, to easily applied regulations. Encouraging development in a recession and in an atmosphere of competition among neighbouring municipalities may mean that cities will be encouraged to drop resources and staff from community development in general, and from anti-violence initiatives specifically. The decline of the community development role in the planning profession, and its replacement by the "professional planner" who needs to know more and more about building codes, planning acts, and city council directives (and who thus needs to spend more time at her or his desk or in meetings with developers, rather than working with communities), is bound to have an impact on the understanding of a neighbourhood, its safety concerns, and the initiatives that can be supported.

It is also possible that urban safety can become one of those places where planning for social change, planning for economic health, and planning for an environmentally sustainable future may coincide. Certainly, Toronto's reputation as a clean and safe city, "New York run by the Swiss," has aided in bringing in tourist dollars.[44] While there is less direct evidence of this, one of Toronto's selling points with international business is its relatively safe downtown.[45]

Lest this article seem to favour the public sector unduly, I should say at some point that enlightened capitalism has its place in planning for a safer city. Some of the worst developments in Toronto were created by governments using philanthropic rhetoric; much of the public housing stock comes to mind. Some of the best projects in Toronto are being stimulated by the profit motive: the transformation of a west-end shopping mall, Dufferin Mall, into a neighbourhood centre, and the creation of a small shopping centre in the east end, Carrot Common, that has added vitality to a major street are good examples. If making Toronto safer is seen as an economic stimulator, if keeping the inner city liveable is seen as an attractor of new development that can help pay for further social programs, then spending time and money on building safer communities can be seen as an investment. Certainly, working with rather than against developers can produce no worse results than many "neighbourhood empowerment" exercises of the 1970s, which as often as not led to the further political marginalization of the poor, the homeless, and non-English speakers.

Similarly, I hope that nothing in this article supports our anonymous gentleman's contention that planning for a safer city means "paving parks." The opposite is true. In many cities, community-based environmental activists have "taken back" the concrete in parks, and made better, safer places. For example, a large schoolyard at Ossington-Old Orchard Public School, outfitted with the usual chain-link fence and concrete, was abandoned after school hours by everyone except the local miscreants. A group of parents spent years battling the school board in order to add a community garden and re-naturalize the space. Now local seniors have garden plots there, benches attract neighbours on summer evenings, and the new park has become a bit of a model for the school board, as well as being a safer place.

Not far from Ossington-Old Orchard is Dufferin Grove, a park in the west end. People living around the park were getting increasingly concerned about the "youth gangs" of male teenagers, mostly refugees from Latin America, hanging out in the park. When a local resident was informed that the owners of Dufferin Mall across the street were willing to donate $25,000 towards improving the park, she and her neighbours (some of whom were parents of the "problem" teens) brainstormed for ideas that would make all ages and cultures happy. The results were a new basketball court, to give the kids something to do besides smoke and look tough; a new sand pit, for younger children to play in; and a fire pit. The fire pit became the site of Friday evening community cookouts, with food provided by the Latin Americans, which led to a breakfast program for the teens as well as some employment constructing these park improvements. While there was a tense moment for some neighbours when the teens arrived one morning bearing axes, communication between the neighbours has been greatly improved. Community "ownership" of the park has been created, and more people feel safe using the park.

In an urban society, the term sustainability has a very complex meaning. Certainly, we need cities that no longer drain good farming land from the surrounding countryside, that stop emitting huge quantities of pollution into the air, land and soil, and that guard the health of citizens and what natural environment remains in the city. But sustainability can also be taken to mean the ability of citizens to sustain an active and happy life in the same community throughout their lives if they wish, with unlimited mobility if they wish. To look at the issue another way, cities are not sustainable if families feel they have to move out to the suburbs to ensure a nice, safe environment for their children, or if people feel they have no choice other than to be ghettoized in a "senior's building" as they age. A city must be safe if it is to sustain itself in this sense, if it is to bear out the medieval adage: "City air makes a person free."

Urban dwellers face the millennium with the knowledge that the year 2000 will probably not bring with it the proverbial "millennium," the perfect society where people will be happy, peaceful, and loving. For the foreseeable future, there will be people with hideous ids living in a class-ridden (and racist and misogynist and homophobic and ...) society. That does not mean that urban planners should not strive to create the new Jerusalem in our green and pleasant land. By focusing on those who are most effected by violence, by combining community development with design improvement, and by listening to what the users of a space say they need, planners can begin to reduce the social and physical conditions that make violence a norm rather than an exception in our society.

I would like to thank my co-authors in this book, as well as Susan Addario, Rose Catallo, and Margo Huxley, for their clear and incisive comments on my drafts.

Notes

1 This article is not intended to represent the views of either the City of Toronto Planning and Development Department or the Safe City Committee.

2 These principles are defined in an earlier article: Carolyn Whitzman, "Taking Back Planning: Promoting Women's Safety in Public Places – the Toronto Experience," *Journal of Architectural and Planning Research* 9, 2 (Summer 1992): 169-79. The phrase "safer for women, safer for everyone" comes from a Metro Toronto Action Committee on Public Violence Against Women and Children (METRAC) pamphlet.

3 A *Toronto Star*-Environics poll published on 10 November 1994, just before the last municipal election, asked the question: "What, in your opinion, is the single most important local problem facing your municipality today?" Thirty-five per cent of voters answered "crime"; 14 per cent answered "unemployment/ economy"; 6 per cent answered "taxes"; "the environment" was mentioned by less than 4 per cent of those polled (Jane Armstrong, "Toronto Race Now Tighter, Poll Says," *Toronto Star* [10 November 1994]). A poll taken just before the previous municipal election in November 1991 showed that 27 per cent of Torontonians rated "crime" as their number one election issue, with 15 per cent choosing unemployment, 7 per cent choosing "high taxes," and 5 per cent "the environment" (Insight Canada Research, quoted in Christina Blizzard, "Crime Considered City's Top Problem," *Toronto Sun* [10 November 1991]).

4 Carolyn Whitzman, "Women, Fear, and Urban Neighbourhoods," MA thesis, University of Toronto, Geography Department, 1988.

5 As reported in "50% Fear Own Neighbourhood, Gallup Finds," *Toronto Star* (20 April 1992).

6 Carl Keane, "Fear of Crime in Canada: An Examination of Concrete and Formless Fear of Victimization, *Canadian Journal of Criminology* (April 1992): 215-24. Although not mentioned, physical ability is also an important factor.

7 See, for instance, Margaret Gordon and Stephanie Riger, *The Female Fear* (New York: The Free Press, 1989).

8 Centre for Criminology, Middlesex Polytechnic, *Second Islington Crime Survey*, 1990.

9 City of Toronto Parks and Recreation Department, *High Park User Survey*, 1987.

10 Statistics Canada, "The Violence Against Women Survey," *The Daily*, catalogue 11-001, (18 November 1993).

11 Ibid.

12 Statistics Canada, "Gender Difference Among Violent Crime Victims," *Juristat Bulletin*, catalogue 85-002, 12,21 (November 1992).

13 Cited in Glenn Chenier, "Statistics on the Problem of Crime in Canada," prepared for the National Crime Prevention Secretariat, September 1994.

14 Nottingham Safer Cities Project, *Community Safety in Nottingham City Centre: Report of the Steering Group*, October 1990.

15 See the chapter on "The Economic Costs of Crime" in Gerda Wekerle and Carolyn Whitzman, *Safe Cities* (New York: Van Nostrand Reinhold, 1995).

16 Goldfarb Consultants poll, as reported in Paul Watson, "Residents Find They're Afraid of Life in 'Toronto the Good,'" *Toronto Star* 17 May 1989.

17 David Dillon, "Fortress America," *Planning* (June 1994): 8-12. See also Jim Schwab, "Home Safe Home?" *Zoning News* (September 1993): 1-14, and Mike Davis, *City of Quartz: Excavating the Future in Los Angeles* (New York: Verso, 1990). Gated communities, of course, are as likely to harbour maniacs and miscreants within their gates. In one anecdotal study of a gated community, a serial rapist, a mass murderer of 23 people, and a man who killed his wife and two stepdaughters were among the happy residents of Green Valley, Nevada (David Guterson, "No Place Like Home", *Harper's Magazine*, November 1992, pp. 55-64).

18 See Richard M. Titus, "Security Works: Shopping Enclaves Bring Hope, Investment to Blighted Inner City Neighbourhoods," *Urban Land* (January 1990): 2-5.

19 Francis Stoks, "Assessing Urban Public Space Environments for Danger of Violent Crime – Especially Rape," doctoral dissertation, Urban Planning Department, University of Washington, 1982.

20 METRAC, Women Plan Toronto, York University Faculty of Environmental Studies, "The WISE (Women in Safe Environments) Report" (Toronto 1987); Gill Valentine, "Women's Fear and the Design of Public Space," *Built Environment* 16, 4 (1990): 288-303.

21 Sally Merry, *Urban Danger* (Philadelphia: Temple University Press, 1981); Dennis Roncek, "Dangerous Places: Crime and Residential Environment," *Social Forces* 60, 1 (1981): 74-96. See also Jane Jacobs, *The Death and Life of Great American Cities* (New York: Vintage Books, 1961), which is still the clearest explanation of these principles.

22 See, for instance, Leslie Weisman, *Discrimination by Design: A Feminist Critique of the Man-Made Environment* (Urbana: University of Illinois Press, 1994).

23 This argument begins to be explored in Carolyn Whitzman, *Planning for a Safer City*, Cityplan Background paper no. 10, (Toronto: City of Toronto Planning and Development Department, 1990) and in Debbie Wise Harris, *A Safer City: The Second Stage Report of the Safe City Committee* (Toronto: City of Toronto Safe City Committee, 1991). For some examples of innovative initiatives, see Rose Catallo, *Lessons from Success Stories: Making Communities Safer* (Toronto: City of Toronto Safe City Committee, 1994).

24 See, for instance, Dennis Rosenbaum, "Community Crime Prevention: A Review and Synthesis of the Literature," *Justice Quarterly* 5, 3 (1988).

25 Presentation by Alice Coleman at "Cities Alive!" Conference, Canadian Housing Renewal Association, May 1993. Alice Coleman's explanation of her theories can be found in *Utopia on Trial: Vision and Reality in Planned Housing* (London: Hilary Shipman, 1980).

26 The Horner Report on *Crime Prevention in Canada: Toward a National Strategy*, Twelfth Report of the Standing Committee on Justice and the Solicitor General,

February 1993, makes a recommendation that 1 per cent a year be allotted to crime prevention activities, with 5 per cent at the end of five years. Unfortunately, this recommendation was not carried forward into the newly (1994) unveiled National Strategy on Crime Prevention.

27 Oscar Newman, *Defensible Space* (New York: The Macmillan Company, 1972).

28 A good example of this analysis is found in Lee Lakeman, *99 Federal Steps Toward an End to Violence Against Women* (Ottawa: National Action Committee on the Status of Women, 1993).

29 See, for instance, Yvonne Korn, *Inspirations for Action: A Practical Guide to Women's Safety* (Swindon, Wiltshire: Crime Concern, 1993).

30 See the annual, *Safer Cities Progress Reports*, produced since 1989 by the Home Office Crime Prevention Unit, London, England.

31 See the section on St. Louis' private streets in Oscar Newman, *Community of Interest* (New York: The Macmillan Company, 1980) and the guidelines on "limiting access to neighbourhoods" and "separating wealthy or middle-class housing from poorer housing" in Barry Poyner, *Design Against Crime: beyond defensible space* (London: Butterworths, 1983).

32 A good example of this argument is found in a blunt article by Jane Jacobs, "Are Planning Departments Useful?" *Ontario Professional Planners Institute Journal* 8, 4 (1993) 2-3.

33 Taskforce on Public Violence Against Women and Children, *Final Report* (Toronto: Government of Metropolitan Toronto, 1984).

34 City of Toronto NDP Caucus, *The Safe City: Municipal Strategies for Preventing Public Violence Against Women* (Toronto: City of Toronto Planning and Development Department, 1989). Adopted by Toronto City Council September 1988.

35 METRAC, *Women's Safety Audit Guide* (Toronto: METRAC, 1989); METRAC, TTC, Metro Toronto Police Force, *Moving Forward: Making Public Transit Safer for Women* (Toronto: TTC, 1989); METRAC, TTC, MTPF, Scarborough Women's Centre, Scarborough Planning Department, *Making Transit Stops Safer for Women: Scarborough Moves Forward* (Toronto: METRAC, 1991).

36 Deborah Hierlihy, *Green Spaces/ Safer Places: Making Parks Safer for Women* (Toronto: City of Toronto Planning and Development Department, 1991).

37 City of Toronto Planning and Development Department, *City of Toronto Official Plan Part I – Cityplan* (Toronto: City of Toronto Planning and Development Department, 1994). Approved by Council 20 July 1993. See also Carolyn Whitzman and Gerda Wekerle, *A Working Guide for Planning and Designing Safer Urban Environments* (Toronto: City of Toronto Planning and Development Department, 1992), the guidelines used by the Planning and Development Department, 1992.

38 See the quarterly *Success Stories* newsletter produced by the Wen-Do Women's Self-Defense Corporation, P.O. Box 139, 260 Adelaide Street East, Toronto, Ontario M5A 1N0, for case studies.

39 There needs to be much more description, analysis, and evaluation of actual initiatives (the information in this paragraph comes from telephone conversations between the author and the co-ordinators of other initiatives). One recent report begins the process: *Building Safer Communities for Women: Municipal and Community Strategies to Reduce Violence Against Women* (Ottawa: Federation of Canadian Municipalities, 1994). Reports that created the initiatives include: Women and

Urban Safety Committee of Ottawa-Carleton, *Women and Urban Safety: A Recommendation for Action* (Ottawa: Women and Urban Safety Committee of Ottawa-Carleton, 1991); Tandem Montreal, *J'Accuse La Peur: Conference Montrealaise sur les Femmes et la Securite Urbaine* (Montreal: Tandem Montreal, 1992); [Edmonton] Mayor's Task Force on Safer Cities, *Toward a Safer Edmonton for All* (Edmonton: City of Edmonton, 1992); Social Planning Council of Winnipeg, *A Safer Winnipeg for Women and Children* (Winnipeg: Social Planning Council of Winnipeg, 1991); Saint John Safe City Committee, *Community Safety: Everyone's Business. The Saint John Safety Audit Report* (Saint John, 1993); [Vancouver] Safer City Taskforce, *Final Report* (Vancouver: City of Vancouver, 1993).

40 One reason may be many books, magazine articles, and reports are found in the popular and professional, rather than the academic, literature. For a good analysis of the relative absence in the academic literature of the issue of violence against women, see Fran Klodowsky, Colleen Lundy, and Caroline Andrew, "Challenging 'Business as Usual' in Housing and Community Planning: The Issue of Violence Against Women," *Canadian Journal of Urban Research* 3, 1 (June 1994): 40-58.

41 A brilliant feminist critique of utopian planning is contained in Elizabeth Wilson, *The Sphinx in the City: Urban Life, the Control of Disorder, and Women* (Berkeley: University of California Press, 1991).

42 Ebenezer Howard, *Garden Cities of Tomorrow* (London: Faber and Faber, 1960); Le Corbusier (Charles Edouard Jeaneret), *Concerning Town Planning* (London: The Architectural Press, 1947).

43 Dolores Hayden, *Reinventing the American Dream: The Future of Housing, Work and Family Life* (Cambridge, MA: MIT Press, 1984).

44 See, for example, "Theatregoers Choosing Toronto over Broadway," *Globe and Mail* (21 October 1993).

45 Recent reports on a survey of cities around the globe by a Geneva-based, international human resources consulting firm stress that Toronto would have been judged the best city in the world to live and work except for a less than perfect score on personal security. Toronto's ranking was fourth, well ahead of major US cities (of which the highest ranked was Boston, at number thirty). Personal safety was deemed the single most important factor in city living, and "American cities would have fared better ... but the presence of violent crime dragged all their scores down." See Bill Schiller, "Toronto Ranks as Fourth-best City to Live in, Survey Says," *Toronto Star* (18 January 1995); and "Three Canadian Cities Among Top 10 in World," *Globe and Mail* (18 January 1995).

SOWING THE SEEDS
OF SUSTAINABILITY:
PLANNING FOR FOOD
SELF-RELIANCE

Connie Guberman

P ART OF the larger vision of more liveable, sustainable cities is planning for food production at the local community level. Growing
food in cities is not a new phenomenon. Dating back at least to early Inca,
Aztec, and Mayan settlements, communities have produced some of their
own food. Urban and rural values were necessarily integrated for survival.
The shape of early towns and villages was determined by their relationship to the cultivated areas. Public open spaces had a functional purpose
and were put to productive use.[1]

The relationship between rural and urban living changed during the
industrialization of the eighteenth and nineteenth centuries in Western
societies. As masses of people migrated from the countryside into the cities for work, the use of open spaces changed. Parks were created as places
of leisure and as refuges from the daily drudgery of factory work. They
were designed to soothe the soul rather than feed the stomach.[2] This
legacy of planning public open space as a beautiful and passive retreat
from the nastiness of city life is still the prevailing value upheld by both
residents and planning professionals.[3]

In order to meet food security needs, we must change the way we look
at where, how, and by whom food is produced and distributed. As a society we are not used to thinking of cities as sustainable landscapes where
food can or should be grown. We assume that productivity happens only
on farmland outside the city and that land in the city is a real estate com-
modity. Yet there are notable precedents for urban food production. For

111

example, during times of emergencies and crises such as war, North American city dwellers have grown vast amounts of fruits and vegetables in all types of city spaces – on railway land, in backyards and schoolyards, in vacant lots, and on balconies and rooftops.

During World War One rural and urban Canadians were encouraged by all levels of government to help with the war effort by growing food wherever possible. In fact, there was moral pressure to produce: "Plant a garden in 1918 and your harvest will include financial gain, a better diet, better health, assistance to our Empire and through it justice and liberty to our world."[4]

Most communities across Canada with populations of more than 10,000 participated in this vacant lot garden movement at the beginning of the century. Governments gave their assistance and support: city councils often paid the cost of renting vacant land, fertilizing, ploughing, and purchasing supplies. There were massive public relations campaigns to encourage the community to get involved, and they were effective. People from a range of socio-economic levels participated through, for example, their religious organizations, ratepayers groups, Women's Institutes, schools, factory workers' groups, and Girl Guides and Boy Scouts groups.

The food growing momentum continued during the second World War with relief or victory gardens. It was estimated that 10 per cent of the food grown in Britain came from urban garden plots. In Montreal, there were 5,000 active garden plots and requests for three times that number. In Vancouver in 1945, residents produced 31,000 tons of fresh fruits and and vegetables. (The market equivalent today would be many millions of dollars).[5]

I am a keen urban gardener both in my own backyard and in a community allotment site, and I strongly believe that cities in Canada today should encourage urban agricultural production to meet a range of food, nutrition, health, and community needs. Taking my own eating culture and habits as a starting point (the first bite?), this chapter explores the importance of and possibilities for planning for urban food self-reliance, the significance of food and nutrition to our personal and collective health and well-being, the quality of the food we eat, the dynamics of the food system, and planning directions for creating a sustainable urban community.

One Friday evening in January, I was particularly tired after a long work week and was looking forward to lingering over supper. But before I could enjoy the meal, I had to shop for the food and then prepare it. I am

Jewish and sometimes I like to acknowledge the Sabbath with a meal that reminds me of dinners held thirty years ago at my grandmother's home with my parents, brother, aunt, uncle, and cousins. Although my cooking is far more modest, the process of preparing the meal, savouring the smells of food cooking, and sharing it with my partner and family of friends fills me with the joy of belonging and community connection, tugs at my cultural memories, and, of course, satisfies my belly.

For most of us, no matter what our heritage, our familial and cultural traditions and social class have a significant impact on the food we buy and the way we prepare and serve it. Globally and historically, human communities have gathered and celebrated around food, as I do on Friday nights. Food is critical to human survival, often integral to our cultural customs, and has an enormous impact on our health and well-being as individuals and communities. Yet most of us are ignorant of how our food is grown and the journey it takes from where it was grown to the stores where we buy it. Most of us are unaware of the political, economic, and environmental dynamics of how our food gets from the fields to our table and the impact these dynamics have on the quality, quantity, and availability of our food.

For dinner at my home on this particular Friday night, the menu was going to be the traditional roasted chicken with potatoes, onions, and carrots, a loaf of challah bread, steamed broccoli, a green salad with tomatoes and herbs, and perhaps baked apple for dessert. This was a balanced meal that met the requirements of three of the four food groups listed in Canada's Food Guide,[6] yet a meal that is inaccessible to a growing number of people in this country.

Hunger and its impacts on health

While few people may starve in Canada from lack of access to food, many people suffer from hunger and inadequate nutrition.

Hundreds of thousands of people in cities across the country do not have access to adequate, appropriate, acceptable, uncontaminated and nutritious food. In 1987 there were more than 2.03 million poor households in Canada according to Statistics Canada.[7] In Toronto, at least one out of twenty of the population of adults and children regularly face involuntary food shortages of varying lengths and intensity.[8] They live under conditions of food "insecurity"; that is, they do not have the means to adequately meet their daily and annual nutrition needs,[9] and they lack access to quality foods or have limited ability to acquire personally acceptable foods.[10]

The dictionary defines hunger as an individual experience of the "need for food [and] the uneasy sensation felt when one has not eaten for some time."[11] Hunger is more than this. Our understanding of it must include not only the personal experience of it, but also a critical analysis of it within the family or household and in the community as a whole.

Access to adequate and nutritious food is a critical and basic prerequisite to our overall health and well-being. Healthy communities are not possible as long as the basic nutrition needs of its citizens are not being met. The health impacts of hunger and inadequate nutrition extend beyond the feeling of discomfort from a grumbling stomach or not meeting daily nutrient needs. Hunger has a range of long-term effects on health resulting in such problems as low birth weight, cardiovascular disease, hypertension, cancer, and diabetes.[12] It affects our intellectual development, growth, work performance, self-esteem, resistance to infection, and general feelings of well-being.

Appallingly, there are no systematically collected national data on the prevalence of hunger or malnutrition, its duration, and its intensity,[13] or on the nutritional status of Canadians.[14] Much of what is known about hunger has been inferred from related research such as data on poverty and social assistance rates, difference in health status and access to food across income levels, surveys on where we spend our food dollars, food bank use, studies of poor children and their families, and local reports of programs that feed school children and promote better nutrition among pregnant women. It is clear, however, that people who are poor and/or people who have limited resources are generally those who experience food insecurity and who, as a consequence, are at greater risk of experiencing poor health. It is estimated that 60 to 70 per cent of diseases have a diet-related dimension.[15] Therefore, poverty may be the most important factor either underlying or causing many preventable short- and long-term health problems.[16]

Women, children, and young families are among the poorest people in Canada. Their situation has been getting worse over the last five years – women, children, and young families are likely to be poorer now than in 1989. In 1994 (ironically, the International Year of the Family) nearly 1.3

million children in Canada lived in poverty – an increase of 35 per cent (or 331,000 children) since 1989. According to a 1991 report published jointly by the Child Poverty Action Group and The Social Planning Council of Metropolitan Toronto, "lone-parent, mother-led families dependent on one income, have a higher chance of ending up in poverty than any other family type."[17] This is particularly serious since the number of poor children who live with single parent mothers has increased over the past ten years. Children of lone parent mothers are disproportionately poor. Poverty rates continue to increase among young families as well. Families that are headed by a person who is under twenty-five years old are 40 per cent more likely to be poor than families in general.[18]

Our health status is clearly related to our income level (or that of our parents) at every stage of life, beginning in the womb. A pregnant woman's deficient diet increases the likelihood of prenatal or neonatal mortality. The death rate for children under twenty years old from families with the lowest income level was 56 per cent higher than children in the wealthiest families,[19] and twice as many low-income children are likely to suffer from health problems than are children who are not poor.[20] Other studies show that the poorer you are, the less healthy you are likely to be over a shorter life time.[21] Poor families are often forced to make a decision about spending to meet their basic necessities – either pay the rent to avoid eviction and retain a place to live, pay the electricity bill,[22] or buy food. The trade offs of such "choices" are devastating and the personal and community consequences long lasting.

One of the relatively recent ways of analyzing the scope of hunger is to look at the number of people using food banks. There are over 450 communities across Canada with at least one food bank.[23] In one winter month in 1992, 14,700 people used the food banks in Metropolitan Toronto. Almost three-quarters of those who were surveyed said they had gone without food because of their lack of money.[24] While they may meet immediate needs, food banks are a system of food charity and they do not address the deeper structural issues of our society which have created and perpetuate poverty and hunger.[25] Food banks depend on donated canned and packaged goods, they do not provide the range of foods required to meet nutritional needs, and cannot be seen as a solution in the long term.

Families on social assistance use foodbanks as a way of supplementing their meagre food budgets. In contrast, my partner and I are in a financial position to choose the food we want to eat. The meal we made at our home cost twenty-eight dollars, a prohibitive cost for a family living on social assistance. We also have the means to make other critical choices concerning our food selection and eating habits: we can buy food where we want to, we can shop at stores which are conveniently close to home but which charge slightly more, and we can afford to pay extra for organic produce which is better for our health and for the health of the environment because it has been grown without chemical fertilizers, pesticides, or additives.

From field to table: Understanding the food system

On an individual or household level, it is possible to satisfy hunger by providing for our immediate calorie needs. But providing for food security, a long-term collective goal, is far more complex. It necessitates looking at the interconnected structural issues of income and economics, housing, education, gender, race, class, health, and the environment. In relation to food needs, food security has at least six interrelated components: access to purchasing quality food, the availability of a variety of foods at a reasonable cost, enough money to buy adequate food for each member of the household, personally appropriate food choice, confidence in the quality of food, and access to information about food and nutrition.[26] Obviously, with the number of people who are hungry and/or malnourished in our country, these needs are not being met. The current food system, which includes the methods by which food is produced, food quality, distribution, accessibility, and retailing, is not working.

Like all critical political, social, and economic issues, the analysis of the origins, scope, and definition of the problem must inform effective strategies for change. It is important to understand where our food is grown, who grows and produces it, and what processes are used to grow and produce it. It is also important to examine the impact of food production on the environment and on farmers both locally and globally. The questions we must ask concern the nutrition content of our food, the health consequences of using chemical additives, and the consequences of genetic construction and manipulation. What happens to our food on its journey from seed to farm to store to kitchen? How is it distributed and who reaps the biggest gains?

To answer these questions about food quality, availability, and choice we must look at how the food system is planned and controlled through corporate profit-making and concentration in food retailing, product marketing and food prices, store size and location, our own shopping patterns, and even how we get food home. In addition, we must look at possible alternatives which involve food production and distribution, preparation and consumption – the processes by which we turn the food (our raw materials) into something we want to eat. Perhaps if people knew the answers to these questions, they would feel compelled to act collectively to regain control over their food choices.

Poisoned to perfection: Food quality

Historically people ate foods that were indigenous to their region. In Canada this meant that we ate a lot of turnips and potatoes in February and looked forward to apple season. Today, most North American consumers expect to have any fresh vegetable at any time of the year, yet most of the food we consume is grown and farmed thousands and thousands of miles away and transported to us. Everything always seems to be in season on our supermarket shelves because plants have been bred specifically to accommodate consumer demand. Many vegetables, such as corn and peas, have been bred to suit supermarket culture. That is, they convert sugars to starch slowly, they retain water longer, and they resist rot and thus have a longer life on supermarket shelves. This form of breeding is known as genetic engineering; it provides the means to slow down or speed up the maturation process of fruits and vegetables so that they appear ripe just at the time they reach the store shelves. The problem is that this process takes a toll on the nutrient value of the food.[27]

For example, the tomato, my favourite ingredient in our dinner salad, was the first genetically altered food to reach the consumer market.[28] It has virtually been poisoned to perfection. Biotechnology techniques have made it possible to design a tomato that is durable and able to travel thousands of miles so that when it arrives in the stores in Canada in midwinter it still looks fresh and pretty – bright red, perfectly round, and blemish-free. But it has very little real food value or flavour because it has been "gassed into a coma"[29] for its journey here.

Growing food in this way has high social, economic, and environmental costs. The consumer indirectly pays for biotechnology research, specialized farm equipment, processing, transportation, and spoilage. The land on which it is grown pays a steep environmental price because it deteriorates in quality. The growers pay a higher price in the deterioration of their personal health due to exposure to the wide variety of toxic fertilizers and pesticides, and the consumer gets a chemical-rich product which is preserved and coloured with those toxins. The nutrient value of the final "product," the tomato, is very low. Analysts have shown that the less real nutrition, the more room for profit.[30] The process of reducing the nutrients even continues in store display bins – when vegetables are sprayed with water to stay crisp and fresh, it causes them to breathe and deteriorate.[31] It is ironic that people think that attractive produce is the freshest and the best, and that they are willing to pay for food that is potentially harmful to their health. Food corporations are cashing in on the myths of the "beauty is everything" generation.

Supermarket shopping: Food availability

Where we buy our food is as important as what we buy. Most of us shop at convenience stores, supermarkets, or superstores.[32] In a study conducted by the trade publication *Canadian Grocer*, nearly half of those surveyed said they had recently switched to shop at a supermarket because it offered lower prices even though they did not like it as much.[33] Studies have shown that for 80 per cent of consumers, price is the most important factor deciding where they shop.

When supermarkets were first designed in the 1950s, they were huge at 5,000 to 30,000 square feet. They were built in malls and other areas people frequented to do other errands. The retailers chose their store locations depending on where the customers were[34] and in the process put a lot of neighbourhood grocers out of business. The logic and cunning are those of the economy of scale – bigger is better and cheaper. Now this neighbourhood supermarket is being replaced by even bigger "superstores" and "supercentres" of 100,000 square feet and more. Planners are changing zoning designations to allow for them. Historically stores have been located in areas where they are likely to be profitable. That is, where there are customers with the money to shop. Supermarket chains are not usually located in low-income neighbourhoods. The people who live in poorer neighbourhoods have few shopping options: either there are only a few stores to choose from or there is a monopoly which often results in even higher prices than those found in higher income areas which have greater competition among stores and a more mobile consumer.[35] People either rely on the corner convenience stores which are usually within walking distance but carry much more expensive and poorer quality produce, or travel miles from their home to shop for food which is less expensive and is better quality.[36] Travelling a long distance to shop means either using a car, which is a prohibitive cost for people on a low-income and environmentally unhealthy, or trekking there and back on public transit or a bicycle loaded with bags of groceries. Just as planners have not traditionally incorporated personal safety into design concerns, they have also not planned neighbourhoods for convenient, affordable, quality shopping.[37]

In Canada, the retail food market is overwhelmingly controlled by five companies. George Weston Ltd., with the Loblaws chain, and Univa Inc., with Provigo, top the list. They provide us with a seemingly endless choice of food items from anywhere and everywhere around the world no matter what the crop or the season – oranges from Morocco, strawberries from Mexico, kiwis from New Zealand or California, coffee from many tropical countries, bananas from Honduras, and so forth. The supermarket is a "veritable palace of consumption."[38]

But what is wrong with this picture? The growing dominance of huge food corporations and their control of all levels of the food industry through the integration of the various stages of production – from growing, processing, packaging, to transporting, distributing and selling – actually reduces consumer choice rather than increases it.[39] It is a myth that there is a lot of brand choice or diversity in the range of available products. This is because the mega-corporations bought out the independent brand names years ago and, because of the small number of distributors, competition is limited. The variety in packaging merely provides the appearance of competition, when in reality the goods may have been produced in the same production plant.

Food corporations like Loblaws mainly buy from the largest food producers and processors and, because of their huge volume and turnover, the prices they pay to suppliers are low. As a result, the farmers who cannot meet the demands of these corporations are at a critical disadvantage. They are being squeezed between the corporate oligopolies that provide them with their raw materials for farming, such as seeds, fertilizer, pesticides, and equipment, and the oligopolies that buy their produce, which are often the same few companies.

119

Since large-scale farming today uses highly technical high energy inputs, it requires a large capital investment for equipment. This means that farmers borrow heavily from the banks to convert and sustain their business, but often cannot keep up with their loan payments. Farm bankruptcies are common. Yet for every farmer who is forced into bankruptcy, seven give it up voluntarily out of despair or frustration.[40] They sell their land to developers because the land has greater market value than their produce does. Not only does this mean personal hardship and the disappearance of a way of life, but it also results in the loss of prime agricultural land, particularly around the larger cities. In addition, it increases the reliance on food grown in countries far away. The farmers who do stay on their land try to compete by reducing costs through adapting less labour-intensive methods. This in turn results in fewer people farming larger areas, the population of rural areas declining, and agricultural output consequently falling.

Several provinces already do not produce enough food to supply their own population. We are importing more and more food from countries where the climate is warmer and labour is cheaper because farm workers are exploited.[41] In 1993 Ontario had a 1.9 billion dollar deficit in agricultural trade, one-third of which was in horticultural products. While some of this deficit is due to our short growing season, "a significant percentage of the crops that comprise this deficit could be produced and stored here if it were a priority of domestic agricultural policy."[42] Canada could be far more self-reliant in meeting our domestic food needs if we developed policies and incentives which encouraged a sustainable food system. Such a system would also need to meet the requirements for food security.

Urban agriculture: Food production

Urban agricultural production or city farming is actively supported today in approximately sixteen cities throughout Africa and Asia where, since the late 1970s, planners and policymakers have been promoting food production as a critical urban function. Governments have even created agencies to encourage and manage food growing activities. Luc Mougeot, of the International Development Research Centre (IDRC) in Ottawa, estimates that "such agriculture often makes a significant contribution to many major cities' food self-reliance."[43] The city farming programs provide the levels of subsidy to those who farm similar to other food assistance and nutrition programs, but at a much lower cost. Cities such as Kathmandu, Karachi, Singapore, Hong Kong, and Shanghai produce between 25 per cent and 85 per cent of their fresh fruits and vegetables with far less space and energy resources available than we have in North America.

There are also current European precedents for integrating agriculture into the city's open space system. In Switzerland and Holland commercial farmers lease space in public parklands surrounding the city to grow crops and raise livestock, while at the same time there are recreational paths for more traditional park users. Visionary landscape architect, Michael Hough, writes in *City Form and Natural Process* that

> these examples show what long tradition and intelligent planning at the municipal level can achieve – a multifunctional, self-sustaining landscape that provides social, environmental and economic benefits. A key ... is that parks systems can be, at least in part economically self-sustaining, contributing in ways other than recreation to the public good.[44]

Canadian cities have food producing histories and have enormous potential to produce again. Urban agriculture is neither a current trendy "green" fad nor a utopian fantasy. It is a practical alternative to many of the urban social and environmental problems that are reaching crisis proportions. The interest in urban agriculture in North America had a resurgence beginning in the 1970s when people were searching for gentler alternatives to living in an increasingly technological society, were increasingly aware of the environmental and health problems caused by food grown with chemicals, and were critical of the traditional approach to parks and open space. In response, community gardening and greening programs were developed throughout the United States and, to a much lesser degree, in Canada.

Community gardening is a form of urban agricultural production and is a general term for gardening and growing together with friends and neighbours. Gardens can range in size, location, and participation; they can be small, local neighbourhood gardens in vacant lots or parks, communal rooftop gardens, or municipally maintained allotment gardens. Whatever form the garden takes, wherever it is located in the city, and whomever owns the land, the process of gardening and growing has many benefits to individual and collective well-being, and to social, economic, and environmental health. It provides individuals with the opportunity to have closer contact with nature and to be directly connected to growing their own food. People save money because they produce their own food, they participate in fulfilling work and physical activity whatever their ability, they develop new skills, and they form new connections on a community level. It contributes to the beautification of the city by putting derelict land to creative and productive use; encourages community participation and neighbourhood control; builds community spirit by sharing knowledge, work, and materials with others; and often results in reduced crime and safer neighbourhoods because of the new sense of shared community concern.[45]

Planning for effective alternatives

Planners do not currently plan for urban land to be used for food production. The agriculture initiatives of the Seaton project which Margrit Eichler describes in her chapter are planning innovations. Community-based projects such as gardens must be seen as viable alternatives to the current system that cannot ensure food quality, accessibility, or affordability. However, in order to develop effective and sustainable alternatives, there are a range of policies, plans, and initiatives which federal departments, provincial ministries, and municipal governments must endorse and implement. In relation to community gardens, these include the four recommendations below.

1) Legitimize diverse open space use

Most planners have been trained or socialized to hold a restrictive sense of how open space should be used, and have set ideas of what is appropriate in a park or garden.[46] Grass lawns which are mowed to an exact height, and immaculate and ordered floral and shrub borders are considered beautiful. These examples of "pedigreed landscapes"[47] demand a high level of water and energy to maintain, lack diversity, and will eventually become sterile. A view of urban open spaces as sustainable landscapes with economic, environmental, social, and cultural benefits should be endorsed and supported. Policymakers should encourage a new attitude to urban open space as diverse and sustainable landscapes and should develop policies to protect open spaces for both traditonal and non-traditonal land uses.

2) Designate permanent land use and zoning

Many community gardens have failed in the long term because they were on temporarily designated or leased land which the city or private owner decided to reclaim. Most gardening groups go from year to year not knowing if they will be able to continue in the garden. Obviously, not knowing if their garden renewal efforts will be covered over with asphalt for a parking lot or high rise has a negative impact on gardeners' commitment. Planning policies are lagging behind popular will. People are supportive of the idea of permanent sites for community vegetable gardens. The Gallup National Gardening Survey of 1983 found that 76 per cent of the eighteen million Americans polled wanted permanent land designated for community growing.[48]

In Canada, only Montreal has land-use zoning for community gardens, whereas in the United States many cities (such as Seattle, New York, Chicago) not only have land zoned for community gardens, but also fund programs to help local groups get established and lease and manage city-owned land specifically for community gardening. In other US cities gardens are being secured in land trusts where philanthropic foundations hold land in trust for the community for as long as one hundred years. The specific zoning designation legitimizes the use of the land for urban food production and ensures garden permanence.

Community gardens should be designated as a priority use in the allocation of city-owned land. Montreal, for example, has successfully integrated a third of their community gardens into public parks so that people can enjoy a range of leisure and productive activities. In addition, the City of Toronto Interdepartmental Technical Working Group on Urban Food Production proposed that

> city zoning and planning policies could reflect the benefits of urban food production by requiring, where ever possible, development plans to include space for community gardening, and guidelines to support community gardening in all social and recreational programmation, development agreements and undertakings, including official and area plans.[49]

Community gardens are not the only landscape or social form that urban agriculture can take. Zoning should also be designated for backyard growing, market gardens, permits for more outdoor markets, and, in some areas, animal husbandry.

3) Provide development, education and research support

Urban food production is not high on the priority list of Agriculture Canada, or, in Ontario, of the Ministry of Agriculture and Food. Their interest in urban agriculture has been marginal and their support minimal. For example, in Ontario in 1990 the government offered a one-time grant to communities that wanted to explore growing gardens in their neighbourhoods. Unfortunately, however, the program was poorly conceived and frustrating to applicants: the grants were to be used only for hiring staff (and not for development), and were issued late in the growing season when gardens were already well under production.

Governments at the federal and provincial levels must take a greater interest and responsibility in furthering urban agriculture initiatives as a form of planning and food provision for security. At the very least, they can support information and education programs, provide start-up funding for individuals and communities who are helping themselves by growing their own food, and encourage further research. While produce from urban agricultural initiatives cannot meet all the food and nutrition needs of urban populations, the initiatives can provide the opportunity for people to be increasingly self-reliant in providing for their food and nutrition needs.

4) Provide maintenance and technical support

Urban agriculture generally, and community gardening specifically, can address a range of community needs, but the land on which the food is grown must be contaminant and radiation-free. Municipalities should take a leadership role in ensuring that food grown in the city is not contaminated with toxins such as lead, by providing information to gardeners about the former land uses of potential growing sites, providing quality soil testing, and offering education and advice around safe gardening practices which in and of themsleves are not contaminating.

Food distribution alternatives

In additition to planning for urban food production alternatives, there are a range of initiatives which challenge other aspects of the food system discussed in this chapter. In Toronto, the community agency FoodShare has taken the lead in offering alternatives to the traditional dynamics of food distribution and production by sponsoring programs that build food security. The programs address health education, nutrition awareness, and community cooking by encouraging "self-sufficiency, community co-operation and creative use of limited resources."[50]

One program, Community Shared Agriculture (CSA),[51] provides urban consumers with a food shopping alternative to the superstores by offering a new form of partnership between farmers and consumers. The urban consumer "shares" the risks (and joys) of farming by paying a local organic farmer in advance for the season's crops. The money goes directly to the farmer who delivers the produce directly to a central location in the purchaser's or "sharer's" neighbourhood each week during the growing season. The consumer shares the risk by sharing whatever the harvest brings as the farmer cannot guarantee that weather, pests, or disease will not affect the bounty.

CSA narrows the distance between producers and consumers and is economically, environmentally, and socially advantageous: "sharers" have access to affordable organic produce; organically grown produce is healthier for consumers to eat, for farmers to grow, and does not pollute the water or soil during farming; farmers can plan their crop more efficiently and reduce waste; the energy used in transporting produce is minimized when it is grown and consumed locally; supporting local farmers helps support the local economy; and CSA promotes a sense of community between farmers and consumers, and within city neighbourhoods.[52] It also means that farmers do not have to wait until the produce is harvested for a return on their labour.

In Field to Table, another of FoodShare's programs, a staff person goes to the Ontario Food Terminal every morning to buy fruits and vegetables directly from the farmers and wholesalers in order to then resell the produce in low-income communities throughout the Metropolitan Toronto area, at cost. Depending on the community's needs, Field to Table can take the format of a market in the lobby of an apartment building; a food buying club; a student nutrition program which helps schools set up nutritious breakfasts, lunches, or snacks; or a monthly food box.

The monthly Good Food Box is a community-based alternative strategy that challenges a range of problems in our food system – food production and distribution, quality, accessibility, and availability. Good Food Box participants pay fifteen dollars at the beginning of the month for delivery of a box of fresh fruits and vegetables in the third week, just when money and food are typically in short supply. Volunteers are responsible for collecting the money and distributing the boxes which are delivered to a central neighbourhood location. The boxes include as much Ontario produce as possible; even in the winter months regionally grown carrots, apples, potatoes, onions, cabbage, and garlic are included.

Conclusion

While food security is a necessity for everyone, poverty and hunger affect women disproportionately. Women, particularly single mothers, are among the poorest, and traditionally it is women who are responsible for making sure their families are fed, housed, and kept healthy. Part of the goal in creating a non-sexist city is to challenge women's role in the home as the primary nurturer and caretaker; but this is a long-term vision of change. In the short-term we must address the needs of providing for food security.

Poverty, hunger, and food availability are not issues which community organizations, individual government departments, or urban planners alone can address. The larger issues of meeting food security needs are both local and national, urban and rural, and are integrated with wider economic, social, health, environmental, and agricultural concerns. A social system which plans for optimal health and nutrition[53] is what is necessary on a national scale and at the community level. But our municipal governments have a critical responsibility for making this happen by supporting and furthering initiatives which work towards the goal of food self-reliance and sustainability.

I would like to thank the co-authors of this book for their comments on drafts of this chapter; Debbie Field, Cathleen Kneen, and Brewster Kneen for sharing their extensive analyses of the food system; and Jill Wigle, Sandy Fox, and Kapri Rabin for their clear and thoughtful editing.

Notes

1 Lewis Mumford, *The City in History: Its Origins, Its Transformations, and Its Prospects* (New York: Harcourt, Brace & World, 1961).

2 As described in Michael Hough, *City Form and Natural Process: Towards a New Urban Vernacular* (New York: Van Nostrand Reinhold, 1984).

3 See Mark Francis, "Some Different Meanings Attached to a City Park and Community Gardens," *Landscape Journal* 6 (1987): 100-112.

4 Edwinna von Bayer, *Rhetoric and Roses: A History of Canadian Gardening*, (Toronto: Fitzhenry & Whiteside, 1984).

5 Hough, *City Form and Natural Process*, 1984.

6 Health and Welfare Canada, *Canada's Food Guide to Healthy Eating* (Ottawa: Health and Welfare Canada, 1993). The four food groups are grain products, vegetables and fruit, milk products, and meat and alternatives. Judy Perkin and Stephanie McCann in their chapter, "Food for Ethnic Americans: Is the Government Trying to Turn the Melting Pot into a One-Dish Dinner," in *Ethnic and Regional Foodways in the United States*, eds. Linda Keller Brown and Kay Mussell (Knoxville: The University of Tennessee Press, 1984), make the critical point that the role of government in determining what people eat has expanded since North Americans have moved away from food self-sufficiency. Nutrition advice reflects the needs of the agricultural industry and is politically and culturally biased.

7 David P. Ross and E. Richard Shillington, *The Canadian Fact Book on Poverty – 1989* (Ottawa: The Canadian Council on Social Development, 1989). This does not include people who live with "self-imposed" starvation such as anorexia.

8 Healthy Toronto 2000 Subcommittee, *Healthy Toronto 2000* (Toronto: Board of Health, 1988).

9 Gary Bellamy (ed.), *The World Food Update* (Ottawa: The World Food Day Association of Canada, October 1994).

10 Cathy Campbell, Stefa Katamay, and Carmen Connolly, "The Role of Nutrition Professionals in the Hunger Debate," *Journal of the Canadian Dietetic Association*, 49, 4 (Autumn 1988): 230-35.

11 *The Oxford Paperback Dictionary*, third edition (Oxford: Oxford University Press, 1988).

12 Healthy Toronto 2000 Subcommittee, *Healthy Toronto 2000*, 1988.

13 Ibid.

14 Campbell, et al., "The Role of Nutrition Professionals in the Hunger Debate" (1988).

15 Toronto Food Policy Council, "Reducing Hunger in Ontario," 1994, p. 27, unpublished report. Statistics reported from the US Surgeon General, 1988.

16 Brigitte Kitchen, Andrew Mitchell, Peter Clutterbuck, and Marvyn Novik, *Unequal Futures: The Legacies of Child Poverty in Canada* (Toronto: The Child Pov-

erty Action Group and The Social Planning Council of Metropolitan Toronto, 1991).

17 Ibid., p. 17.

18 Project Team, *The Outsiders: A Report on the Prospects for Young Families in Metro Toronto* (Toronto: Social Planning Council of Metropolitan Toronto, 1994).

19 Healthy Toronto 2000 Subcommittee, *Healthy Toronto 2000*, 1988.

20 Kitchen, et al., *Unequal Futures*, 1991.

21 Ibid.

22 Kathryn MacDonald and Mary Lou Morgan, *The Farm and Country Cookbook* (Toronto: Second Story Press, 1994).

23 Countdown 94, *Campaign 2000: Child Poverty in Canada. Report Card 1994* (Ottawa: Canadian Council on Social Development, 1994).

24 Board of Health, *The Economy and Health in the City of Toronto*, Public Health Department Annual Statement 1992, (Toronto: City Clerk's Department, City of Toronto, 1992).

25 See Toronto Food Policy Council, *Reducing Urban Hunger in Ontario: Policy Responses to Support the Transition from Food Charity to Local Food Security*, Discussion Paper 1 (Toronto Food Policy Council Discussion Paper Series, 1994) for a further discussion of food banks as a system of food charity.

26 Campbell, et al., "The Role of Nutrition Professionals in the Hunger Debate" (1988).

27 Brewster Kneen, *From Land to Mouth: Understanding the Food System*, second edition (Toronto: NC Press, 1993).

28 John Seabrook, "Tremors in the Hothouse," *New Yorker* (July 1993).

29 Kneen, *From Land to Mouth*, 1991, p. 47.

30 Kneen, *From Land to Mouth*, 1991.

31 Ibid.

32 Toronto Food Policy Council, *Reducing Urban Hunger in Ontario*, 1994.

33 From the *Canadian Grocer*, June 1982, as in Michael Czerny and Jamie Swift, *Getting Started on Social Analysis in Canada* (Toronto: Between the Lines, 1984).

34 Kneen, *From Land to Mouth*, 1991.

35 Toronto Food Policy Council, *Reducing Urban Hunger in Ontario*, 1994.

36 FoodShare, "Field to Table," Information Brochure.

37 This analysis was brought to my attention by Debbie Field, Executive Director of FoodShare.

38 Philip White, *Supermarket Tour* (Toronto: Public Interest Research Group, 1990), p. 5.

39 White, *Supermarket Tour*, 1990; and Kneen, *From Land to Mouth*, 1991.

40 White, *Supermarket Tour*, 1990.

41 Gary Lawrence Fairbarin, *Will the Bounty End: The Uncertain Future of Canada's Food Supply* (Saskatoon: Western Producer Prairie Books, 1984).

42 Toronto Food Policy Council, *Reducing Urban Hunger in Ontario*, 1994, p. 23.

43 Luc J.A. Mougeot, "Urban Food Self-Reliance: Significance and Prospects," *IDRC Reports* 211, 3 (1993): 3.

44 Hough, *City Form and Natural Process*, 1984, p. 229.

45 Francis, "Some Different Meanings" (1987).

46 See Moura Quayle, "The Changing Community Garden: Legitimizing Non-Traditional Open Space," *Landscape Architectural Review* 10, 2 (May 1989): 23-7.

In this article she reports the findings of her survey of planners regarding community gardens. Respondents found that "community gardens tend to look seedy."

47 Michael Hough uses this term in *City Form and Natural Process*, 1984. He contrasts pedigreed landscapes with non-pedigreed landscapes which are generally self-maintaining, productive, and sustainable.

48 As described in Mark Frances, Lisa Cashdan, and Lynn Paxson, *Community Open Spaces: Greening Neighborhoods Through Community Action and Land Conservation* (Washington, DC: Island Press, 1984), p. 21.

49 City of Toronto Interdepartmental Technical Working Group on Urban Food Production, "City of Toronto Support for Urban Food Production: Creating a Garden City," a proposal, April 1993, p. 16.

50 FoodShare Brochure entitled, "Field to Table." FoodShare was established in 1985. Its mandate is "working with communities to end hunger by improving access to affordable nutritious food." For further information on food security initiatives, contact: FoodShare, 238 Queen Street West, Lower Level, Toronto, Ontario, M5V 1Z7.

51 Community Shared Agriculture is a new concept in Canada. The first CSA farm was established in 1992 near Winnipeg by Dan Wiens. In 1994 there were more than thirty CSA farms across the country.

52 Community Shared Agriculture information brochure.

53 See Toronto Food Policy Council, *Reducing Urban Hunger in Ontario*, 1994, for a further discussion of the need for the development of a social agenda which integrates economic, health, nutrition, environment, and agriculture concerns.

ACCESS OVER EXCESS: TRANSCENDING CAPTIVITY AND TRANSPORTATION DISADVANTAGE

Sue Zielinski

EVERY ONCE in a while a term will crop up that seems to capture the essence of a situation. But I must admit I hesitate to celebrate the day I hit the jackpot with not one, but two such telling terms. While the chance discovery of two glorious golden nuggets of cultural representation more than tickled my sense of irony, I knew right away that this transportation chapter was not going to be the linear, academic piece of work that I perhaps too often strive to achieve. It was going to move in its own direction, and I was decidedly the passenger. Let me tell you how it all started.

I was invited to contribute to this book because of my work on sustainable transportation and because of my not-so-secret feminist leanings. Excited by the prospect of bringing two passions together, I began the research process with a routine scan of my transportation planning files. That was when I ran across the aforementioned nuggets: "transportation disadvantaged" and "captive."[1] Both of these terms are actual technical classifications that boil down to meaning "unfortunately car-less."

The first term, "transportation disadvantage," comes from the planning profession and is used to describe, label, and count the people in a city who have limited access to a car or have not yet achieved the state of car ownership and/or drivership. The second term, "captive," summons up an even more graphic, almost Victorian image. It is used by transit planners and transit marketers to analyze and describe the state of being trapped on public transit as the sad result of not having a car. (Only recently have the Victorian undertones been updated by a cinematic thriller entitled *Speed* in which transit riders are truly held "captive" by a deranged man in a bus that will blow up if it goes below fifty miles an hour.)

Perhaps not surprisingly, given women's general economic and social situation,[2] "transportation disadvantaged captives" are more likely to be women than men. Fewer women than men own cars, and more women than men are regularly found trapped on the transit system. Judging by the most recent car ads,[3] it would seem that the car companies are anxious to remedy this inequitable situation by getting more women into cars. They will provide child seats, air bags, cellular phones, vanity mirrors, cool sales guys – anything to prevent women from getting the short end of the stickshift. The problem is, the private automobile is not by any means the vehicle to equity – gender-based or otherwise. Getting more women into cars is not the route to a non-sexist city. In fact, quite the opposite is true.

More often than not, the car frees women to chauffeur their kids to hockey, babysitting jobs, and daycare, to taxi their aging parents to doctor's appointments, to drive to the shopping centre, to drive to work to make money to help pay for their car, to scurry through poorly lit underground parking lots, and to sit in traffic for hours on end.[4]

What is more, all the infrastructure required to afford drivers this "freedom" has made it next to impossible to get around the city in any other way, thus compounding the inequity. In cities built and sprawled for cars, it is too far to walk, too dangerous and difficult to manoeuvre a wheelchair, too frightening and polluted to cycle, too unreliable to take transit, and for many, too expensive or demanding to drive. This leaves a significant proportion of the population with literally NO options. The result: people with cars are forced to drive, and the people without cars are stuck.

My gut response to this situation, and the auto-centric terms used to describe it, came to me spontaneously in the form of a dialogue between two women. Soon the dialogue grew into a short, somewhat fanciful play called *Telling Terms*, which is included in the following pages. It is accompanied by explanatory text outlining principles for planning sustainable, equitable, accessible cities, along with some real live success stories for inspiration and "do-ability" value.

Telling Terms was written in the spirit that fun unlocks the imagination

– a necessary building tool for the feminist city. In keeping with this spirit, I made the events in the play larger than life for dramatic effect. Or so I thought at the time. It was only after completing the second draft that I actually met a woman who told me she had left her psychotherapist because he hassled her for not having a car. Needless to say I faxed the woman – who shall remain nameless – a copy of the draft, and felt even more humbled by the extent of our society's addiction to private car travel.

Telling Terms: A Three-Act Play About Women and Mobility
ACT ONE, Scene One: Diagnosis

(Scene: At the general practitioner's office. It's Karen's annual check-up. GP is furrowing his brow at complicated looking charts.)

Karen: Wh- wh- what is it, Doc? I want to know the truth.

Doctor: Well, Karen, you may want to sit down for this. I'm afraid you're ... TRANSPORTATION DISADVANTAGED.

Karen: Oh no! What could be worse?

Doctor: Well, you're also CAPTIVE.

Karen: Oh God. Is it fatal?

Doctor: Dammit, Karen, I'm a DOCTOR, not a transportation expert!

Karen: But can't you at least tell me what it means to be TRANSPORTA-
TION DISADVANTAGED and CAPTIVE? Will I live a normal life? Will I be able to play the piano? Will it hurt? How long have I got? Do you need to operate?

Doctor: Why don't you put your clothes back on, Karen, and I'll meet you back in my office and give you several glossy, superficial brochures on TD and we'll talk about prescribing something for you.

Karen: (Now in his office) This prescription says I have to get a CAT? But I'm allergic. Why would I need to ...

Doctor: No – a CAR. You need to get a CAR. That's an "R" at the end. And, by the way, the car's not covered by OHIP.[5] And I have no free samples left. Do you have a medical plan at work?

Karen: W-W-Well yes I do, but ...

Doctor: Fine then. Call my secretary if you have any problems or side ef-
fects and take this Prozac regularly to calm you down. *(Looking out the door)* Dorothy, can you send in my next patient? *(To Karen, with a glazed smile)* Bye now!

Act One, Scene Two: Seeking Treatment

(In Karen's living room. She's reading the glossy brochures to herself and looking confused.)

Karen: Hmm ... here it is ... *(she reads)* TRANSPORTATION DISADVAN-TAGED (TD): "A term used to describe the painful and unfortunate condition of NOT HAVING A CAR." Oh, and here's CAPTIVE *(she reads)*, "A term used to describe the painful and unfortunate condition of being trapped into taking transit because of NOT HAVING A CAR. KNOWN CURES: Take one to two cars daily."

Uh Oh! – *(she reads)* "Despite some reported side effects of car use, notably death, injury, respiratory disorders, aggression, and psychiatric complications, it is the only known and proven method for reversing TD and CAPTIVITY." Ho boy. This is all I need. And I just got rid of my yeast infection last week.

What's this? *(she reads)* "... the condition is far more common among women, but this trend is reversing as the result of an aggressive car cure campaign aimed at the female population. Experts are hopeful that before the beginning of the next century, the difference between women and men will be virtually erased *(she turns the brochure over to read the other side)* in terms of the incidence of TD and Captivity."

(The doorbell rings. She opens the door and it's her friend Linda.)

Linda: Hi Karen, what's up?

Karen: Not me, that's for sure. I've got some women's disease that's supposed to be really bad, but the cure is pretty bad, too, maybe even worse and it's expensive if you're not covered ...

Linda: When did all THIS happen? What do they say you've got?

Karen: *(Handing the brochure to Linda)* Here. It's all in here.

(Linda reads the brochure and looks puzzled.)

Linda: Oh wow. This looks bad. What are you going to do?

Karen: I guess I'll have to take some time off work and go to the car dealership tomorrow. Know anything about cars?

Linda: Not much, but I've heard they're addictive. You know this kind of reminds me of when they told me I was suffering from LDD back when you were living in Ottawa.

Karen: LDD?

Linda: Yeah, Living Downtown Disease. They said my best bet was to move to the suburbs to protect myself from the city. They figured since I already had a car I was halfway there.

Karen: What were the symptoms?

Linda: I had some trouble breathing, but mostly it was that I was getting angry all the time. You know. I'd be taking Poopee for a walk, and suddenly I'd flare up. Like I remember getting ballistic this one time, when this old woman was walking across at the lights, and she couldn't quite make it across in time, and all these cars – they saw her there – they started going anyway. They could have killed her. So I jumped in front of her and made like a traffic cop. And they stopped. But then once she was across, I stayed there and started to scream at them. I asked them if they had an elderly parent or two at home they were ALSO trying to kill. They all started honking and revving and I would have stayed there yelling at them – I really would have.

Karen: So what happened?

Linda: Well, I guess luckily for me, Poopee decided to prove his name, right there in the middle of the intersection. It must have been all the excitement. So of course I had to stoop and scoop, and by that time, all the cars just drove around me.

Karen: But everybody flares up every once in a while. If those were your only symptoms ...

Linda: No, but that was just the beginning. It would happen all the time. It was getting embarrassing ...

Karen: But what does all that have to do with living downtown? It could have happened anywhere.

Linda: They said it was a problem of controlling myself. Apparently, since I live downtown but don't drive my car downtown, I expose myself to stressful situations that I can't handle. If I'd been in a car – protected – I wouldn't have experienced those upsetting things. I would have been listening to calming music or books on tape or something. They also said that I was obviously under stress and maybe trying to build a career was getting to me. They suggested a bunch of things. Like the pill to regulate my hormonal fluctuations. And maybe moving to the suburbs where it was less stimulating. It was sort of a car therapy.

Karen: So what did you do?

Linda: I had no choice, really. I couldn't move to the suburbs because I'm allergic to pesticides. My allergies don't act up down here, since there's no green space. Good thing I'm not allergic to ground level ozone and carbon monoxide. Anyway, I stayed down here and took up welding. It channels my anger. But I'm apparently still suffering from LDD. Anyway, I'm already late for my lunch, but let's talk more when we meet tomorrow.

Karen: Yeah sure, see you then.

(Karen leans against the open door frame pensively, well after the little talking elevator voice and security beeps have faded away. Finally she scuffs across the room and flops into her stuffed chair and sighs. She takes the pamphlet from the side table, and reads it again. This time she sees something she'd missed before. She draws it closer to her wire-rimmed glasses.)

Karen: (She reads) "For a speedier recovery, visit the Corpcoma - Moltinati Privatized Healing Clinic and register for your choice of intensive Bigthrea Therapy programs. All credit cards accepted." Hmm. Worth a try. *(She picks up the phone and dials.)*

Phone: (Beep. A soft throaty machine voice, strikingly similar to the elevator woman's voice answers.) HELLO, you have reached the Corpcoma-Moltinati Privatized Medical Healing Clinic. If you would like information on ANY ONE of our one hundred and fifty three Intensive Bigthrea Healing Programs, please stay on the line. For Anorexia Shop-osa, please press "ONE"...; for Living Downtown Disease, or LDD, please press "TWO".... For those suffering from CODS – Community Over-Dependence Syndrome, please press "THREE"...; for Topofilia, please press "FOUR"...; for TD, or Transportation Disadvantage, please press "FIVE"...;"

Phone: "Hello. You pressed FIVE. You have reached the TD Helpline for those suffering from Transportation Disadvantage. Please hold for assistance.

(Music comes on, and it's a car ad on a loop. The car ad cuts off. A velvety male radio voice cuts in.)

Phone: "Hello. Can I help you?"

Karen: (Caught off guard by a real human) Uh. Yes. Uh. I was wondering – how do I find out about your TD program?

Phone: We have an opening tomorrow at 2:00. Can you come to the clinic?

Karen: Uh. Sure. How exactly do I get there?

Phone: I'm sorry. Since I'm speaking to you from the Global Information

Network Free Trade Zone in Atlanta, I wouldn't be able to tell you where your local CM Bigthrea Therapy Clinic is located, however, I will connect you with our global mapping centre when I've extracted your details. Please hold ...

What do the telling terms tell us? or,
transportation = necessary = cars

Assuming that language – even technical language – is socially constructed,[6] what do terms like "transportation disadvantaged" and "captive" tell us about the way we are thinking? My guess is that the idea of "transportation disadvantage" can only emerge from a society which perceives transportation – "the conveyance (of things or persons) from one place to another"[7] – as the primary and necessary way of meeting needs. If you want something, you will have to travel to get it or ship it from long distances. It is unlikely to be close by. Transportation is always necessary.

Along the same lines, that "transportation disadvantaged" and "captive" are understood to mean not having a car must emerge from a society which equates transportation with cars. If it is not a car, it is not transportation. If you do not have a car, you are transportation disadvantaged.

When these two cultural assumptions are merged, a syllogism results. Transportation is necessary. Transportation is cars. Cars are necessary. Although unstated, this has been a lucrative syllogism for the car industry – the purveyors of the theory that the right to drive should be one of the basic tenets of women's emancipation. It serves the multiple purpose of selling more cars to more women (and others) while creating a demand for more car-based infrastructure which, in turn, serves to squeeze out other options which, in turn, necessitates selling more cars.

But the economic advantage does not stop there. If cars equal transportation, solving transportation problems equals making cars better. Such a stroke of algebraic genius means that any problems identified as transportation-related must naturally be solved by improving on cars.

Hence, in the experimental labs of our present society, our best and brightest have their work cut out for them. They are working on alternative fuels and interior vacuum filters to solve "the pollution problem," air bags, cellular phones, and anti-skid brakes to solve "the safety problem," computerized locks and car alarms to solve "the crime problem," and smart cars to solve "the congestion problem."[8]

Despite its drawbacks, there is popular support for the car-based fix, not only because it seems simpler, but also because any other approach seems impossible. For example, within the transportation = necessary = cars paradigm which our North American society has internalized, it would be unfair to just take people's cars away. Faced with the current car infrastructures, physical and cultural, banning cars would only add to the growing number of people who are car-less and paralysed in the midst of a car-based environment. It would leave even more people with little or no access to their basic needs.

For this reason, if we are to envision and create a truly equitable and sustainable city, we will need no less than a new guiding logic and a new way of organizing our cities.

Act Two: A Brush with Therapy

(The Bigthrea Clinic. It is rather pleasant – a bit like an ad agency. It has a track lighting glow to it, and is tastefully adorned with original artwork, framed award-winning ads, trickling fountains, and sculptures. There are grand and elegant tinted windows and green everywhere – lush plants which are probably not plastic.

Dr. Freemarket is a youngish chiselled man who has had his hair tinted at the ends to achieve a quiet, hip-yet-sophisticated and credible look. He wears an elegantly cut white coat over an expensive casual sweater, loose linen pants, and Italian leather shoes.)

Dr. Freemarket: Hello Karen, Welcome to CM. Please come in.

(Karen sinks into the luxurious leather bucket seat client chair and a look of ecstasy comes over her face. As she examines the chair for the source of her ecstasy, a cappuccino is placed on the table beside her. Soft, beautiful quadrophonic sound surrounds her.)

Dr. Freemarket: Sugar?

Karen: No thanks, this is perfect. How did you know I love cappuccino?

Dr. Freemarket: Oh, Karen, I'd love to tell you we just had a feeling, or we read your mind, but I'll be honest. To make our clients comfortable, we keep "happy files" on current and potential clients. We believe in partnerships, and our partnership with the major credit card companies lets us know what you buy and when you buy it. Needless to say, cappuccino came up a few times for you. You see, this market partnership helps us give clients what they want.

Karen: Oh.

Dr. Freemarket: But enough about us, how about you? I see your charts indicate TRANSPORTATION DISADVANTAGE and CAPTIVITY. I'm so sorry.

Karen: Well, I'm only captive on transit in the dead of winter, when it's too snowy to ride my bike and too far to walk. But it IS true I don't have a car. Although sometimes I rent a car to go to the cottage, or I borrow my parents' car.

Dr. Freemarket: I see. Now Karen, what about shopping? How do you get to the mall?

Karen: Well I don't really go to the mall I guess. I get my food close by. I pick up a few things here and there. I've gotten to know the storekeepers in my neighbourhood. And mostly I can carry things on my bike.

Dr. Freemarket: Oh you poor thing. Such sacrifices. Having to get all sweaty, and being kept from the wide choice of consumer items at the mall. Risking your life out on the street. Not to mention how embarrassed you must feel when people SEE you walking or cycling. This must be devastating to your career, not to mention to your social life. Have you had a problem getting a job? Or getting a date? *(He twinkles his glassy blue eyes at her.)*

Karen: Well no, actually. I live in one of the last remaining neighbourhoods. My job at the library is close to my home. I have wonderful friends. I play music with them once a week. I actually, um, I guess I like my life. And I feel like in some way, I'm treading lightly on the earth, which also makes me feel good.

Dr. Freemarket: (Aside, with his back to Karen, as he is flipping through the files in his teak filing cabinet) Oh goody. I mean – oh dear. This is worse than I suspected. Could mean years of therapy.

Karen: Pardon?

Dr. Freemarket: Oh nothing ...

Karen: Anyway, I suppose I can't think of how any of it is really a sacrifice. I love using my own energy to get around. I love the street life. I don't really like shopping unless I need something. I enjoy meeting my neighbours. That's kind of why I found it so confusing when I was diagnosed with TD. I mean, I'm sure there are some people who suffer from it, but I don't really feel the symptoms. Maybe that's a problem. You're the expert. What should I do?

Dr.. Freemarket: Well, I hate to break this to you, Karen, because you are such a sweet and bright young lady. But your symptoms are so advanced that you've internalized them into your life. Do you know what "internalized" means? Let me rephrase this. You are in "denial" *(he makes a quotation gesture with his manicured hands).* In other words, you don't even know what your own body needs any more.

Karen: Wow. So then what do you suggest? I mean, I guess I ...

Dr.. Freemarket: Intensive physical and psychological therapy is your only hope. But rather than explaining what's involved, please allow me to SHOW you some of our treatment approaches *(he buzzes the machine on his desk).*

Machine voice: Yes Dr. Freemarket?

Dr. Freemarket: Ada, we're coming through for a tour.

(As they wind though the building on the way to the TD therapy lab, Karen peeks surreptitiously through the two-way mirrors exposing therapeutic labs in session. One lab is a simulated department store, and people seem to be wired to a machine that gives pleasure when they buy an item, and shocks them when they put it down. At the next window, rows and rows of people are wearing helmets with goggles and writhing in response to the images that are projected through them. The sign says "Television Anti-Deprivation and Daycare Training." At the next window, some people are wearing gloves and spraying pesticides, others seem to be getting lawn mowing lessons. Through the next window, marked "Community Over-Dependence," people are sitting in comfortable cubicles by themselves watching television screens with beautiful images. They finally get to the window marked "TD Therapy.")

Karen: Okay, don't tell me, let me guess. It's driving school.

Dr. Freemarket: You catch on quickly, Karen. In a sense, yes. We feel that this one is central to our overall therapy program. It promotes independence and freedom from others, and it gets people back on track with their consumer patterns by providing automotive access to the mall. We call it "Automotivational Therapy." This lab takes people on speedy car rides through beautiful countryside in the safety of their lab seats. We recently added music and an aromatherapy component so that people can experience that great outdoors scent accented with a pinch of burning rubber and leather. It shows them what a sensual and freeing experience it is to drive a car.

Karen: But ... I don't understand. People don't usually get to drive in those situations. They're usually stuck in traffic on their way to work. Or they're taxiing their kids halfway across the city to school and hockey and babysitting for hours on end.

(Suddenly an alarm shrieks, and a huge air bag bursts open, knocking Karen unconscious and catapulting her into another one of those sensual leather bucket seats. When she wakes up, she struggles to free herself from the locked seatbelts, but is unsuccessful.)

Karen: Ahh! What happened?

Dr. Freemarket: (Appears from the next room) Oh, Karen, I'm sorry I didn't get a chance to mention it, but around here, air bags are for dangerous situations, and you were getting into some dangerous territory. We call it a "negative epiphany," in other words, realizations based on negative values. When that happens, we're forced to take drastic action. We don't usually do it until after people have signed on with us, but this was serious so we took the liberty.

Karen: What was I saying?

Dr. Freemarket: Uh – I can't remember. It didn't make a lot of sense, dear. You were confused. Just rest up and you should be okay. In the meantime, I hope this means you'll stay with us. You really need help!

Karen: Actually, what time is it? I promised my friend I'd meet her this afternoon.

Dr. Freemarket: Don't worry your sweet little head about that. Just rest now.

Karen: No thank you, I feel fine. Let me go.

Dr. Freemarket: Get ahold of yourself Karen, you're out of control. Here, take these *(he hands her some pills)*.

Karen: No! Let me go! *(Thanks to her yoga classes, in a fit of concentration, she wriggles out of the seatbelts and makes a break for the door. A sequence of negative epiphany air bags inflates one by one in her wake, tripping up the entire CM staff. In a flash, her bike is unlocked, and she's gliding off into the night. She is long gone before the therapists reach their cars breathlessly and head for the bumper to bumper traffic in pursuit of their cappuccino client. Karen's head is spinning like the wheels of her bike and her eyes are wide open. It's night-time, so she must have been inside that place all day long. It is a full moon and the streets are acting up to prove it. She pedals past a bus and there is a big racket, a few screams, and repetitive ringing. Karen looks back and there is a woman trying to pull a twin baby carriage, and the twins, back into the bus. The doors have closed on the carriage, suspending one of the twins outside of the bus, while one of them, and the mother, is still inside, barely hanging on. She pushes the twin into the bus, and gets back on her bike. As she silently glides on, a woman who had been walking down the poorly lit street hits the deck and sprays mace mistaking Karen for an attacker. Karen apologizes and rides on, and is suddenly forced to leave the bike lane to avoid the guy who is parked in it eating his submarine sandwich, then gets cut off by a speeding car, swerves, and accidentally sets off someone's perimeter violation car alarm. The police are on the scene in seconds. It is a property violation, but not just property – somebody's car! And the key to the situation is obvious. It was an attempted ride-by stealing! When Karen hears the police sirens, she assumes the worst – she's being chased – and she steps on it.)*

Revamping the transportation planner's job description

Questioning the dominance of the private automobile is not new. Since it was invented, thoughtful writers and thinkers have been predicting the kinds of noisy, dangerous, polluted, sprawling, and inequitable scenarios we experience today. But generally such questioning has been muted by passionate promises of North America's collective – yet strangely individual – car ride to progress, status, democracy, and economic growth. These promises are financially supported by an annual five billion dollar car advertising budget and philosophically supported by our North American auto culture.

Hence, grappling with cars means grappling with no less than our frontier history, our car-based culture, our car-based infrastructure, and our generalized loss of imagination. In other words, questioning cars and their needs, although essential, is only one aspect of a larger, more integrated and imaginative approach to providing for people, cities, and *their* needs.

It could be said that one of the biggest problems in thinking about transportation is thinking too much about transportation. In the context of the transportation = cars = necessary paradigm, we currently live in a car-dominated culture in which those who challenge car-domination challenge cars. But what if we take a step back and ask what would happen if, rather than challenging cars, we challenged the domination of transportation itself.

As an example, imagine that you were made the transportation planner, and you were charged with the responsibility of meeting a city's transportation needs. Your product is the transportation system, so the job of moving people and things around – using the prescribed transportation modes – defines the scope of your mission. Theoretically,[9] you can be highly creative within the bounds of moving people and goods from A to B and back. But you can venture no further.

On the other hand, suppose you were charged with a different task. Suppose you were asked to help people gain access to their basic needs within a city, such as food, shelter, employment, community, and recreation. Your job description could involve any number of ideas and systems, including transportation, but it would not be limited to transportation, and it would not necessarily require transportation. The transportation system would be the means of meeting personal and societal needs, not the goal.

Within this framework, your first step would probably be to talk to the community involved, and together with them, identify their needs. Depending on their needs, you may find collective ways to move things closer to each other. If work and shopping were close enough to home, people could walk or cycle and would not have to rely on motorized forms of transportation. If speeds were reduced and traffic were calmed within neighbourhoods, more use could be made of the street and the neighbourhood for recreation and social life.[10] If people could hook up with each other by computer rather than drive across the city, they could eliminate a certain amount of work-related transportation.[11] If seniors could walk the neighbourhood children to school as part of a community "walking bus,"[12] the children's taxi service could be eliminated. If you could safely park your bicycle at the transit stations,[13] you could go longer distances without a car, provided that there was reliable transit service. If you could put your bicycle on the train at the local train station,[14] you could even get out of the city without relying on a car.

Few of these viable options fall within traditional transportation planning. Or, if they do, they receive minimal attention and even fewer resources. Under the new access-based job description, planning to meet people's basic needs and assure equity and environmental sustainability means making transportation, and therefore private automobile travel, the option of last resort,[15] not the priority in policy, action, and especially investment.

Such a reorientation of priorities is not just wishful thinking. Cities like Portland, Oregon, Amsterdam, in the Netherlands, and Copenhagen, Denmark, are already reaping the social, ecological, and economic advantages of favouring the needs of people over the needs of cars.[16]

Act Three: Revelations

(Karen's first thought is to get to the library, where she works. It's closed, but she has her smart card. Even though it's not far, and she's lit up like a Christmas tree, she still manages to be screamed at and ogled at through half-open tinted windows a few times before reaching the library steps. She zips down the slope and around to the back door, inserts her card, and brings her bike right in. It is 11:30 p.m. and she can still hear that car alarm. Time passes, the clock strikes 2:00 a.m. and Karen has been researching since she got to the library. The buzzer goes. It's Linda. Karen runs up the stairs to open the door. The car alarm is still on.)

Linda: It's crazy out there.

Karen: Tell me about it. Why, what happened to you?

Linda: Let's see. Drunk drivers. No street lighting. Speeding cars. You know, the usual. Never mind. How are you doing?

Karen: I'm okay now. Thanks for cycling over here so late. I need your help. Tell me if I'm losing my mind. I went to that clinic this morning, and ... *(they continue talking as they walk down the stairs...)*

Karen: ... so anyway, that's how I ended up here, and I'm scared to leave in case the cops, or worse, those therapists, are staking me out.

Linda: But you didn't do anything.

Karen: I know but it's been such a crazy day. Anyway it doesn't matter, I've got a whole bunch of stuff to show you. Am I keeping you from anything?

Linda: Just sleep.

Karen: Oh yeah. You should go.

Linda: No. I'm here. What do you want to show me?

Karen: Well, I got to thinking about this transportation disadvantage thing. And how screwed up it all seems to be, so I started looking up reports and studies. Because it hit me as I was riding tonight that I've never felt "disadvantaged" because I live so close to where I work, and because my bike lets me go almost anywhere, even at night. And my neighbourhood is lively and I know all the people at the local shops and the cafes and they look out for me.

Linda: Yeah. You've got it made, for the most part.

Karen: But really, it's hell for women who work shifts and have to walk down scary streets at night, and deal with bus drivers who won't open the door long enough for the kids to get out safely, and people in wheelchairs can't even GET IN to the subway. And getting from downtown to the suburbs is impossible. If I lived in the suburbs there's no way I'd try to take transit. All those people really are disadvantaged because they don't have a car. It's ass backwards. People should be rewarded, not punished, for not driving cars. Look at these stats:

- Approximately 47,000 people are killed each year on US roads, similar to the number that died in the entire Vietnam war. Also in the US, 30,000 additional deaths per year are caused by motor vehicle emissions.[17] In Ontario, there are 1,200 traffic fatalities, and almost 120,000 injuries annually.[18]

- During the average Canadian summer, over half of all Canadians are exposed for some time to concentrations of ground level ozone termed "unacceptable" by Health and Welfare Canada.[19]

- Over the last twenty years, almost 60 per cent of Canada's urban growth was onto high quality farmland.[20]

- Subsidies to defend the oil supply cost the United States $15 billion per year, or $23.50 per barrel, which is more than the current market price of a barrel of oil.[21]

- People in the province of Ontario spend approximately $5 billion annually to pay for imported automobiles. Combined with the $2.8 billion lost to the economy each year for motor fuels, this is equivalent to losing at least 133,000 jobs each year.[22]

Linda: Wow. Where did you find all that stuff?

Karen: It wasn't easy, but I was trying to look up alternative cures for Transportation Disadvantage, and the only thing I could find was a line in one article that put alternative research down to quackery verging on conspiracy theory. Then I logged on to the Internet and downloaded this stuff.

Linda: When you say alternative cures, do you mean like alternative fuels?

Karen: No. In fact you may think I've really lost it but I'm beginning to think alternative fuels are all part of it.

Linda: Part of what?

Karen: Part of keeping cars as the only way.

Linda: What do you mean?

Karen: Well, even if all the cars in the world are running on alternative fuels, they're still killing people, and they're still driving everyone crazy with noise, and they're still the reason why my grandfather's farm got paved over by roads and suburbs, and they're still breaking up neighbourhoods with their speed and their tinted windows, and they're still the second most popular place for women to get raped after the home.[23]

Linda: Yeah, but what else is there? I mean, what are people going to do for transportation if they don't have cars? Things are so far away. You want to go back to horses? Or make everybody ride a bike out to the suburbs? It's not going to happen, especially if they have kids to schlepp around.

Karen: That's the thing. There's no other choice because of cars. Because of cars, things are so far away. Look at my life – it's so easy because almost everything I need is close by. I live in a community, in a neighbourhood that was built before cars. I can get everything I want easily, on foot, or by bike. If the transit service was better, I'd even take that more often. But cars force people to travel long distances for things. And they allow the big cheeses to screw up cities so you HAVE to go long distances for things.

Linda: Aw, come on. Cars can't force people to do things. It's like there's a car with an Arnold Schwarzenegger voice that drives in to your living room and says "okay we are going for a ride. A vewy long ride."

Karen: Well maybe not the car itself, but the whole idea that the car is King, and it's freedom, and it's the only way to go. All the car ads that say the car is cool and it's going to get men dates, and conquer nature. And the way that outside our neighbourhood, there are hardly any sidewalks any more – there's no choice. There's no way of doing anything different. That's why they're telling me I'm sick. And that's why they told you you're sick with LDD. You were RIGHT to get mad at the way things are. You're not sick, THEY are.

Linda: Yeah, yeah. But you still haven't answered my question about what people are going to do in this city if they don't have cars. Will it be camels? Helicopters? Yogic Flying?

Karen: No, that's the thing. If we didn't need so much transportation, we wouldn't need cars. Let me put it this way. If things like work and home and school and shops were built closer together, we wouldn't need so much transportation. Hence, not so many cars!

Linda: I think I get it. You want to completely reorganize the city. That shouldn't take long. How about putting casters on people's houses so that they can move their houses closer to where they work?

Karen: Yeah, sort of.

Linda: You HAVE lost it.

Karen: But you'd also have to move a few other things around, so that people would have everything they need, not just work. That's one of the big problems. Most of these roads were designed for the workforce of the fifties, which at the time was mostly men. So women were stuck with no transit and no cars ...

Linda: So what else is new, eh? Don't you think that's always going to be the way? You're saying maybe we could do better?

Karen: Exactly!

Linda: Oh boy.

Karen: You know, today at the clinic, while I was waiting for my Dr. Freemarket appointment, I got talking to this woman in the waiting room. She'd been sent to the clinic for "Delusions of Grandeur" because she read about this group in Eugene, Oregon, that tried to do things differently. She proposed the same thing to some local planners and politicians and the next thing you know she's sent to the clinic for therapy, as if SHE's sick.

Linda: You're saying she's not? And the professionals are wrong?

Karen: Maybe. Look. This is what the Eugene group did. I got this off the Freenet. ... The Watershed Sentinel reports that the City of Eugene, Oregon, proposes to spend $157 million over the next seven years on four new highways. A group called Auto Relief did some research and found that the same amount could be used to purchase all of the following:

- free bus transportation to the year 2000, including a one million dollar per year administrative budget increase
- a ten-fold increase in funding for ride-share programs

- a free bicycle for every resident over age eleven, complete with lock, helmet, and rain gear
- bike racks around the city
- ten thousand free bike-carrying racks for cars
- ten thousand free bike trailers
- forty-eight kilometers of bike paths
- total elimination of the projected municipal deficit to the year 2000
- a one hundred dollar rebate to every citizen
- a $7.1 million surplus, which could go towards other publicly funded projects, or to reduce taxes. Left out of this equation are added health benefits, from both reduced nitrogen oxide (NOX) emissions contributing to ground-level ozone, and more physical exercise. Another benefit is reduced greenhouse gas emissions (CO_2).[24]

See, those people had the imagination and the gumption to envision what could be instead of putting up with what was. And they're not professionals. They're average Joe's, like us.

Linda: Speak for yourself.

Karen: Anyway ...

Linda: (She's examining the Eugene print-out) You know, I hate to admit it, but this really is kind of cool. It's a bit scary though, because I'm beginning to see your point. It must be really late.

Karen: Great! So are you in? Are you with me?

Linda: I guess so. But the thing is, that woman was sent to the clinic for even suggesting this, so even if we wanted to do something like it, they'd send us there, too. We'd be ridiculed and told we're sick. They'd probably have us committed, and not to a cause, if you know what I mean ...

Karen: Yeah, I know. It seems impossible. It was almost easier before my "negative epiphany." But I figure there must be others like us. You know, I bet if we got hold of some of the other dropouts from the clinic, we'd find a few sympathetic souls at least. There are probably even a few sympathetic big cheeses around, if we really look.

Linda: And they'd call two people, and they'd call two people...?

Karen: If there were enough of us, we could reorganize our own community. Maybe we've just got to start by imagining what we want, and what's possible, and how we're going to get it ...

(Suddenly, Karen and Linda are being transported through the air, on a great

winged tandem rolodex over to the other side of the Grand Canyon,[25] *where new friends and children are busy widening sidewalks, planting trees where through-ways once were, erecting bike racks, tearing up parking lots for gardens, talking to each other, carting compost in human powered trailers, and laying down bright purple and green recycled plastic paving stones ...)*

– THE END, AND THE BEGINNING –

Principles for re-organizing

Our story suggests a set of principles which might be applied to rethinking and reorganizing a city for equity and ecological sustainability. These principles – People-Centred Planning, Appropriate Technology, and Community-Led Planning – favour access over transportation and favour people over cars. A description of each principle follows.

1. People-centred planning

ACCESS OVER TRANSPORTATION. Closer, more convenient access to the basics means reducing the length and number of trips people need to take. An access-based approach is more socially equitable than a transportation-based approach because it downplays the need for costly transportation, and prioritizes the needs of people who are the least advantaged, or cannot or choose not to drive. From a planning point of view, local access is becoming a more practical, economically viable option because more people live in urban centres where access-based service provision is becoming not only feasible but necessary. In Canada, most people live in urban centres.

REORIENTATION OF THE HIERARCHY OF TRANSPORTATION.[26] Transportation planners and engineers are trained to channel the greatest number of cars and trucks along the straightest roads in the shortest amount of time. This priority forms the basis of a hierarchy which begins with cars and trucks. Reorienting towards a "feet first" or human powered focus means that priority in policies, education, and investment is given first and foremost to access by foot (the mode used by most people during every trip), and wheelchair, then to bicycle facilities, then to transit and trains, and THEN to private motorized travel.

INCREASED RATE OF EXCHANGE OVER INCREASED SPEED OF TRAVEL, OR ACCESS OVER EXCESS.[27] Cities and towns that favour access by foot, bicycle, and transit typically legislate speed restrictions and street design in favour of safe use of the streets as public spaces. They also typically have more vibrant local economies because the emphasis is placed on participation in the city – socializing, shopping, playing – rather than speeding from destination to destination.[28] This is an access over excess approach. Such priority on street exchanges also has a positive effect on crime levels. Scandinavian studies have shown that on streets where there is heavy auto traffic, people socialize less and retire to the backs of their houses, resulting eventually in reduced street life and increased crime.[29]

INTEGRATION OF ALL TRANSPORTATION MODES AND SYSTEMS. Integrating local, regional, national, and international transportation options is essential to efficiency, sustainability, and economy. If people are deterred from using a combination of sustainable options because of inadequate service or connections, they will revert to less sustainable, more costly modes. Integration of modes increases the possibility for "mixed mode" trips which provide safe and equitable options to combine walking, cycling, and car pooling with transit and train travel. This possibility increases the size of the area that transit and trains can serve well.[30] Mixed mode options also increase the possibility for connecting trucks with trains to allow for delivery of train freight inside and outside localities.

INTEGRATION OF TRANSPORTATION WITH OTHER SECTORS AND CONCERNS. Transportation relates directly to housing, health, land use, economy, technology, environment, social services, and education, among other sectors. For example, it is short-sighted to build affordable housing so far away from essential services that people are forced to spend money on travel to meet their basic needs. In Toronto, one of the greatest barriers to getting food from the food banks to the people is transportation.[31]

2. Appropriate technology

The discussion of which technologies are "appropriate technologies" within the realm of access and transportation is complex, and goes beyond the scope of this paper. However, there are some general principles which can inform the process of planning appropriate technologies for equitable and sustainable communities and cities.[32]

In general, technologies which serve to increase private car use or make car use more convenient (including the car itself) are less appropriate than technologies which serve to increase access to basic needs without the use of the automobile.

This framework intentionally downplays the notion of so-called "transition technologies" which focus on improving car travel, or making car travel more convenient, more appealing, or seemingly more environmentally sustainable. In general "transition technologies" applied to private automobiles only reinforce the "transition" to increased car use, and its inequitable and unsustainable consequences.[33]

On the other hand, new developments in alternative fuels that are applied to private automobiles are less appropriate than alternative fuels for taxis, transit vehicles, delivery vehicles, and vehicles which provide alternatives to private car use. In general, however, the belief that clean fuel will solve all our problems is short-sighted, inequitable, and environmentally unsustainable. First, this mythology sees air pollution as the only problem with cars, and completely ignores the much larger land use, health, social, and economic problems caused by overdependence on the private automobile. Second, the common belief that alternative fuels will solve our problems means that more people drive more, with a clearer conscience. Earlier attempts at cleaning the air with emission controls demonstrate the problem with this thinking.[34] While individual cars are purported to have become "cleaner," we have ever increasing numbers of them and we are driving them further and further. The number of motor vehicles crossing the Metro Toronto boundary daily has increased by 150 per cent since 1975, a rate which is disproportionate to the increase in population.[35]

The same prinicple applies to "smart car" technologies which purport to make driving cleaner, safer, faster, and cheaper, but which actually serve to get more cars on the roads.[36]

3. Community-led planning

Planning for improving access and transportation options is not a set of transferable techniques as much as it is a process.[37] It is a process in which people who will be effected by access and transportation decisions have a major role in making all aspects of those decisions – economic, social, and ecological. This is to be distinguished from the more traditional "community-based planning" in which planners lead, and often pre-scribe, rather than facilitate the process.

Of course, this process needs to evolve. A community-led process might result in a number of sustainable transportation options which are not necessarily equitable. For example, women's transportation needs are in part proportional to the options they have available to them, a fact which underlines the need for in depth needs assessments. As well, an equitable, community-led planning process is only one small step to-wards a less patriarchal society in which women would be free to move around a city without fear, and without having to wonder "how am I go-ing to get home?" [38]

Such an evolution requires at minimum a commitment to imagine saner, more equitable, more enjoyable options, and to begin to work col-lectively to put those options in place. Working for equity and access does not just mean gaining access to our streets as they exist now. It also means gaining access to our deep, serious, practical, and fanciful visions of what a sustainable and equitable city could be.

Just a few success stories

- "The idea of calming a street started in Holland about thirty years ago. After the third child had been run over in a residential neighbourhood of Delft, and after authorities refused to take action, local residents took matters into their own hands. They organized a night raid with picks and shovels to reconstruct their streets in line with a new idea, the concept of Woonerf (literally, a "living-yard"). When the authori-ties arrived with police and bulldozers to reconstruct the street, the residents stood their ground and protected their new layout."[39] In the same spirit, neighbourhoods across Toronto are getting together to draw up their own plans for "traffic calming" their streets and commu-nities.

- In Denmark, when a road becomes too congested with traffic, traffic engineers remove a lane rather than adding one.[40]

- In Toronto, a group called Women On Wheels is working with the Community Bicycle Network (CBN) to provide bicycle riding and bike mechanics skills that lead to independent mobility for women and children through a City of Toronto initiative called Breaking the Cycle of Violence. On a more ongoing basis, through the Community Bicycle Network, community-based bicycle recycling and repair centres are working to reduce landfill and provide cheap, sustainable transportation by restoring old bicycles and getting them to people who could not otherwise afford one. The CBN also works to stimulate community economic development (CED) related to bicycle transportation.[41]

- In the Bathurst Quay and St. Lawrence communities of Toronto, local citizens worked succesfully with local councillor Olivia Chow to lobby to keep their bus route. This inspired the formation of a network of Transit User Groups (TUGs) across Ontario.[42]

- In Australia, seniors walk children to school every day rather than driving them, as part of a community "walking bus" project.[43]

- In Toronto, a group called Transportation Options runs a Car Use Reduction Program, which is akin to a twelve-step program for people who are car dependent. People get together on a regular basis with neighbours or colleagues to find and apply ways to support each other in reducing their car use.[44]

- In New York, Portland, and now in Toronto, Centres for Appropriate Transportation have formed to provide a creative space for innovation, design, and manufacture of human-powered transportation technologies to take place.[45]

- In Toronto, a project called the Green Tourism Partnership is working to provide electronic information and services to people who are seeking ways to get around and out of Toronto without using a private automobile.[46]

- In Curitiba, Brazil, 75 per cent of all commuters ride the efficient, clean, wheelchair-accessible buses which charge a flat forty cent "social" fare. The bus system competes in performance with subways, but it is five hundred times cheaper to build and run. The Curitiba system is not subsidized and is run by a mix of public and private enterprise.[47]

These stories represent only a smattering of inspirational examples which show that change can happen, and is happening. Please allow them to inspire you to visions and actions in your own community.

Notes

1 See Gerda Wekerle and Brent Rutherford, "Employed Women in the Suburbs: Transportation Disadvantage in a Car-Centred Environment," *Alternatives* 14, 3 (1987): 49-54, for a definition elaboration of transportation disadvantage and transit captivity among women and minorities.

2 See Gerda Wekerle and Brent Rutherford, "The Mobility of Capital and the Immobility of Female Labour: Responses to Economic Restructuring," in *The Power of Geography: How Territory Shapes Social Life*, eds. J. Welch and M. Dear (Boston: Unwin Hyman, 1987) for an explanation of the relationship between women's travel patterns and their social and economic situation.

3 See description of Saturn and other ads in Jody Berland "Cars: Have We Been Seduced?" speech made at the St. Lawrence Public Forum in Car Culture, Toronto, September 1994.

4 See MacGregor's chapter in this volume for an elaboration on women's double day.

5 OHIP is the Ontario Hospital Insurance Plan.

6 The relationship between language, culture, and technology is explored by Dr. Ursula Franklin in *The Real World of Technology*, (Toronto: CBC Enterprises, 1990).

7 Compact Edition of the *Oxford English Dictionary*, volume 2, (London: Oxford University Press, 1971), p. 277.

8 See the chapter entitled "The Future of the Automobile" in *Beyond The Car*, eds. S. Zielinski and G. Laird (Toronto: Steel Rail Press, 1995).

9 I say theoretically because this creativity in transportation planning has been the exception rather than the rule.

10 See the chapter by Egan entitled "Calming Traffic, Exciting People" in *Beyond the Car*, eds. Zielinski and Laird, 1995.

11 See the Telecommuting and Economy section of "Transporting Ourselves to Sustainable Economic Growth" in S. Zielinski, "Transporting Ourselves to Sustainable Economic Growth," paper presented for the International Institute for Sustainable Development Employment and Sustainable Development Meeting, Winnipeg, 1994, IISD, p. 17.

12 In D. Engwicht, *Reclaiming Our Cities and Towns: Better Living With Less Traffic* (Gabriola Island, BC: New Society Publishers, 1993).

13 The Toronto Transit Commission has recently initiated a major Bike 'n Ride Program to encourage mixed mode opportunities in the Greater Toronto area. The program includes provision of safe parking and increased possibilities for bikes on buses and trains.

14 This service is already available in a number of European cities, and throughout Scotland.

15 See Bradshaw's chapter on walkability in *Beyond the Car*, eds. Zielinski and Laird, 1995.

16 See M.D. Lowe, "Alternatives to the Automobile: Transport for Livable Cities," *Worldwatch Paper 98*, (October 1990).

17 According to the Alliance for a Paving Moratorium, P.O. Box 4347, Arcata, California, 95521, US.

18 In Pollution Probe's report "Costs of The Car," (October 1991).

19 In Canada's Green Plan, Government of Canada, 1990.

20 Environment Canada, *State of Canada's Environment* (Ottawa: Environment Canada, 1991).

21 According to the Alliance for a Paving Moratorium.

22 In Stillich, Udo, *The Liveable Toronto Area: Transforming Transportation for Prosperity and Sustainability* (Toronto: Environmentalists Plan Transportation, February 1994).

23 Cited at the Cars and Patriarchy workshop at the Second International Conference On Auto Free Cities in May 1992.

24 From *Earthkeeper Magazine* (February/March 1994).

25 This Thelma and Louise fantasy is borrowed from P. Zimmerman's chapter entitled "Boys and Their Toys" in *Beyond the Car*, eds. Zielinski and Laird, 1995; and in *TRANSmission*, the magazine of Transportation Options.

26 In Bradshaw's walkability chapter in *Beyond the Car*, eds. Zielinski and Laird, 1995.

27 The notion of exchange is explored in detail in Engwicht, *Reclaiming Our Cities and Towns*, 1993.

28 In a survey of 105 town centres worldwide, where auto traffic has been restricted, the Organization for Economic Co-operation and Development found that retail sales rose in half the cities and fell in only two. "Facts and Arguments," *Globe and Mail* (16 August 1994): A18.

29 See Whitzman's chapter in this volume, and Jan Gehl, *Life Between Buildings: Using Public Space* (New York: Van Nostrand Reinhold, 1987).

30 See Michael Replogle, *Bicycles and Public Transportation: New Links to Suburban Transit Markets* (Washington, DC: The Bicycle Federation, 1988), on integrating bicycles and public transportation.

31 From an interview with Debbie Field, of FoodShare in Toronto. See also Guberman in this volume.

32 See Ursula Franklin's checklist for public and policy decisions related to technology in Franklin, *The Real World of Technology*, 1990.

33 See Zielinski's chapter entitled "The Future of Automobile" in *Beyond the Car*, eds. Zielinski and Laird, 1995.

34 See Ellen Schwartzel, "Car Control in Canada: The Current Scene," notes from a slide presentation (Toronto: Pollution Probe, June 1993).

35 Ibid.

36 In Zielinski, "The Future of the Automobile," 1995.

37 According to transportation expert Lisa Caton of Transportation Options in Toronto.

38 According to Lisa Caton of Transportation Options.

39 See Wolfgang Zuckerman, *The End of the Road: The World Car Crisis and How We Can Solve It* (Post Mills, VT: Chelsea Green Publishing, 1991).

40 According to Marc Baraness, Director of Urban Design, City of Toronto.

41 From the Community Bicycle Network, 427 Bloor Street West, Suite 205, Toronto, Ontario, M5S 1X7. Telephone: (416) 323-0897.

42 Information from Metro Councillor Olivia Chow. Telephone: (416) 392-4044.

43 See Engwicht, *Reclaiming Our Cities and Towns*, 1993.

44 From the Car Reduction Kit, c/o Transportation Options, 427 Bloor Street West, Suite 205, Toronto, Ontario, M5S 1X7. Telephone: (416) 960-0026.

45 From Centre for Appropriate Transportation in Toronto, c/o the CBN, Telephone: (416) 323-0897.

46 From Transportation Options. Telephone: (416) 960-0026.

47 In David Engwicht, *The Reclaiming Tour: USA, Canada, and Brazil – Antidotes and Lessons* (Australia: Engwicht, 1994).

PLANNING CHANGE:
NOT AN END
BUT A BEGINNING

Sherilyn MacGregor

THIS BOOK is the product of a collective process. Over the course of several months, seven of us came together to discuss our respective chapters and the progress of the book. We gave each other feedback on drafts and encouragement when putting words down on paper seemed impossible. We shared ideas, experiences, visions, food, and sometimes wine. And when it came time to write a final chapter we all agreed that it should be based on a group dialogue expressing our collective reflections about the book and its themes.

The discussion took place in Margrit Eichler's living room on a cold mid-December afternoon. Cuddled up in an eclectic mix of easy chairs (Margrit was conserving energy), we began throwing out questions about what else we could have included in the book. After coming to terms with the fact that we could not have covered it all, we turned our attention to the range of positive solutions we have presented to address the environmental and social problems that confront our communities. We also tried to identify the common ideas that run through our different chapters.

I was given the task of synthesizing all that we discussed that afternoon into something that resembles a conclusion. The result seems to raise more questions than it answers. From the outset we knew that, with the exception of gender inequality, many of the issues we address in our book are the difficult ones with which planners have been struggling for decades. But since our intention is to bring about a change in how people think about planning, sustainability, food security, housing, transportation, safety, and human health, we hope that challenging questions will inspire others to pick up where we leave off.

The limits of personal experience

One of the main themes articulated in our book is that planners have not done a very good job of asking "Who and what has been left out?" Rather, they often work from a base of experience that is shared only by a small and privileged segment of society. Feminists and other social justice groups have been vocal in demanding that public decisionmakers find ways to include a diversity of perspectives in their work. Planners are being asked to listen to people and learn about their concerns rather than speak for them or make assumptions about a common public interest. An important first step in becoming more inclusive is for planners to recognize personal privilege and be aware of how limiting professional approaches can be.

At one point in our discussion we had to look around the room and admit that our own personal experiences have had a big impact on which issues we chose to write about and how we have conceptualized those issues. We have written our chapters at a specific point in time and from a body of experience that is neither complete nor static. But these experiences do not include a cross-section of those found in most Canadian communities. As Carolyn Whitzman observed, "We're not the world's most heterogeneous group." As a result, we have not included the specific concerns that would be raised by children, teenagers, seniors, people with disabilities, new Canadians, people of colour, homeless people – the list could go on and on. We also have been rather Toronto-centric because that is where all but one of us live and work. While we recognize that people from other regions in Canada and the world will have more and different concerns, we hope that the issues we discuss in our chapters are broad enough to resonate with their experiences as well.

What is missing?

A community is sustainable if it meets the needs of all its living members without in any way jeopardizing the capacity of future generations to do the same. This definition points to the *inter*-generational aspect of sustainability: that one generation must practice moderation and forethought for the sake of future generations. It is unreasonable, however, to expect all members of a generation to preserve the environment for the next if many cannot meet their immediate needs and lack the power to control their own lives. Therefore we also must be concerned with the *intra*-generational distribution of resources and opportunity. Unless there is intra-generational equity today, the goal of environmental sustainability in the long term will not be realized.[1]

There are many interconnected elements of sustainability. Although we have touched on many issues and problems that pertain to contemporary urban life, we by no means offer an exhaustive list. There are many topics we could have included that merit additional chapters unto themselves. Some of the issues that we think should be included in a more thorough discussion of environmentally *and socially* sustainable cities are outlined below.

Work

A crucial component of sustainable communities is that every person has meaningful work. This requires a reorganization and redistribution of both paid and unpaid work. What kinds of work arrangements would exist in the equitable communities we envisage? How can we ensure that subsequent generations will have meaningful work? In a non-sexist community the division of labour must be more egalitarian. In what ways can this be achieved? Who will do the unpleasant, but necessary, work (i.e., washing dishes, sweeping sidewalks, and cleaning toilets)? Another important question is: If everyone had equal access to meaningful work, would there still exist a sex trade (i.e., prostitution) in the non-sexist city?

Cultural diversity

We did not explore issues of race and how cultural diversity shapes our neighbourhoods, nor did we consider the impacts of racism on planning and policy decisions. Only communities that foster equitable relationships among diverse people are socially sustainable. What kinds of changes can we move towards in order to bring about an acceptance and celebration of difference?

Public art

Another aspect of culture involves public art and cultural heritage. What role can and do artists play in the life of a city? Are beautiful places also less frightening places? Would a non-sexist city include pornography as part of its culture? What kinds of erotic images would be included in the culture of a non-sexist city?

Communication and information technology

What impact will technologies like the "information super-highway" have on communities? Will they help us to share information, reduce the need to travel, or create a society of people who no longer know how to talk to their neighbours over the proverbial back fence? Will the ability to work at home/on-line lessen or increase the double day for women?

Environmental issues

Even though ecological sustainability is a key theme in the book, we have only scratched the surface of all the environmental issues that relate to urban environments and urban planning. There are many questions that require answers if we are to achieve truly sustainable communities. How can cities take responsibility for their own waste within their own boundaries? How can we preserve irreplaceable environmental resources from consumption in times of economic crisis and high unemployment? Do some earth-friendly practices simply create more work for already over-burdened women (i.e., separation of household waste, the use of cloth diapers, replacing chemical cleansers with good old elbow grease)?

Resource distribution and municipal finance

Some readers will wonder how we expect municipalities to implement our ideas given the current economic realities. Are taxpayers willing to accept ecologically sound technologies and equitable social policies if it means increased costs?

A reply to such concerns requires an in depth analysis of how resources are distributed and the ways in which municipal economies are managed. It can be argued that if our economies were based on full-cost accounting in which the entire range of costs over the long term were calculated, it would become obvious that we cannot afford to maintain the status quo. In other words, we cannot afford not to be sustainable. We already pay enormous social and environmental costs that are not factored into planners' cost-benefit analyses. Many of these, such as clean-up costs, medical costs, and lost opportunity, would be significantly reduced if a sustainability approach were implemented. In addition, there are many inefficiencies in our market-driven system that create undue costs in the name of increased corporate profit – often masked by the concept of "global efficiency." For example, how reasonable is it for governments to subsidize food and shelter through a publicly funded welfare system when local farmers are forced to destroy their surplus produce and buildings stand vacant?

The question, then, should not be how do we pay, but rather how can resources be distributed more sustainably and equitably, and how can municipal economies be restructured in order to effect the kinds of changes that are necessary?

Globalization

Any discussion of environmental and social problems today has to include an analysis of the impact of current global trends on the types of solutions that are possible. Although communities are getting more active in their drive to exert local control, transnational corporations and international free trade agreements are changing the rules of the game. It has become increasingly difficult to implement environmental and social alternatives that run counter to corporate interests. How can communities take control over their own destiny and provide for their own needs? What are the implications of our decisions on women, men, children, and ecosystems in developing countries? Can we learn from the examples of non-Western, non-Northern communities that are fighting the effects of corporate and cultural imperialism?

Community-led planning is more important than ever

It is somewhat paradoxical that interest in local communities is growing in an era of rapid globalization. We have supposedly moved into a new world order where free trade and fibre optics are "king," national borders are blurred, and the time-space continuum has collapsed into an ever-present Now.[2] But these changes (some call them advances) are making it almost impossible for us to exercise control over our environment and economy at the provincial and federal levels. Regions, cities, and neighbourhoods seem to be the only places left where citizens can exercise some degree of control over public decision-making.

The growth in local initiatives is having a profound effect on the planning and public policy agenda. All over Canada grass-roots groups are mobilizing to fight for positive, proactive changes in their lifestyles and in the way their communities are being developed. These include some of the groups mentioned in preceding chapters, such as the Seaton

Community Group, the Niagara Neighbourhood Association, Foodshare, Women Plan Toronto, METRAC, and the Community Bicycle Network.

However, these successes have occurred *in spite of* the conditions that exist in most communities. There are enormous economic, political, and social barriers to community-driven change. Municipal governments face crippling debt loads and a reduction of transfer payments at a time when they are being asked to take on more responsibilities. Furthermore, federal and provincial governments still exercise a great degree of control over how money is spent at the local level. There remains a tendency towards big, glitzy capital expenditures – mega-projects like Skydomes and freeways – that attract positive media attention for the "parties" involved, but that do not necessarily improve the quality of life for the community at large.

Meanwhile, growing numbers of community groups vie for shrinking resources, and small innovations get thwarted by bureaucratic red tape and regulations. When community groups do get support, it is often because they are seen to be an effective way for governments to off-load their responsibilities and to quell public dissent. Further, local initiatives require the kinds of collective structures that have not been built into the design of our cities. People are alienated from each other in so many ways that it is not surprising that privacy and individual property are protected more often than collective goods and community bonds. After all, what are apartments "ment" to do but keep people "apart"?

While it is true that much depends on macroeconomic forces, our book has stressed the need to create an infrastructure that facilitates and supports community. A socially and environmentally sustainable city requires that communities find their own solutions to community problems. They must be given the resources and information necessary to plan change and be empowered to improve the quality of their lives.

Change of Plans presents many positive ideas about how to create a physical and social infrastructure that meets community needs, allows people to make choices about how they want to live, and creates an environment that fosters a sense of collective purpose. For example, we have emphasized the consumption of locally produced food; advocated a wide range of housing choices that support a variety of living arrangements; and suggested citizen advisory councils and public education programs to ensure that people make informed contributions to the planning process.

Visions that sustain us

Our discussion also included the sharing of positive feelings about the cities we live in and the cities we dream of. After months of talking about what is wrong with the way cities have been planned, and how insurmountable the prospect of change seems to be, it was refreshing to shift the focus to more sustaining visions. We all have some ideal notions of what makes a city livable, ranging from the practical to the whimsical. These visions guide our practice and keep us inspired to work for change. They also remind us that some of our dreams are not as unattainable as might be expected. Our sustaining visions of ideal cities are summarized below.

The chia city
A whole city covered with lush green foliage, flowers, and trees. Unsightly concrete buildings brought to life by a blanket of vines.

The beautiful city
At every turn there is something pleasing to the senses: elegant architecture, fragrant gardens, street musicians, artisans, children playing freely in the park, colourful murals rather than billboards. A city full of surprises – treasures of a diverse sort.

The integrated city
All areas of the city have multiple uses, and every space is usable space. The village within the city. People could live their entire lives in the same place if they so desired.

The diverse city
A city with a rich blend of cultures and lifestyles that is constantly changing. A wide variety of restaurants, stores, galleries, and bookstores. There is a celebration of difference and an absence of racial hierarchy.

The user-friendly city
A city that comes with easily accessible operating instructions. Newcomers, tourists, and long-time residents need only look at signs or tap into a database to find answers to their questions: How can I get around the city cheaply and environmentally? What housing co-ops have vacancies? Where can I get a cold frame greenhouse? Historical walking tours with maps and guides, service directories, and public art inventories would be available.

The safe and equitable city

Many of the above ideals have been elaborated before by urban visionaries like Ebenezer Howard, Le Corbusier, and Jane Jacobs. However, few utopian thinkers included gender equity or the freedom from violence as part of their ideal cities. In contrast, we argue that beauty, diversity, and natural abundance mean little if over half of the population is too afraid for their personal safety to enjoy them, or if a large percentage are not physically able to access them. Safety, accessibility, and equity are the foundations upon which a non-sexist city must be built. Only if cities meet these criteria will they be socially sustainable.

The real and the ideal: Seaton revisited

This book is introduced with an extremely atypical example of a planning process. Initiated by a community group, guided by sustainability principles, and designed by fourteen unrepresentative "planners," the Eco-City described by Margrit Eichler also sounds utopian. Not only does it start from scratch, but it is to be built on publicly-owned land, and there are no politicians or citizens around to oppose its innovative proposals. Further, had Margrit not been a participant, it is questionable whether many of the gender-related ideas would have been incorporated into the plan.

The value of the Seaton planning exercise, and our "sustaining visions," is that they generate new ideas and help us to identify a direction in which we want our communities to move. As Margrit explained, "the act of envisaging what might be makes us better able to critique what is." Our book seeks to fuel this type of intellectual project because it is an integral part of the process of urban change.

In reality, however, opportunities for building an ideal city are few and far between. Half of the world's population lives in cities that are growing and decaying simultaneously. And even if building a new town were possible, it would probably come at the expense of precious agricultural land, or an established community would have to be displaced through an "urban renewal" program. So the question must be asked: What do we do with cities that already exist? Our ideas for a non-sexist and sustainable city are inspirational, but how would we implement them in cities like Toronto and Vancouver, let alone Los Angeles and New York City?

When this question was asked in our discussion, silence fell over the group as we struggled to find answers. After a long period of reflection, we came back to what has been a consistent argument in our chapters. Change will not happen quickly or easily, but if it is to happen at all it must start at the local level and be driven by community residents. People must be empowered to make changes, no matter how small, in the way they interact with each other and the earth.

We also recognize that the community-building process alone will not achieve the structural transformations required to create social and environmental sustainability. Community members can make changes in the way they live their daily lives, but it will be difficult to break free of the government policies, the economic trends, and the corporate control that limit their options. Similarly, women may come together to support each other in a quest for gender equity, but we will still face the effects of patriarchy on a worldwide scale. It is therefore imperative that local-level change be coupled with fundamental structural and ideological change. The "power paradigm"[3] which is based on market competition, individualism, sexism, racism, and anthropocentrism, must be replaced by a new paradigm based on more communitarian and life-affirming values.

How will this come about? There is no "right" answer to this question. But, if people are willing to implement the communicative and empowering processes, the self-generating economies, and the physical infrastructure needed to transform their neighbourhoods, perhaps this experience will serve as a model and an impetus for restructuring on a larger scale.

The role of planners

Finally, we are left with the question of what role planners have, or should have, in the quest for non-sexist and sustainable cities. While planners are just one of many players in the urban development process, they are in a unique position to help create a municipal environment that fosters successful innovation. In particular, they have a role in alleviating the barriers to innovation by reducing the costs and time delays involved with the approval of new community-led projects. By playing the role of "honest broker," they also can try to ensure that public participation processes are controlled by all citizens, not just those who stand to gain in the short term.

Further, if community action is the foundation of our vision, then planners will need to play a supportive/catalyst role rather than authoritarian/expert role in public decision-making. This will require different skills and approaches than those that have been used traditionally. Planners will need to practice mediation, negotiation, facilitation, and conflict resolution. They will need to respect other forms of knowledge and find ways to base decisions on collaboration and consensus rather than adversity and argumentation.[4]

But this emphasis on public participation assumes that, left to make their own decisions, community members will choose the course of action most beneficial to the community. What if after a lengthy public participation process people decide that they do not want to build a composting centre or a community green house? What if they *choose* to build walls around their neighbourhood to keep the criminals out? Some studies have shown that a large percentage of Canadian home buyers still equate single detached homes with a high standard of living.[5] Planners who have a commitment to social and environmental sustainability might find it difficult to reconcile the benefits of community participation with the desire to change the status quo.

Although it is rather naive to think that people will embrace half-way houses with open arms no matter how involved they are in the planning process, in many cases, "bad" (i.e., unsustainable) decisions are made because people lack resources, information, and choices. For example, the single detached home may be the shelter of choice primarily because people do not know what other options are possible or what the advantages of alternative living arrangements might be. In fact, where alternatives have been provided, studies show an increased interest in them – the success of Montreal's Grow Homes and Ottawa's freehold row housing are two cases in point.[6] A lack of options can keep people coming back to the same solutions that have created social and environmental problems in the first place.

This highlights the need for planners to take on the role of public educator not only to expand the range of ideas that get considered, but also to incite citizens/consumers to demand a greater range of choices. Communities need to be aware of all the alternatives that are available to them if they are going to make informed choices about their future. Sue Zielinski gave the example that if people knew they could recycle their plastic waste into brightly-coloured paving stones, maybe they would choose such an option: "We could have purple streets! Why not?" Planners should play a key role in changing the way we think about the form and function of our public spaces and how we choose to act within them. This of course requires that planners themselves be open to creative ideas and that they have the latitude to be able to act on them.

The creation of an infrastructure that strengthens intra-community connections, preserves the ecosystem, and fosters social equity is the key to achieving sustainable cities. If we are to realize this goal, for the sake of future generations as well as our own, then we require a radical change of plans.

Notes

1 The distinction between inter- and intra-generational sustainability is discussed by Margrit Eichler in "The Need for Feminist Eco-Sociology: Results of a Voyage of Discovery," in *As Canadian as Possible Under the Circumstances: Issues of Women, Canada and the Environment* (working title) eds. Marilyn Macdonald, Rebecca Raglan and Melody Hessing, (Vancouver: UBC Press, forthcoming).

2 J. Friedmann, "Educating the Next Generation of Planners," paper presented at the 34th Annual Association of Collegiate Schools of Planning Conference, Columbus Ohio, October 1992.

3 J. Birkeland, "An Ecofeminist Critique of Manstream Planning," *The Trumpeter: Journal of Ecosophy* 8,2: (1991). For a discussion, see also S. MacGregor earlier in this volume.

4 S. Hendler and S. MacGregor, "Engendering Planning Theory Discourse," *Plan Canada* (July 1994): 104-12.

5 D. Chamberland, "The Social Challenges of Sustainable Community Planning," *Plan Canada* (July 1994): 137-43.

6 Ibid.

REFERENCES

Ackelsberg, Martha. "Communities, Resistance, and Women's Activism: Some Implications for a Democratic Polity." In *Women and the Politics of Empowerment*, eds. A. Bookman and S. Morgan, 297-313. Philadelphia: Temple University Press, 1988.

Adams, Carol J. *The Sexual Politics of Meat. A Feminist-Vegetarian Critical Theory*. New York: Continuum, 1991.

Adams, Patricia. *Odious Debts: Loose Lending, Corruption, and the Third World's Environmental Legacy*. (Probe International) London, Toronto: Earthscan, 1991.

Advisory Committee on Environmental Standards. *A Standard for Tritium: A Recommendation to the Minister of the Environment and Energy*. Toronto: Advisory Committee on Environmental Standards, May 1994.

Ahrentzen, Sherry. Introduction to *New Households New Housing*, eds. K. Franck and S. Ahrentzen, xi-xv. New York: Van Nostrand Reinhold, 1989.

Alexander, Ernest R. *Approaches to Planning: Introducing Current Planning Theories, Concepts, and Issues*. New York: Gordon and Breach Science Publishers, 1986.

Andrew, Caroline. "The Feminist City." In *Public Arrangements: Power and the City*, ed. Henri Lustiger-Thaler, 109-22. Montreal: Black Rose Books, 1992.

Andrew, Caroline and Beth Moore Milroy, eds. *Life Spaces: Gender, Household, Employment*. Vancouver: UBC Press, 1988.

Armstrong, Jane. "Toronto Race Now Tighter, Poll Says." *The Toronto Star*, 10 November 1994.

Armstrong, Pat and Hugh Armstrong. *The Double Ghetto: Canadian Women and their Segregated Work*. 3rd ed. Toronto: McClelland and Stewart, 1994.

Bacher, John. *Keeping to the Marketplace: The Evolution of Canadian Housing Policy*. Montreal: McGill-Queen's University Press, 1993.

Barrett, Michèle and Mary McIntosh. *The Anti-Social Family*. London: Verso, 1982.

Beauregard, Robert A. "Introduction." *Planning Theory* 7/8 (1992): 9-12.

Belenky, Mary Field, Blythe McVicker Clinchy, Nancy Rule Goldberger, and Jill Mattuck Tarule. *Women's Ways of Knowing: The Development of Self, Voice and Mind*. New York: Basic Books, 1986.

Bellamy, Gary, ed. *The World Food Update*. Ottawa: The World Food Day Association of Canada, October 1994.

Berger, K.T. *Where the Road and the Sky Collide*. New York: Henry Holt & Co., 1993.

Berland, Jody. "Cars: Have We Been Seduced?" Speech made at the St. Lawrence Public Forum on Car Culture, September 1994.

Bertell, Rosalie. *No Immediate Danger? Prognosis for a Radioactive Earth*. Toronto: Women's Educational Press, 1985.

Birkeland, Janis. "An Ecofeminist Critique of Manstream Planning." *The Trumpeter, Journal of Ecosophy* 8, no. 2 (Spring 1991): 72-84.

Blizzard, Christina. "Crime Considered City's Top Problem." *The Toronto Sun*, 10 November 1991.

Board of Health. *The Economy and Health in the City of Toronto.* Toronto: Public Health Department Annual Statement, 1992.

Boivin, Robert and Jean François Pronovost. *The Bicycle: Global Perspectives.* Paper presented at the Conférence Vélo Mondiale, Montréal, 13-17 September 1992.

Boles, Janet K. "The Feminist Reshaping of Urban Services." *Women and Environments* 9, no. 2 (1987): 20-23.

Braaten, Jane. "Towards a Feminist Reassessment of Intellectual Virtue," *Hypatia* 5, no. 3 (1990): 1-14.

Bradshaw, Chris, "Walkability." In *Beyond the Car*, eds. S. Zielinski and G. Laird. Toronto: Steel Rail Press, 1995.

Bricklin, Mark and Maggie Spilman, eds. *Preventions: Practical Encyclopaedia of Walking for Health.* Emmaus, Pennsylvania: Rodale Press, 1992.

Brown, Lester R., Christopher Flavin, and Sandra Postel. "Picturing a Sustainable Society." In *State of the World 1990.* Report of the World Watch Institute, eds. Lester R. Brown, C. Flavin, and S. Postel, 173-90, 237-41. New York: W.W. Norton, 1990.

Brown, Lester and Jodi Jacobson. *The Future of Urbanization: Facing the Ecological and Economic Constraints.* Worldwatch Paper #77. Washington: Worldwatch, 1987.

Burke, Mary Anne. "Loss Of Prime Agricultural Land, The Example of Southern Ontario." In *Canadian Social Trends*, eds. Craig McKie and Keith Thompson. Ottawa: Minister of Supplies and Services; and Toronto: Thompson Educational Publishing, 1990.

Burke, Mary Anne. "People in Co-operative Housing." *Canadian Social Trends* (Autumn 1990): 27-31.

Burnell, Barbara S. "Images of Women: An Economic Perspective." In *Foundations for a Feminist Restructuring of the Academic Disciplines*, eds. M. Paludi and G. Steuernagel, 127-65. New York: The Hawthorne Press, 1990.

Campbell, Cathy, Stefa Katamay, and Carmen Connolly. "The Role of Nutrition Professionals in the Hunger Debate." *Journal of the Canadian Dietetic Association.* 49, no. 4 (Autumn 1988): 230-35.

Canada. *Canada's Food Guide to Healthy Eating.* Ottawa: Health and Welfare Canada, 1993.

Canada. *The State of Canada's Environment.* Ottawa: Minster of Supply and Services, 1991.

Canada Mortgage and Housing Corporation. *Changing Canadian Households, 1971-91.* Ottawa: CMHC, Research and Development Highlights, Issue 14, March 1994.

Canada Mortgage and Housing Corporation. *Low Income, Labour Force Participation and Women in Housing Need, 1991.* Ottawa: CMHC, Research and Development Highlights, Issue 16, 1994.

Canada Mortgage and Housing Corporation. *Sustainable Residential Developments: Planning, Design and Construction Principles (Greening the "Grow Home").* Ottawa: CMHC, Research and Development Highlights, Issue 15, July 1994.

Canadian Advisory Committee on the Status of Women. *110 Canadian Statistics on Work and Family – Background Paper.* Ottawa: Canada Communication Group, 1994.

Canadian Automobile Association. *Car Costs.* Toronto: Canadian Automobile Association, 1991-92.

Canadian Urban Transit Association. *The Environmental Benefits of Urban Transit, a Report of the Transit/Environmental Task Force.* Toronto: Canadian Urban Transit Association, April 1990.

Carnegie Mellon University. *Electric and Magnetic Fields From 60 Ez Electric Power: What do we Know about the Possible Health Risks?* Pittsburgh, PA: Department of Engineering and Public Policy, 1989.

Castells, Manuel. *City, Class and Power.* London: Macmillan Publishers, 1972.

Catallo, Rose. *Lessons from Success Stories: Making Communities Safer.* Toronto: City of Toronto Safe City Committee, 1994.

Centre for Criminology. *Second Islington Crime Survey.* Middlesex: Middlesex Polytechnic, 1990.

Chamberland, Denys. "The Social Challenges of Sustainable Community Planning." *Plan Canada* (July 1994): 137-43.

Charland, Michele. *J'Accuse La Peur: Conférence Montréalaise sur les Femmes et la Securité Urbaine.* Montreal: Tandem Montreal, 1992.

Chenier, Glenn. "Statistics on the Problem of Crime in Canada." Prepared for the National Crime Prevention Secretariat, September 1994.

Cichocki, Mary K. "Women's Travel Patterns in a Suburban Development." In *New Space for Women,* eds. G. Wekerle, R. Peterson, and D. Morley, 151-63. Boulder, CO: Westview Press, 1980.

City of Toronto. *Toronto Declaration on the Environment.* Toronto: City Council, July 1991.

City of Toronto. *Zero Discharge Statement of Principles.* Toronto: City Council, June 1991.

City of Toronto Department of Public Health. *Outdoor Air Quality in Toronto: Issues and Concerns.* Perry Kendall, MBBS, MSc, FRCPC, Medical Officer of Health. Toronto: City of Toronto, October 1993. Principle Author: Monica Campbell, Ph.D.

City of Toronto Department of Public Health. *Policy Respecting Electric and Magnetic Fields (EMFs).* Toronto: Toronto Board of Health, 6 October 1993.

City of Toronto Housing Department. *ATARATIRI: Draft Environmental Evaluation Study Report.* Toronto: City of Toronto Housing Department, September 1991.

City of Toronto Interdepartmental Technical Working Group on Urban Food Production. "City of Toronto Support for Urban Food Production: Creating a Garden City." A proposal. April 1993.

City of Toronto NDP Caucus. *The Safe City: Municipal Strategies for Preventing Public Violence Against Women.* Toronto: City of Toronto Planning and Development Department, 1989.

City of Toronto Parks and Recreation Department. "High Park User Survey." Unpublished report. 1987.

City of Toronto Planning and Development Department. *City of Toronto Official Plan Part 1 – Cityplan (By-law 423-93).* Toronto: City Council, 20 July 1993.

Clapham, David, Peter Kemp, and Susan J. Smith. *Housing and Social Policy.* London: Macmillan Education, 1990.

Clark, Clifford E. Jr. *The American Family Home, 1800-1960.* Chapel Hill: The University of North Carolina Press, 1986.

Code, Lorraine. "Feminist Theory." In *Changing Patterns: Women in Canada,* eds. S. Burt, L. Code, and L. Dorney, 18-50. Toronto: McClelland and Stewart, 1988.

Code, Lorraine. *What Can She Know? Feminist Theory and the Construction of Knowledge.* Ithica: Cornell University Press, 1991.

Coleman, Alice. *Utopia on Trial: Vision and Reality in Planned Housing.* London: Hilary Shipman, 1980.

Coleman, Alice. Presentation at "Cities Alive!" Conference, Canadian Housing Renewal Association, May 1993.

Comité Logement Rosemont. *Discrimination, Harcèlement et Harcèlement Sexuel.* Montréal, Front d'Action Populaire en réaménagement urbain, Avril 1986.

Cool, Julie. "Co-ops: Creating Violence-free Communities." *Vis-À-Vis: A National Newsletter on Family Violence* 12 (Fall 1994): 1, 4.

Co-operative Housing Federation of Canada. "Members To Take On Domestic Violence." *Co-opservations* (September 1991): 5.

Countdown 94. *Campaign 2000: Child Poverty In Canada. Report Card 1994*, Ottawa: Canadian Council on Social Development, 1994.

Czerny, Michael, and Jamie Swift. *Getting Started on Social Analysis in Canada.* Toronto: Between the Lines, 1984.

Daly H.E. and J.B. Cobb. *For The Common Good: Redirecting The Economy Toward Community, the Environment and the Sustainable Future.* Boston: Beacon, 1989.

Davis, Mike. *City of Quartz: Excavating the Future in Los Angeles.* New York: Verso, 1990.

Decision Research. *Health Risk Perception in Canada.* Ottawa: Health and Welfare Canada, 1993.

Devon County Council. *Traffic Calming Guidelines.* Exeter: Devon County Council, 1991. Available from Engineering and Planning Department, County Hall, Topsham Road, Exeter EX2 4QD, UK.

Diamond, Irene and Gloria Feman Orenstein, eds. *Reweaving the World: The Emergence of Ecofeminism.* San Francisco: Sierra Club, 1990.

Dillon, David. "Fortress America." *Planning* (June 1994): 8–12.

[Edmonton] Mayor's Task Force on Safer Cities. *Toward a Safer Edmonton for All.* Edmonton: City of Edmonton, 1992.

Egan, Daniel. "Calming Traffic, Exciting People." In *Beyond the Car*, eds. S. Zielinski and G. Laird. Toronto: Steel Rail Press, 1995.

Eichler, Margrit. "Designing Eco-City in North America." In *Change of Plans: Towards a Non-Sexist Sustainable City*, ed. M. Eichler. Toronto: Garamond Press, 1995.

Eichler, Margrit. *Families in Canada Today: Recent Changes and their Policy Consequences.* 2nd ed. Toronto: Gage, 1988.

Eichler, Margrit. "Family Policy in Canada: From Where to Where?" In *Justice Beyond Orwell*, eds. Rosalie S. Abella and Melvin L. Rothman, 353-63. Montreal: Les Éditions Yvon Blais, 1985.

Eichler, Margrit. "Grasping the Ungraspable: Socio-Legal Definitions of the Family in the Context of Sexuality." In *Transactions of the Royal Society of Canada*, Series VI, vol. III, 3-15. Ottawa: Royal Society of Canada, 1993.

Eichler, Margrit. "The Need for Feminist Eco-Sociology." In *As Canadian as Possible Under the Circumstances: Issues of Women, Canada and the Environment* (working title), eds. Marilyn Macdonald, Rebecca Raglan and Melody Hessing. Vancouver: UBC Press, forthcoming.

Eichler, Margrit. "Social Policy Concerning Women." In *Canadian Social Policy*, 2nd ed., ed. Shankar A. Yelaja, 139-56. Waterloo: Wilfrid Laurier University Press, 1987.

Eichler, Margrit. "Umwelt als soziologisches Problem." *Das Argument. Zeitschrift fuer Philosophie und Sozialwissenschaften* 36, no. 3 (1994): 359-76.

Engels, Frederick. *The Origin of the Family, Private Property, and the State.* New York: International Publishers, 1942.

Engwicht, David. *Reclaiming Our Cities and Towns: Better Living with Less Traffic.* Gabriola Island, BC: New Society Publishers, 1993.

Engwicht, David. *The Reclaiming Tour: USA, Canada, and Brazil – Antidotes and Lessons.* Australia: Engwicht, 1994.

Fainstein, Susan S. "Planning in a Different Voice." *Planning Theory* 7/8 (1992): 27-31.

Fairbairn, Gary Lawrence. *Will the Bounty End: The Uncertain Future of Canada's Food Supply.* Saskatoon: Western Producer Prairie Books, 1984.

Farland, William and Daniel Krewski. "Risk Management in Canada and the United States: A Comparative Analysis." St. Catharine's, ON: Background Paper prepared for the International Joint Commission Workshop on Risk Assessment, 1-2 February 1993.

Fava, Sylvia. "Women's Place in the New Suburbia." In *New Space for Women*, eds. G. Wekerle, R. Peterson, and D. Morley, 129-50. Boulder, CO: Westview Press, 1980.

Federation of Canadian Municipalities. *Building Safer Communities for Women: Municipal and Community Strategies to Reduce Violence Against Women.* Ottawa: Federation of Canadian Municipalities, 1994.

Ferguson, Kathy. *The Feminist Case Against Bureaucracy.* Philadelphia: Temple University Press, 1984.

Ferrier, Mercia. "Sexism in Australian Cities: Barrier to Employment Opportunities." *Women's Studies International Forum* 6, no. 1 (1983): 73-84.

"50% fear own neighbourhood, Gallup finds." *The Toronto Star*, 20 April 1992.

Finnie, Ross. "Women, Men, and the Economic Consequences of Divorce: Evidence from Canadian Longitudinal Data." *The Canadian Review of Sociology and Anthropology* 30 (May 1993): 205-41.

Fox Keller, Evelyn. *Reflections on Gender and Science.* New Haven: Yale University Press, 1985.

Francis, Mark. "Some Different Meanings Attached to a City Park and Community Gardens." *Landscape Journal* 6 (1987): 100-112.

Francis, Mark, Lisa Cashdan, and Lynn Paxson. *Community Open Spaces. Greening Neighbourhoods Through Community Action and Land Conservation.* Washington, DC: Island Press, 1984.

Franck, Karen A. "Social Construction of the Physical Environment: The Case of Gender." *Sociological Focus* 18, no. 2 (1985): 143-60.

Franklin, Ursula. *The Real World of Technology.* Toronto, CBC Enterprises, 1990.

Frazer, Elizabeth and Nicola Lacey. *The Politics of Community: A Feminist Critique of the Liberal-Communitarian Debate.* London: Harvester Wheatsheaf, 1993.

Freund, Peter, and George Martin. *The Ecology of the Automobile.* Montreal: Black Rose Books, 1993.

Friedan, Betty. *The Feminine Mystique.* New York: Dell, 1963.

Friedmann, John. "Educating the Next Generation of Planners." Paper presented at the 34th Annual Association of Collegiate Schools of Planning Conference, Columbus, Ohio, 1992.

Friedmann, John. "Feminist and Planning Theories: The Epistemological Connection." *Planning Theory* 7/8 (1992): 40-43.

Friedmann, John. *Planning in the Public Domain: From Knowledge to Action*. Princeton: Princeton University Press, 1987.

Fromm, Dorit. *Collaborative Communities: Cohousing, Central Living, and other New Forms of Housing with Shared Facilities*. New York: Van Nostrand Reinhold, 1991.

Gaudet, C. *A Framework for Ecological Risk Assessment at Contaminated Sites in Canada: Review and Recommendations*. Ottawa: Environment Canada, 1994.

Gehl, Jan. *Life Between Buildings: Using Public Space*. New York: Van Nostrand Reinhold, 1987.

Gelb, Joyce and Marilyn Gittel. "Seeking Equality: The Role of Activist Women in Cities." In *The Egalitarian City*, ed. J.K. Boles, 93-110. New York: Praeger Publishers, 1986.

George, Susan. *How The Other Half Dies: The Reason For World Hunger*. New York: Penguin Books, 1976.

George, Susan. *Feeding The Few: Corporate Control of Food*. Washington: The Institute of Policy Studies, 1979.

Gilligan, Carol. *In a Different Voice: Psychological Theory and Women's Development*. Cambridge: Harvard University Press, 1982.

Ginsburg, Robert. "Quantitative Risk Assessment and the Illusion of Safety." *New Solutions: A Journal of Environmental and Occupational Health Policy*. (Winter 1993): 8-15.

Golden, Stephanie. *The Women Outside: Meanings and Myths of Homelessness*. Berkeley, CA: University of California Press, 1992.

Goldenthal, Howard. "Declaration Makes Co-op Violence-Free." *Now* (22-28 November 1990): 27.

Gordon, Margaret and Stephanie Riger. *The Female Fear*. New York: The Free Press, 1989.

Great Lakes Water Quality Board Report to the International Joint Commission. "Risk Assessment, Communication and Management in the Great Lakes Basin." Proceedings of an International Joint Commission Workshop on Risk Assessment. St. Catharine's, ON: International Joint Commission, 1-2 February 1993.

Guberman, Connie. "Sowing the Seeds of Sustainability: Planning for Food Self-Reliance." In *Change of Plans: Towards a Non-Sexist Sustainable City*, ed. M. Eichler. Toronto: Garamond Press, 1995.

Guterson, David. "No Place Like Home." *Harper's Magazine*, (November 1992): 55–64.

Guth, Joseph H. *Presentation to the American Public Health Association 1992 Annual Meeting*. Washington, DC: Natural Resources Defense Council, 1992.

Hamilton, Roberta. "Feminist Theories." *Left History: An Interdisciplinary Journal of Historical Inquiry and Debate* 1, no. 1 (1993): 9-33.

Hapgood, K. and J. Getzels, eds. *Planning, Women, and Change*. Chicago: American Society of Planning Officials, 1974.

Harding, Sandra. "The Instability of the Analytical Categories of Feminist Theory." In *Feminist Theory in Practice and Process*, eds. M. Malson, J. O'Barr, S. Westphail-Whihl, and M. Wyer, 15-34. Chicago: The University of Chicago Press, 1986.

Harding, Sandra. *The Science Question in Feminism*. Ithaca: Cornell University Press, 1986.

Hayden, Dolores. *The Grand Domestic Revolution: A History of Feminist Designs for American Homes, Neighbourhoods, and Cities*. Cambridge, MA: The MIT Press, 1981.

Hayden, Dolores. *Redesigning the American Dream: The Future of Housing, Work, and Family Life*. New York: W.W. Norton, 1984.

Hayden, Dolores. "What Would a Non-Sexist City Be Like? Speculations on Housing, Urban Design, and Human Work." *Signs* 5, no. 3 Supplm. (Spring 1980): S170-87. Also in: *Women and the American City*, ed. C. Stimpson, E. Dixler, M. Nelson, and K. Yatrikis, 167-84. Chicago: The University of Chicago Press, 1980.

Health and Welfare Canada, National Child Care Information Centre, Child Care Programs Division. *Status of Day Care in Canada*. Ottawa: Health and Welfare Canada, 1991.

Healthy City Office, City of Toronto and the Technical Working Group on Traffic Calming and Vehicle Emission Reduction. *Evaluating the Role of The Automobile: A Municipal Strategy*. Toronto: City of Toronto, September 1991.

Healthy Public Policy Committee. *Nurturing Health: A Framework On The Determinants of Health*. Toronto: Premier's Council on Health Strategy, 1991.

Healthy Toronto 2000 Subcommittee. *Healthy Toronto 2000*. Toronto: City of Toronto, Board of Health, 1988.

Hendler, Sue and Sherilyn MacGregor. "Engendering Planning Theory Discourse." *Plan Canada* (July 1994): 104-12.

Henry, Frances. *Housing and Racial Discrimination in Canada: A Preliminary Assessment of Current Initiatives and Information*. Toronto: Equal Opportunity Consultants, August 1989.

Hierlihy, Deborah. *Green Spaces/Safer Places: Making Parks Safer for Women*. Toronto: City of Toronto Planning and Development Department, 1991.

Hillman, Mayer, John Adams, and John Whitelegg. *One False Move: A Study of Children's Mobility*. London: Policy Studies Institute, 1990.

Hjortland, Christine, Audun Moflag, Randi Skjerven, and Anne Grimsrud. *Mobilizing Women in Local Planning and Decision-Making: A Guide to How and Why*. Oslo, Norway: Ministry of Foreign Affairs, 1991.

Home Office Crime Prevention Unit. *Safer Cities Progress Reports*. London: Home Office, 1990, 1991, 1992, 1993, 1994.

hooks, bell. "Homeplace: A Site of Resistance." In *Yearning: Race, Gender, and Cultural Politics*. Toronto: Between the Lines, 1990.

Horner Report. *Crime Prevention in Canada: Toward a National Strategy*. Twelfth Report of the Standing Committee on Justice and the Solicitor General. Ottawa: Government of Canada, February 1993.

Hough, Michael. *City Form and Natural Process. Towards a New Urban Vernacular*. New York: Van Nostrand Reinhold, 1984.

Hulchanski, David. "Barriers to Equal Access in the Housing Market: The Role of Discrimination on the Basis of Race and Gender." A Report prepared for the Ontario Human Rights Commission, June 1993.

Hynes, H. Patricia, ed. *Reconstructing Babylon: Essays on Women and Technology*. Bloomington: Indiana University Press, 1991.

Hynes, H. Patricia. *The Recurring Silent Spring*. New York: Pergamon Press, 1989.

Illich, Ivan. "Energy and Equity". *Toward a History of Needs*. New York: Pantheon, 1978.

Jabanoski, Jeanne. "At Risk: The Person Behind the Assumptions – Planning to Protect Human Health." In *Change of Plans: Towards a Non-Sexist Sustainable City*, ed. M. Eichler. Toronto: Garamond Press, 1995.

Jabanoski, Jeanne. "CITIZEN SCIENCE: The Toronto Refiners and Smelters Site Remediation Project." Presentation to the Ministry of Environment and Energy Conference, The New Economy: Green Needs and Opportunities. Toronto: November 1994.

Jacobs, Jane. "Are Planning Departments Useful?" *Ontario Professional Planners Institute Journal* 8, no. 4 (1993): 2–3.

Jacobs, Jane. *The Death and Life of Great American Cities*. New York: Vintage Books, 1961/Modern Library Edition, 1993.

Johnston, Barbara Rose and Gregory Button. "Human Environmental Rights Issues and the Multinational Corporation: Industrial Development in the Free Trade Zone." In *Who Pays the Price? The Sociocultural Context of Environmental Crisis*, ed. Barbara Rose Johnston, 206-16. Washington, DC: Society for Applied Anthropology, Committee on Human Rights and the Environment, 1994.

Karhoff, Brigitte, Rosemarie Ring, and Helga Steinmaier. *Frauen veraendern ihre Stadt. Selbstorganisierte Projekte der sozialen und oekologischen Stadterneuerung: Vom Frauenstadthaus bis zur Umplanung einer Grossiedlung*. (Hrsg. by Feministische Organisation von Planerinnen und Architektinnen.) Goettingen: Verlag die Werkstatt, 1993.

Kaufman, Jerome. "An Approach to Planning for Women." In *Planning, Women, and Change*, eds. K. Hapgood and J. Getzels, 73-77. Chicago: American Society of Planning Officials, 1974.

Kay, Jane Holtz. "The Day The Traffic Died." *The Nation*. 28 February 1994.

Keane, Carl. "Fear of Crime in Canada: An Examination of Concrete and Formless Fear of Victimatization." *Canadian Journal of Criminology* (April 1992): 215–24.

Kelly, Liz. *Surviving Sexual Violence*. Minneapolis: University of Minnesota Press, 1988.

Ketcham, Brian and Charles Komanoff. "Win-Win Transportation: A No-Losers Approach to Financing Transport in New York City and the Region." Available from: Komanoff Energy Associates, 270 Lafayette #400, New York, NY 10012, USA. Tel: 212-334-9767.

Kitchen, Brigitte, Andrew Mitchell, Peter Clutterbuck, and Marvyn Novick. *Unequal Futures. The Legacies of Child Poverty in Canada*. Toronto: The Child Poverty Action Group and The Social Planning Council of Metropolitan Toronto, 1991.

Klodowsky, Fran, Colleen Lundy, and Caroline Andrew. "Challenging 'Business as Usual' in Housing and Community Planning: The Issue of Violence Against Women." *Canadian Journal of Urban Research* 3, no. 1 (June 1994): 40–58.

Klodawsky, Fran and Aron Spector. "New Families, New Housing Needs, New Urban Environments: The Case of Single-Parent Families." In *Life Spaces*, eds. C. Andrew and B. Moore Milroy, 141-58. Vancouver: UBC Press, 1988.

Klodawsky, Fran, Aron Spector, and Damaris Rose. *Single Parent Families and Canadian Housing Policies: How Mothers Lose*. Ottawa: Canada Mortgage and Housing Corporation, 1985.

Kneen, Brewster. *From Land To Mouth. Understanding the Food System.* 2nd ed. Toronto: NC Press, 1993.

Kneen, Brewster. "The Story of Farmer Dan." *The Ram's Horn* 100 (December 1992): 6-8.

Kneen, Cathleen. "Women and the Food System." *Healthsharing* 8, no. 2 (Spring 1987): 10-13.

Korn, Yvonne. *Inspirations for Action: A Practical Guide to Women's Safety.* Swindon, Wiltshire: Crime Concern, 1993.

Ladner Birch, Eugenie. "From Civic Worker to City Planner: Women in Planning, 1880-1980." In *The American Planner: Biographies and Recollections*, ed. D.A. Krueckeberg, 396-427. New York: Methuen, 1983.

Lakeman, Lee. *99 Federal Steps Toward an End to Violence Against Women.* Toronto: National Action Committee on the Status of Women, 1993.

Lappé, Frances Moore. *Diet for a Small Planet.* Rev. ed., book I. Toronto: Random House, 1982.

Lappé, Frances Moore, Joseph Collins, and Cary Fowler. *Food First: Beyond The Myth of Scarcity.* New York: Ballantine, 1977.

Leavitt, Jacqueline. "Feminist Advocacy Planning in the 1980s." In *Strategic Perspectives in Planning Practice*, ed. B. Checkoway, 181-93. Lexington: Lexington Books, 1986.

Leiss, William, ed. *Prospects and Problems in Risk Communication.* Waterloo, ON: University of Waterloo Press, 1989.

Liebow, Elliot. *Tell Them Who I Am: The Lives of Homeless Women.* New York: The Free Press, 1993.

Liggett, Helen. "Knowing Women/Planning Theory." *Planning Theory* 7/8 (1992): 21-26.

Light, Beth and Ruth Roach Pierson. *No Easy Road: Women in Canada 1920s to 1960s.* (Documents in Canadian Women's History III). Toronto: New Hogtown Press, 1990.

Little, Jo, Linda Peake, and Pat Richardson, eds. *Women in Cities: Gender and the Urban Environment.* London: Macmillan Publishers, 1988.

Littman, Tod. "Transportation Cost Survey." Available from: 1112 May Street, Victoria, BC, V8V 2S5.

Lowe, Marcia D. "Alternatives to the Automobile: Transport for Livable Cities." *Worldwatch Paper 98.* Washington, DC: Worldwatch Institute, October 1990.

Lowe, Marcia D. "The Bicycle: Vehicle for a Small Planet." *Worldwatch Paper 90.* Washington, DC: Worldwatch Institute, September 1989.

Luxton, Meg. *More Than a Labour of Love: Three Generations of Women's Work in the Home.* Toronto: Women's Press, 1980.

Macdonald, Doug. *The Politics of Pollution: Why Canadians Are Failing Their Environment.* Toronto: McClelland and Stewart, 1991.

MacDonald, Kathryn and Mary Lou Morgan. *The Farm And Country Cookbook.* Toronto: Second Story Press, 1994.

MacGregor, Sherilyn. "Planning Change: Not an End But a Beginning." In *Change of Plans: Towards a Non-Sexist Sustainable City*, ed. M. Eichler. Toronto: Garamond Press, 1995.

MacGregor, Sherilyn. "Deconstructing the Man Made City: Feminist Critiques of Planning Thought and Action." In *Change of Plans: Towards a Non-Sexist Sustainable City*, ed. M. Eichler. Toronto: Garamond Press, 1995.

MacGregor, Sherilyn. "Feminist Approaches to Planning Thought and Action: Practical Lessons from Women Plan Toronto." MA Thesis, School of Urban and Regional Planning, Queen's University, ON, 1994.

MacKenzie, James, Roger Dower, and Donald Chen. "The Going Rate: What it Really Costs To Drive." Available from: World Resources Institute, 1709 New York Ave. NW, Washington, DC 20006, US. June 1992.

MacKenzie, Suzanne. "Building Women, Building Cities: Toward Gender Sensitive Theory in the Environmental Disciplines." In *Life Spaces*, eds. C. Andrew and B. Moore Milroy, 13-30. Vancouver: UBC Press, 1988.

MacKenzie, Suzanne. "Women's Responses to Economic Restructuring: Changing Gender, Changing Space." In *The Politics of Diversity: Feminism, Marxism and Nationalism*, eds. R. Hamilton and M. Barrett, 81-100. Montreal: Book Centre, 1986.

McCamant, Kathryn and Charles Durrett. *Cohousing: A Contemporary Approach to Housing Ourselves*. Berkeley: Habitat Press, 1988.

McClain, Janet and Cassie Doyle. *Women and Housing: Changing Needs and the Failure or Policy*. Ottawa: Canadian Council on Social Development and Lorimer, 1984.

Meeker-Lowry, Susan. *Economics as If the Earth Really Mattered*. Gabriola Island, BC: New Society Publishers, 1988.

Merchant, Carolyn. *The Death of Nature: Women, Ecology, and the Scientific Revolution*. New York: Harper and Row, 1983, 1990.

Merchant, Carolyn. *Ecological Revolutions: Nature, Gender and Science in New England*. Chapel Hill: University of North Carolina Press, 1989.

Merry, Sally. *Urban Danger*. Philadelphia: Temple University Press, 1981.

METRAC (Metro Action Committee on Public Violence Against Women and Children). *Women's Safety Audit Guide*. Toronto: METRAC, 1989.

METRAC, Toronto Transit Commission, Metro Toronto Police Force. *Moving Forward: Making Public Transit Safer for Women*. Toronto: Toronto Transit Commission, 1989.

METRAC, Toronto Transit Commission, Metro Toronto Police Force, Scarborough Women's Centre, Scarborough Planning Department. *Making Transit Stops Safer for Women: Scarborough Moves Forward*. Toronto: METRAC, 1991.

METRAC, Women Plan Toronto, York University Faculty of Environmental Studies. *The WISE (Women in Safe Environments) Report*. Toronto: METRAC, 1987.

[Metro Toronto] Taskforce on Public Violence Against Women and Children. *Final Report*. Toronto: Government of Metropolitan Toronto, 1984.

Michelson, William. "Divergent Convergence: The Daily Routines of Employed Spouses as a Public Affairs Agenda." In *Life Spaces*, eds. C. Andrew and B. Moore Milroy, 81-101. Vancouver: UBC Press, 1988.

Michelson, William. *From Sun to Sun: Daily Obligations and Community Structure in the Lives of Employed Women and Their Families*. Totowa, NJ: Rowman and Allanheld, 1985.

Mies, Maria and Vandana Shiva. *Ecofeminism*. Halifax: Fernwood and London: Zed Books, 1993.

Minard, Richard Jr. *A Practitioner's Guide to Comparative Risk – and how we got here*. Toronto: Resources for The Future, 1 June 1994.

Ministry of Housing of the Province of Ontario. *Special Priority Policy for Assaulted Women: New Revised Guidelines and Implementation Strategies*. Toronto: Tenant Support Services, Ministry of Housing, 1990.

Moffat, John and Peter Miller. "The Price of Mobility." Available from: Natural Resources Defence Council, 71 Stevenson Place #1825, San Francisco, CA 94105, US. Tel: 415-777-0220. October 1993.

Moore Milroy, Beth. "Some Thoughts About Difference and Pluralism." *Planning Theory* 7/8 (1992): 33-43.

Moore Milroy, Beth. "Taking Stock of Planning, Space, and Gender." *Journal of Planning Literature* 6, no. 1 (1991): 3-15.

Morris, Jenny and Martin Winn. *Housing and Social Inequality*. London: Hilary Shipman, 1990.

Moser, Caroline. "Women, Human Settlements, and Housing: A Conceptual Framework for Analysis and Policy-Making." In *Women, Human Settlements, and Housing*, eds. C. Moser and L. Peake, 12-32. London: Tavistock Publications, 1987.

Moudon, Anne V. and Pierre Laconte. "Streets as Public Property: Opportunities for Public/Private Interaction in Planning and Design." Proceedings of an International Interaction. Seattle, WA, University of Washington, 1983.

Mougeot, Luc J.A. "Urban Food Self-Reliance: Significance and Prospects." *IDRC Reports* 21, no. 3 (1993): 1-5.

Mumford, Lewis. *The City in History: Its Origins, Its Transformations, and Its Prospects*. New York: Harcourt, Brace and World, 1961.

Munro, Moira and Susan J. Smith. "Gender and Housing: Broadening the Debate." *Housing Studies* 4 (1989): 3-17.

Murdie, Robert. *Social Housing in Transition: The Changing Social Composition of Public Sector Housing in Metropolitan Toronto*. Ottawa: Canada Mortgage and Housing Corporation, 1992.

National Council of Welfare. *Poverty Profile 1992*. Ottawa: Minister of Supply and Services Canada, 1994.

National Council of Welfare. *Women and Poverty Revisited*. Ottawa: Minister of Supply and Services, 1990.

Newman, Oscar. *Community of Interest*. New York: The Macmillan Company, 1980.

Newman, Oscar. *Defensible Space*. New York: The Macmillan Company, 1972.

Newman, Peter and Jeff Kenworthy. *Cities and Automobile Dependence: An International Sourcebook*. Brookfield, VT: Gower, 1989.

Newman, Peter, and Jeff Kenworthy with Les Robinson. *Winning Back the Cities*. Marrickville, NSW, Australia: Australian Consumers' Association, 1992.

Nottingham Safer Cities Project. *Community Safety in Nottingham City Centre: Report of the Steering Group*. Nottingham: Safer Cities Project, October 1990.

Novac, Sylvia. "Not Seen, Not Heard: Women and Housing Policy." *Canadian Woman Studies* 11 (1990): 53-57.

Novac, Sylvia. "Seeking Shelter: Feminist Home Truths." In *Change of Plans: Towards a Non-Sexist Sustainable City*, ed. M. Eichler. Toronto: Garamond Press, 1995.

Novac, Sylvia and Associates. *A Place To Call One's Own: New Voices of Dislocation and Dispossession*. Ottawa: Advisory Council on the Status of Women, forthcoming.

Novac, Sylvia and Associates. *The Security of Her Person: Tenants' Experiences of Sexual Harassment*. Toronto: Ontario Women's Directorate, forthcoming.

Nozick, Marcia. *No Place Like Home: Building Sustainable Communities*. Ottawa: Canadian Council on Social Development, 1992.

"Oak Street Co-op Takes Action Against Domestic Violence." *The Circuit*, 14 (Summer 1992): 1.

O'Brien, Mary H. "Alternatives to Risk Assessment: The Example of Dioxin." *New Solutions: A Journal of Environmental and Occupational Health Policy* (Winter 1993): 39-42.

Ontario Association of Interval and Transition Houses. "Balance the Power: Background Report, Annual Lobby." Unpublished report. November 1990.

Ontario Ministry of Transportation. *The Social Cost of Motor Vehicle Crashes in Ontario.* Toronto: Safety Research Office, Safety Policy Branch in Co-operation with the Research and Development Branch, March 1994.

Orloff, Ann Shola. "Gender and the Social Rights of Citizenship: The Comparative Analysis of Gender Relations and Welfare States." *American Sociological Review* 58 (1993): 303-27.

Oxford Paperback Dictionary. 3rd ed. Oxford: Oxford University Press, 1988.

Pascall, Gillian. *Social Policy: A Feminist Analysis.* London: Tavistock Publications, 1986.

Peattie, L., S. Cornell, and M. Rein. "Development Planning as the Only Game in Town." *Journal of Planning Education and Research* 5, no. 1 (1986): 17-25.

Perkin, Judy and Stephanie F. McCann. "Food For Ethnic Americans: Is the Government Trying to Turn the Melting Pot into a One-Dish Dinner?" In *Ethnic and Regional Foodways in the United States: The Performance of Group Identity,* eds. Linda Keller Brown and Kay Mussell. Knoxville, TN: The University of Tennessee Press, 1984.

Peters, Suzanne, Mary-Jean Wason, and Rachel Grasham. *Voices Of Young Families.* Toronto: Social Planning Council of Metropolitan Toronto, 1994.

Pharoah, Tim. *Less Traffic, Better Towns.* London: Friends of the Earth Trust Limited, 1992.

Piche, Denise. "Interacting with the Urban Environment: Two Case Studies of Women's and Female Adolescents' Leisure Activities." In *Life Spaces,* eds. C. Andrew and B. Moore Milroy, 159-75. Vancouver: UBC Press, 1988.

Plant, Christopher and Judith Plant, eds. *Green Business: Hope or Hoax?* Philadelphia: New Society Publishers, 1991.

Pollock Shea, Cynthia. *Employment and Sustainable Development: Opportunities for Canada.* Winnipeg: International Institute for Sustainable Development, 1994.

Pollution Probe. *The Costs of the Car: A Preliminary Study of the Environmental and Social Costs Associated with Private Car Use in Ontario.* Toronto: Pollution Probe, 1991.

Poyner, Barry. *Design Against Crime: Beyond Defensible Space.* London: Butterworths, 1983.

Project Team. *The Outsiders, A Report On The Prospects for Young Families in Metro Toronto.* Toronto: Social Planning Council of Metropolitan Toronto, 1994.

Quayle, Moura. "Canadian Community Gardens. A Sustainable Landscape Legacy." *Landscape Architectural Review* (March 1989): 17-20.

Quayle, Moura. "The Changing Community Garden. Legitimizing Non-Traditional Open Space." *Landscape Architectural Review* 10, no. 2 (May 1989): 23-27.

Renner, Michael. "Rethinking the Role of the Automobile." *Worldwatch Paper 84.* Washington, DC: Worldwatch, 1988.

Renner, Michael. "Rethinking Transportation." *State of The World.* Washington, DC: Worldwatch, 1989.

Replogle, Michael. *Bicycles and Public Transportation: New Links to Suburban Transit Markets.* Washington, DC: The Bicycle Federation, 1988.

Ritzdorf, Marsha. "Feminist Thoughts on the Theory and Practice of Planning." *Planning Theory* 7/8 (1992): 13-19.

Ritzdorf, Marsha. "Women and the City: Land Use and Zoning Issues." *Journal of Urban Resources* 3, no. 2 (1986): 23-27.

Ritzdorf, Marsha. "Zoning Barriers to Housing Innovations." *Journal of Planning Education and Research* 4, no. 3 (1985b): 177-84.

Ritzdorf, Marsha. "Zoning Ordinances Out of Touch with Changing American Demography." *Urban and Housing Research Report* 85, no. 11 (1985a): 1.

Roberts, John, Johanna Cleary, Kerry Hamilton, and Judith Hanna, eds. *Travel Sickness*. London, UK: Lawrence and Wishart, 1992.

Roberts, Wayne, John Bacher, and Brian Nelson. *Get a Life! A Green Cure for Canada's Economic Blues*. Toronto: Get a Life Publishing House, 1993.

Robertson, James. *The Sane Alternative: Signposts to a Self-Fulfilling Future*. London: Villiers Publishing, 1978.

Roncek, Dennis. "Dangerous Places: Crime and Residential Environment." *Social Forces* 60, no. 1 (1981): 74–96.

Rosenbaum, Dennis. "Community Crime Prevention: A Review and Synthesis of the Literature." *Justice Quarterly* 5, no. 3 (1988).

Ross, David P. and E. Richard Shillington. *The Canadian Fact Book on Poverty – 1989*. Ottawa: The Canadian Council on Social Development, 1989.

Rothblatt, Donald, Daniel Garr, and Jo Sprague. *The Suburban Environment and Women*. New York: Praeger Publishers, 1979.

Rutherford, Brent M. and Gerda R. Wekerle. "Captive Rider, Captive Labour: Spatial Constraints and Women's Employment." *Urban Geography* 9, no. 2 (1989): 116-37.

Rutherford, Brent M. and Gerda R. Wekerle. *Equity Issues in Women's Accessibility To Employment: Transportation, Location, and Policy*. Toronto: Institute on Women and Work, City of Toronto, 1987, revised 1988.

Rutherford, Brent M. and Gerda R. Wekerle. "Single Parents in the Suburbs: Journey-to-Work and Access to Transportation." *Spec. Trans. Plan. and Pract.* 3, no. 3 (1989).

Sacchetti, Clara and Todd Dufresne. "President's Choice Through The Looking Glass, Loblaws, Nichol and Specular Consumption." *Fuse Magazine* 17, no. 4 (May/June 1994): 22-31.

Sachs, Wolfgang. *For Love of the Automobile – Looking Back into the History of Our Desires*. Berkeley: University of California Press, 1992.

Saegert, Susan. "The Androgenous City: From Critique to Practice." *Sociological Focus* 18, no. 2 (1985): 161-76.

Saint John Safe City Committee. *Community Safety: Everyone's Business*. The Saint John Safety Audit Report. Saint John: City of Saint John, 1993.

Sale, Kirkpatrick. *Human Scale*. New York: Coward, McCann, & Geoghegan, 1980.

Salem, Greta. "Gender Equity and the Urban Environment." In *The Egalitarian City*, ed. J.K. Boles, 152-61. New York: Praeger Publishers, 1986.

Sandercock, Leonie and Ann Forsyth. "Feminist Theory and Planning Theory: Epistemological Linkages." *Planning Theory* 7/8 (1992): 45-49.

Sandercock, Leonie and Ann Forsyth. "Gender: A New Agenda for Planning Theory." *Planning Theory* 4 (1990): 61-92.

Schantz, Faith. "The Fresh Connection." *Country Journal* 22, no.1 (January/February 1995): 70-75.

Schiller, Bill. "Toronto ranks as fourth–best city to live in, survey says." *The Toronto Star* (18 January 1995).

Schneekloth, Lynda. "Advances in Practice in Environment, Behaviour, and Design." In *Advances in Environment, Behaviour, and Design.* Vol. 1, eds. E.H. Zube and G.T. Moore, 307-34. New York: Plenum Press, 1987.

Schumacher, E.F. *Small is Beautiful: A Study of Economics as if People Mattered.* 2nd ed. London: Arcus, 1978.

Schwab, Jim. "Home Safe Home?" *Zoning News* (September 1993): 1–14.

Schwartzel, Ellen. "Car Control in Canada: the Current Scene." Notes from a slide presentation. Toronto: Pollution Probe, June 1993.

Seabrook, John. "Tremors In The HotHouse." *New Yorker* (July 1993).

Seager, Joni. *Earth Follies: Coming to Feminist Terms with the Global Environmental Crisis.* New York: Routledge, 1993.

Seaton Advisory Committee. "Seaton Planning and Design Exercise Phase 3 Design Brief" (draft), 4 July 1994.

Seaton Team Dunker. *Seaton Handbook.* Toronto: Dunker Associates, 1994.

Shaw, Helen. "Elite Women in Canada: A Study of Women in the Key Positions of the Corporate and Political Sectors of Canadian Society." Ph.D. thesis, University of Toronto, Department of Educational Theory, OISE, 1994.

Shiva, Vandana. *Staying Alive: Women, Ecology and Development.* London: Zed Books, 1989.

Smith, Malcolm, "Environmental Implications of the Automobile." *A State of the Environment Fact Sheet.* Ottawa: Environment Canada, 1993.

Smith, Susan. "Income, Housing Wealth and Gender Inequality." *Urban Studies* 27 (February 1990): 67-88.

Social Planning Council of Metropolitan Toronto. *Losing a Home: Experiences Under Ontario's Rental Housing Protection Act.* Toronto: Federation of Metro Tenants' Associations, 1988.

Social Planning Council of Winnipeg. *A Safer Winnipeg for Women and Children.* Winnipeg: Social Planning Council of Winnipeg, 1991.

Spain, Daphne. *Gendered Spaces.* Chapel Hill: The University of North Carolina Press, 1992.

Spender, Dale. *Man Made Language.* 2nd ed. London: Routledge and Kegan Paul, 1985.

Spirn, Anne Whiston. *The Granite Garden, Urban Design and Human Design.* New York: Basic Books, 1984.

Stanbury, W.T. and John D. Todd. "Landlords as Economic Prisoners of War." *Canadian Public Policy* (1990): 399-417.

Statistics Canada. "Gender Difference Among Violent Crime Victims." *Juristat Bulletin* 12, no. 21 (November 1992). Catalogue 85–002.

Statistics Canada. *A Portrait of Families in Canada.* Target groups project. Ottawa: Minister of Industry, Science and Technology, 1993. Catalogue 89-523E.

Statistics Canada. *Violence Against Women Survey, 1993: Shelf Tables 1-25.* Ottawa: Minister of Industry, Science and Technology, November 1993.

Statistics Canada. "The Violence Against Women Survey." *The Daily,* (18 November 1993). Catalogue 11–001.

Stewart, Dana and Freda Steel. *The Economic Consequences of Divorce on Families Owning A Marital Home.* Ottawa: Canada Mortgage and Housing Corporation, 1990.

Stocker, Midge, ed. *Cancer as a Women's Issue: Scratching the Surface*. Chicago: Third Side Press, 1991.

Stoks, Francis. "Assessing Urban Public Space Environments for Danger of Violent Crime – Especially Rape." Unpublished Ph.D. dissertation, Urban Planning Department, University of Washington, 1982.

TEST. *Quality Streets*. London: TEST, 1989.

"Theatregoers choosing Toronto over Broadway." *The Globe and Mail*, 21 October 1993.

"Three Canadian Cities among top 10 in world," *The Globe and Mail*, 18 January 1995.

Titus, Richard M. "Security Works: Shopping Enclaves Bring Hope, Investment to Blighted Inner City Neighbourhoods." *Urban Land* (January 1990): 2–5.

Todd, Nancy and John Todd. *From Ecocities to Living Machines: Principles of Ecological Design*. Berkeley: Northatlantic Books, 1994.

Tolley, Rodney. *Calming Traffic In Residential Areas*. Brefi Press, 1989.

Toronto City Council. *Toronto's First State of the City Report*. Toronto: Department of the City Clerk, Information and Communications Services Division, 1993.

Toronto Food Policy Council. *Reducing Urban Hunger in Ontario: Policy Responses to Support the Transition from Food Charity to Local Food Security*. Discussion Paper no. 1. Toronto: Toronto Food Policy Council, 1994.

United States Environmental Protection Agency. *Risk Assessment Guidance for Superfund. Volume I: Human Health Evaluation Manual (Part A)*. Springfield, VA: US Department of Commerce, December 1989.

United States Environmental Protection Agency. *Risk Assessment Guidance for Superfund. Volume II: Environmental Evaluation Manual*. Washington, DC: Office of Solid Waste and Emergency Response, March 1989.

Valentine, Gill. "Women's Fear and the Design of Public Space." *Built Environment* 16, no. 4 (1990): 288–303.

[Vancouver] Safer City Taskforce. *Final Report*. Vancouver: City of Vancouver, 1993.

Van Vliet, Willem. "Communities and Built Environments Supporting Women's Changing Roles." *Sociological Focus* 18, no. 2 (1985): 73-77.

von Bayer, Edwinna. *Rhetoric and Roses. A History of Canadian Gardening*. Toronto: Fitzhenry & Whiteside, 1984.

Vorhees, Michael. "The True Costs of the Automobile to Society." Available from: 3131 Bell Drive, Boulder, CO 80301, US. Tel: 303-449-9067. January 1992.

Walby, Sylvia. *Theorizing Patriarchy*. Oxford: Basil Blackwell, 1990.

Walter, Bob, Lois Arkin, and Richard Crenshaw, eds. *Sustainable Cities, Concepts and Strategies for Eco-City Development*. Los Angeles: Eco-Home Media, 1992.

Waring, Marilyn. *If Women Counted: A New Feminist Economics*. San Francisco: Harper and Row, 1988.

Warren, Karen J. "Feminism and Ecology: Making Connections." *Environmental Ethics* 9, no. 1 (1987): 3-20.

Warren, Karen J. "The Power and the Promise of Ecological Feminism." *Environmental Ethics* 12, no. 2 (1990): 125-46.

Wartenberg, Daniel and Caron Chess. "The Risk Wars: Assessing Risk Assessment." In *New Solutions: A Journal of Environmental and Occupational Health Policy* (Winter 1993).

Watson, Paul. "Residents find they're afraid of life in 'Toronto the Good.'" *The Toronto Star* (17 May 1989).

Watson, Sophie. *Playing the State: Australian Feminist Interventions.* London: Verso, 1990.

Watson, Sophie with Helen Austerberry. *Housing and Homelessness: A Feminist Perspective.* London: Routledge and Kegan Paul, 1986.

Weedon, Chris. *Feminist Practice and Poststructuralist Theory.* Oxford: Blackwell, 1987.

Weisman, Leslie. *Discrimination by Design: A Feminist Critique of the Man–Made Environment.* Urbana, IL: University of Illinois Press, 1994.

Wekerle, Gerda. "Responding to Diversity: Housing Developed by and for Women." In *Shelter, Women and Development: First and Third World Perspectives,* ed. Hemalata Dandekar, 178-86. Ann Arbor, MI: George Wahr Publishing, 1993.

Wekerle, Gerda and Sylvia Novac. "Developing Two Women's Co-operatives." In *New Households New Housing,* eds. Karen Franck and Sherry Ahrentzen, 223-42. New York: Van Nostrand Reinhold, 1989.

Wekerle, Gerda and Sylvia Novac. *Gender and Housing in Toronto.* Toronto: Equal Opportunity Division, Institute on Women and Work, 1991.

Wekerle, Gerda, Rebecca Peterson, and David Morley, eds. *New Space for Women.* Boulder, CO: Westview Press, 1980.

Wekerle, Gerda and Brent Rutherford. "Employed Women in the Suburbs: Transportation Disadvantage in a Car-Centred Environment." *Alternatives* 14, no. 3 (1987): 49-54.

Wekerle, Gerda and Brent Rutherford. "The Mobility of Capital and the Immobility of Female Labour: Responses to Economic Restructuring." In *The Power of Geography: How Territory Shapes Social Life,* eds. Jennifer Wolch and Michael Dear. Boston: Unwin Hyman, 1987.

Wekerle, Gerda and Carolyn Whitzman. *Safe Cities.* New York: Van Nostrand Reinhold, 1995.

Wen–Do Women's Self–Defense Corporation. *Success Stories* newsletter. Available from: Wen–Do Women's Self–Defense Corporation, PO Box 139, 260 Adelaide Street East, Toronto, Ontario M5A 1N0.

Weninger, Jane. "Public Participation in Decommissioning and Site Clean-up: A Look at the Ataratiri Project." Presented at the symposium sponsored by the Institute for Social Impact Assessment, Toronto, 1990.

White, Philip. *Supermarket Tour.* Toronto: Ontario Public Interest Research Group, 1990.

Whitzman, Carolyn. *Planning for a Safer City,* Cityplan Background paper no. 10. Toronto: City of Toronto Planning and Development Department, 1990.

Whitzman, Carolyn. "Taking Back Planning: Promoting Women's Safety in Public Places – the Toronto Experience." *Journal of Architectural and Planning Research* 9, no. 2 (Summer 1992): 169–79.

Whitzman, Carolyn. "What Do You Want to Do? Pave Parks? Urban Planning and the Prevention of Violence." In *Change of Plans: Towards a Non-Sexist Sustainable City,* ed. M. Eichler. Toronto: Garamond Press, 1995.

Whitzman, Carolyn. "Women, Fear, and Urban Neighbourhoods." MA Thesis, University of Toronto Geography Department, 1988.

Whitzman, Carolyn and Gerda Wekerle. *A Working Guide for Planning and Designing*

Safer Urban Environments. Toronto: City of Toronto Planning and Development Department, 1992.

Wilson, Alexander. *The Culture of Nature, North American Landscape from Disney to the Exxon Valdez.* Toronto: Between The Lines, 1991.

Wilson, Elizabeth. *The Sphinx in the City: Urban Life, the Control of Disorder, and Women.* Berkeley: University of California Press, 1991.

Wise Harris, Debbie. *A Safer City: The Second Stage Report of the Safe City Committee.* Toronto: City of Toronto Safe City Committee, 1991.

Women and Urban Safety Committee of Ottawa-Carleton. *Women and Urban Safety: A Recommendation for Action.* Ottawa: Regional Government of Ottawa-Carleton, 1991.

Zielinski, Susan. "Access Over Excess: Transcending Captivity and Transportation Disadvantage." In *Change of Plans: Towards a Non-Sexist Sustainable City*, ed. M. Eichler. Toronto: Garamond Press, 1995.

Zielinski, Susan. "Transporting Ourselves to Sustainable Economic Growth." Paper submitted for the International Institute for Sustainable Development Employment and Sustainable Development Meeting, Winnipeg, 1994.

Zielinski, Susan and Gordon Laird, eds. *Beyond the Car.* Toronto: Steel Rail Press, 1995.

Zimmerman, Patricia. "Boys and their Toys." In *Beyond the Car*, eds. S. Zielinski and G. Laird. Toronto: Steel Rail Press, 1995.

Zuckerman, Wolfgang. *End of the Road. The World Car Crisis and How We Can Solve It.* Cambridge: Lutterworth Press, 1991.

• Cap-Saint-Ignace
• Sainte-Marie (Beauce)
Québec, Canada
1995